State Business Incentives: Trends and Options for the Future

Second Edition

by Keon S. Chi and Daniel J. Hofmann

2000

WITHDRAWN

APR 30 ...

WDC LIB - STACKS

The Council of State Governments

2760 Research Park Drive
P.O. Box 11910
Lexington, KY 40578-1910
Phone: (859) 244-8000
Fax: (859) 244-8001
Internet: www.csg.org

⌷CSG⌷ The Council of State Governments

The Council of State Governments, a multibranch association of the states and U.S. territories, works with state leaders across the nation and through its regions to put the best ideas and solutions into practice. To this end, The Council of State Governments:
- Builds leadership skills to improve decision-making;
- Advocates multistate problem-solving and partnerships;
- Interprets changing national and international conditions to prepare states for the future; and
- Promotes the sovereignty of the states and their role in the American federal system.

CSG's **C**enter for **L**eadership, **I**nnovation and **P**olicy (**CLIP**) serves the state government community by promoting policy development and leadership training and by recognizing innovative state programs. With CSG's membership and regional leadership conferences as a foundation, **CLIP** is uniquely positioned to develop and execute critical state problem-solving initiatives with intergovernmental, philanthropic and corporate partners.

CSG Officers:
   Chair: Deputy Minority Leader Rep. Tom Ryder, Ill.
   Chair-Elect: Senate President Pro Tempore
           Manny M. Aragon, N.M.
   Vice Chair: Sen. John Chichester, Va.

President: Gov. Paul Patton, Ky.
President-Elect: Gov. Dirk Kempthorne, Idaho
Vice President: Gov. Parris Glendening, Md.

Headquarters:
2760 Research Park Drive
P.O. Box 11910
Lexington, KY 40578-1910
(859) 244-8000
Fax: (859) 244-8001
E-mail: info@csg.org
Internet: www.csg.org

Daniel M. Sprague, *Executive Director*
Bob Silvanik, *Deputy Executive Director*
Howard Moyes, *Assistant Director*

Eastern:
 Alan V. Sokolow, *Director*
5 World Trade Center, Suite 9241
New York, NY 10048, (212) 912-0128
Fax: (212) 912-0549
E-mail: csge@csg.org

Midwestern:
Michael H. McCabe, *Director*
641 E. Butterfield Road, Suite 401
Lombard, IL 60148, (630) 810-0210
Fax: (630) 810-0145
E-mail: csg-midwest@csg.org

Southern:
 Colleen Cousineau, *Director*
3355 Lenox Road, Suite 1050
Atlanta, GA 30326, (404) 266-1271
Fax: (404) 266-1273
E-mail: slc@csg.org

Western:
Kent Briggs, *Director*
121 Second Street, 4th Floor
San Francisco, CA 94105
(415) 974-6422
Fax: (415) 974-1747
E-mail: csgw@csg.org
Denver, CO: (303) 572-5454
Fax (303) 572-5499

Washington:
Jim Brown, *General Counsel and Director*
444 N. Capitol Street, NW, Suite 401
Washington, DC 20001
(202) 624-5460
Fax: (202) 624-5452
E-mail: dcinfo@csg.org

Copyright 2000
The Council of State Governments
Manufactured in the United States of America
Order # STBUSIINCEN99
ISBN # 0-87292-876-4
Price: $60.00

All rights reserved. Inquiries for use of any material should be directed to:
The Council of State Governments
2760 Research Park Drive • P.O. Box 11910
Lexington, Kentucky 40578-1910
(859) 244-8000

Publication Sales Order Department
1-800-800-1910

Table of Contents

State and Territory Profiles

Table of Contents (continued)

Acknowledgments

Funding for *State Business Incentives: Trends and Options for the Future, Second Edition* was provided in part by The Council of State Governments 21st Century Fund. The 21st Century Fund is an internal foundation operating within the Council's 501(c)(3) organization. The purpose of the Fund is to strengthen the Council's policy and research capacity by "supporting" innovative and entrepreneurial approaches to product development.

Corporate contributors include:
- American Express Company
- BP America
- DuPont
- Eastman Kodak Company
- Glaxo Wellcome Inc.
- Metabolife International, Inc.
- Pfizer Inc.
- Pharmacia & Upjohn, Inc.
- Philip Morris Management Corporation
- The Procter and Gamble Company
- 3M Company
- United Parcel Service
- Volvo North American Company
- Wyeth-Ayerst Laboratories

Foreword

Since the 1970s, the number of states with business incentive programs to promote economic development has increased steadily. As a result, interstate competition has intensified. Recently, however, policy-makers in many states are raising questions about the effectiveness and opportunity costs of such incentive programs.

I am pleased to release this report on state tax and financial incentive programs and options for state policy-makers to consider when pondering future courses of action. Based on CSG's 1994, 1996 and 1999 surveys of state economic development agencies and other sources, this report presents the most recent information and data on business incentive programs in the 50 states and U.S. territories.

In view of the ongoing debates on the effectiveness of tax and financial incentive programs, I believe this report will be an invaluable resource for policy-makers across the states. On behalf of the CSG staff who played a role in the production of this report, I want to acknowledge and thank state economic development agency officials who responded to CSG's surveys and provided useful documents. Without their support, this report would not have been possible.

Finally, I would like to extend a special appreciation to the corporate donors to CSG's 21st Century Fund and its board members for supporting this timely project.

Daniel M. Sprague
Executive Director
The Council of State Governments

Executive Summary

- In the past two decades, the number of states with tax incentives for businesses steadily increased. By 1998, more than 40 states offered tax concessions or credits for equipment, inventories and job creation. Other tax exemption programs offered by more than 30 states are linked to corporate and personal income and research and development.

- The number of states with financial incentive programs also increased over the past 20 years. By 1998, more than 40 states offered low-interest loans for building construction, equipment, machinery, plant expansion and industrial plants in high-unemployment areas.

- In the past five years, 32 states increased their number of business incentive programs, while the number of such incentives remained the same in 14 states. In 1994, 38 states said their incentive programs increased and 10 states did not increase the number of incentive programs in the previous five years.

- In the next five years, a majority of the states are likely to maintain their incentive programs at current levels, according to the 1999 CSG survey. Thirteen states said they would increase the number of incentives, but 35 states said the number would stay the same.

- In the 1999 CSG survey, several states reported that some of their business incentives programs have been successful in luring and creating jobs in the past five years. Such programs relate workforce development, job-creation tax credits and enterprise zone programs.

- Many states still do not use written guidelines to determine the offering of business incentives. They should evaluate cost-benefits of such incentives, gather sufficient information for decision-making, and develop options for interstate competition for job creation.

- State leaders and managers can consider three courses of action in dealing with interstate competition in job creation: status quo, federal intervention, and interstate and intergovernmental cooperation.

INTRODUCTION

During the past two decades, states have offered various business incentive programs to create, retain or expand jobs. In addition to tax and financial incentives, some states have used customized, company-specific incentives to engage in bidding wars with other states. Others have offered incentives to recruit business from abroad. Interstate competition for industries and businesses has become increasingly intense.

Researchers link causes of interstate competition for job creation to various factors, such as high unemployment rates, promotional efforts by state economic development agencies, innovation diffusion among states and interest group politics. Proponents of business incentives maintain business incentives have a positive effect on business-location decisions, finance job creation, are cost-effective, help foster competitiveness and are politically popular. Opponents say that tax and financial incentives are not necessarily the most important factor considered in business-location decisions. Critics say that such incentives are ineffective in creating jobs; raise questions about equity in the treatment of existing businesses; pull dollars away from the improvement of public services, such as education and infrastructure; and create a self-defeating zero-sum game between states.

Recently, state and local government officials and observers of business incentive practices have raised important questions about the effectiveness and impact of using incentives. Some have suggested general principles and standards of fair competition for job creation. State and local policy-makers are pondering future courses of action regarding the use of business incentives and the overall improvement of their jurisdictions' business climate to create jobs.

To help state policy-makers make informed decisions, The Council of State Governments in 1989 published *The States and Business Incentives: An Inventory of Tax and Financial Incentive Programs*. In 1994, CSG published "State Business Incentives: Options for the Future" in its *State Trends & Forecasts* publication series. An updated and expanded version of these two CSG publications on state business incentives was published in 1997 as *State Business Incentives: Trends and Options for the Future*.

This report is the second edition of *State Business Incentives*. It contains information and data on state business incentives offered by states; legislative actions on business incentives; examples of successful incentive programs; arguments for and against the use of business incentives; issues when offering business incentives; and policy options and courses of action for state policy-makers to consider for the future.

The report also contains several tables designed to give comparative analysis of job-training programs (Appendix B), enterprise-zone programs (Appendix C), public- and private-partnership programs (Appendix D) and tax rates for all 50 states (Appendix E). The information and data contained in this report are based on a national survey of economic development and business incentive leaders in the 50 states and U.S. territories conducted by CSG staff in 1996 and 1999, documents and promotional materials published by state economic development agencies, and information on "legislative climates" and state business incentives extracted from selected issues of *Site Selection*, published by Conway Data, Inc.

In this report, the term "business incentives" is broadly defined as public subsidies, including, but not limited to, tax abatement and financial assistance programs, designed to create, retain or lure businesses for job creation. The term is used interchangeably as "industrial" or "development incentives." The term "tax incentives" broadly refers to any credits or abatements of corporate income, personal income, sales-and-use, property or other taxes to create, retain or lure business. The term "financial incentives" broadly refers to any type of direct loan, loan guarantee grant, infrastructure development, or job training assistance offered to help create, retain or lure businesses.

TRENDS IN STATE BUSINESS INCENTIVES

In the past 20 years:

Since the 1970s, the number of states providing tax incentives to businesses steadily increased. By 1998, more than 40 states offered tax concessions or credits to businesses for equipment and machinery, goods in transition, manufacturers' inventories, raw materials in manufacturing and job creation. Other tax exemption programs becoming increasingly popular in the states are linked to corporate income, personal income, and research and development (see Tables 1 and 3). Figure 1 shows an increase in the number of states with tax incentive programs over a 20-year period.

Similarly, the number of states with financial-incentive programs also increased over the past two decades, as shown in Tables 2 and 4. By 1998, more than 40 states offered special low-interest loans for building construction, equipment, machinery, plant expansion and establishment of industrial plants in areas of high unemployment. Figure 2 illustrates a 20-year trend in financial incentives offered by states.

In the past five years:

In response to the 1999 CSG survey, respondents from 32 states said their states increased the number of business incentive programs in the past five years, while the number of such incentive programs remained unchanged in 14 states. Two states (Arizona and New York) decreased the number of business incentives (see Map 1). These figures can be compared with the 1994 CSG survey data: 38 states had an increase in business incentives; 10 states' activities remained the same and two states experienced a decrease during the previous five years (Page 2 - Map 1: Trends in State Business Incentive Programs in the Past 5 Years).

The 1999 CSG survey shows that a majority of states offer tax and financial incentives for foreign investment

(29 states), export assistance program (43), incentives for certain business sectors (36), day care facilities (29), and regulatory relief (26 states).

In the next five years:

In the next five years, a majority of the states are likely to maintain their incentive activities at current levels. In responding to the 1999 CSG survey, 13 state economic development officials said the number of business incentives would increase in their states, 35 said the number would stay the same, and no state predicted a decrease (two states did not respond to the survey) (see Map 2). In responding to the 1994 CSG survey, 18 state economic development officials said they would increase business incentives, 25 said they would stay the same, and two predicted the activity would decrease (This page - Map 2: Trends in State Business Incentive Programs in the next 5 years).

LEGISLATIVE ACTIONS ON BUSINESS INCENTIVES

In recent years, most state legislatures have enacted laws to create more jobs in their states by strengthening business incentive programs. More than 30 states each year have enacted legislation to create or retain jobs. Legislative actions have centered around tax and financial incentives, new economic development organizations, economic zones and worker's compensation (see Appendix A for year-by-year and state-specific highlights).

SUCCESSFUL BUSINESS INCENTIVES

The 1999 CSG survey asked state economic development officials to describe one or two customized business incentives programs that have been successful in creating jobs in the past five years. Examples of responses include American Honda Motor Co. in Alabama; AstraZeneca in Delaware; Advanced Silicon Materials, Inc. in Montana; Federal Express, Nucor and Wisconsin Tissues in North Carolina; American International Insurance Company in New Jersey; Brother International and Federal Express in Tennessee; and Hewlett Packard in Washington state.

In addition, survey respondents from more than 20 states identified tax and financial programs that have been especially successful in job creation in their states:

Arkansas	Enterprise Zone Create Rebate
Colorado	Economic Development Commission
Connecticut	Manufacturing Assistance Act
Florida	Qualified Target Industry Tax Refund Program
Hawaii	General Excise Tax/Use Tax Abatement
Idaho	Workforce Development Training Fund Program
Illinois	DCCA's Capital Access Program
Iowa	New Jobs and Income Program

TRENDS IN STATE BUSINESS INCENTIVE PROGRAMS

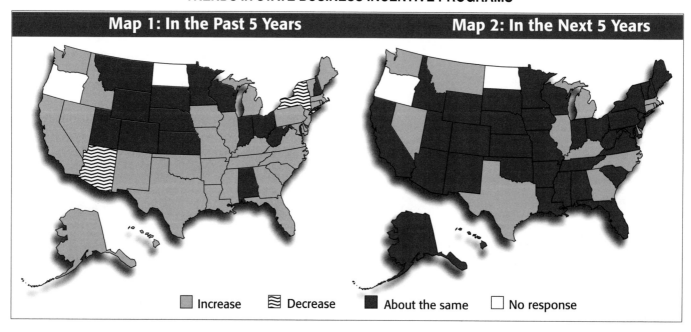

Past Five Years	Number of States
Increased	32
Decreased	2
About the Same	14

Next Five Years	Number of States
Increased	13
Decreased	0
About the Same	35

Source: Compiled by The Council of State Governments from CSG's 1999 national survey of state economic development and business-incentive leaders (50 states and three territories responding).

Kentucky	Tourism Development Act
Maine	Tax Increment Financing; Employment Tax Increment Financing
Maryland	Maryland Job Creation Tax Credit Program
Massachusetts	Economic Development Incentive Program
Michigan	Renaissance Zone Program
Nebraska	Production Tax Credit
New Jersey	Business Employment Incentive Program
New Mexico	Industrial Revenue Bond
Oklahoma	Quality Job Program
Pennsylvania	Opportunity Grant Program; Job Creation Tax Credit
Texas	Smart Jobs Fund Program; Economic Development Sales Tax
Utah	Industrial Assistance Fund; Enterprise Zone Program
West Virginia	Governor's Guaranteed Workforce Program

ARGUMENTS FOR AND AGAINST BUSINESS INCENTIVES

Proponents of state business incentives argue:

• Incentives have a positive effect on business location decisions. Since corporate income, sales and property tax incentives directly affect businesses, they cannot be ignored in decisions on business location.

TABLE 1

STATE TAX INCENTIVES FOR BUSINESS: CHANGES BETWEEN 1988-98, 1990-98

Types of Tax Incentives	1988	1989	1990	1991	1992	1993	1995	1996	1998	Changes between 1988-98	Changes between 1990-98
Corporate Income Tax Exemption	31	32	34	35	35	36	36	37	37	+6	+3
Personal Income Tax Exemption	28	32	32	32	32	32	32	33	34	+6	+2
Excise Tax Exemption	19	21	22	22	22	23	23	24	25	+6	+3
Tax Exemption or Moratorium on Land, Capital Improvements	35	35	35	36	36	36	37	37	38	+3	+3
Tax Exemption or Moratorium on Equipment, Machinery	39	41	41	41	41	41	42	42	42	+3	+1
Inventory Tax Exemption on Goods in Transit (Freeport)	48	48	49	49	49	49	49	49	49	+1	0
Tax Exemption on Manufacturers' Inventories	44	45	45	46	46	46	46	46	47	+3	+2
Sales/Use Tax Exemptions on New Equipment	44	45	46	47	47	47	47	47	47	+3	+1
Tax Exemption on Raw Materials Used in Manufacturing	45	47	48	48	49	49	49	49	50	+5	+2
Tax Incentive for Creation of Jobs	35	39	40	43	44	44	44	44	43	+8	+3
Tax Incentive for Industrial Investment	32	33	35	36	37	37	39	39	43	+11	+8
Tax Credits for Use of Specified State Products	7	5	4	4	4	4	4	6	7	0	+3
Tax Stabilization Agreements for Specified Industries	5	6	6	7	7	7	8	8	9	+4	+3
Tax Exemptions to Encourage Research and Development	25	27	28	31	31	34	36	36	39	+14	+11
Accelerated Depreciation of Industrial Equipment	35	36	39	39	39	40	41	41	41	+6	+2

Source: Compiled by The Council of State Governments from October 1988-1998 issues of *Site Selection*, Conway Data, Inc. (Data unavailable for 1994 and 1997).

• Incentives finance job creation. Low taxes and low-interest financing are necessary to create or expand businesses and recruit businesses from other states or foreign countries. These businesses create jobs.

• Incentives are cost-effective. Business incentives are less costly than they appear. Tax, financial and other incentives are effective and efficient tools for economic development, and benefits outweigh costs in the long run. Moreover, incentives have spin-off or multiplier effects that pay off over time.

• Incentives help foster competitiveness. States tend to replicate what other states, especially neighbors, offer to prevent existing firms from leaving or to lure firms away from other states. States frequently find themselves in bidding wars, competing with each other for jobs and economic development.

• Incentives have a political element. Elected officials, as well as administrators responsible for economic development, are under public pressure to attract businesses. The temptation to offer business incentives is great, espe-

TABLE 2

STATE FINANCIAL INCENTIVES FOR BUSINESS: CHANGES BETWEEN 1988-98, 1990-98

Types of Financial Incentives	1988	1989	1990	1991	1992	1993	1995	1996	1998	Changes between 1988-98	Changes between 1990-98
State-Sponsored Industrial Development Authority	38	38	40	40	40	40	42	42	42	+4	+2
Privately-Sponsored Development Credit Corporation	37	37	36	38	38	39	39	39	39	+2	+3
State Authority or Agency Revenue Bond Financing	44	44	44	43	44	4	44	44	45	+1	+1
State Authority or Agency General Obligation Bond Financing	15	15	18	19	20	20	20	21	24	+9	+6
City and/or County Revenue Bond Financing	49	49	49	49	49	49	49	49	49	0	0
City and/or County General Obligation Bond Financing	33	3	37	36	37	37	37	37	40	+7	+3
State Loans for Building Construction	38	40	40	41	40	40	41	42	42	+4	+2
State Loans for Equipment, Machinery	37	39	42	42	41	42	43	43	43	+6	+1
City and/or County Loans for Building Construction	34	37	39	41	44	45	46	46	47	+13	+9
City and/or County Loans for Equipment, Machinery	32	35	38	41	44	45	46	46	47	+15	+9
State Loan Guarantees for Building Construction	25	25	28	25	26	28	27	28	27	+2	-1
State Loan Guarantees for Equipment, Machinery	26	25	29	28	28	31	30	30	29	+3	0
State Financing Aid for Existing Plant Expansion	42	43	44	44	44	44	44	44	44	+2	0
State Matching Funds for City and/or County Industrial Financing Programs	20	21	22	22	25	26	26	26	27	+7	+5
State Incentives for Establishing Industrial Plants in Areas of High Unemployment	31	33	36	40	41	41	41	41	43	+12	+7
City and/or County Incentives for Establishing Industrial Plants in Areas of High Unemployment	30	30	32	33	35	35	35	36	36	+6	+4

Source: Compiled by The Council of State Governments from October 1988-1998 issues of Site Selection, Conway Data, Inc. (Data unavailable for 1994 and 1997).

FIGURE 1

STATE TAX INCENTIVES FOR BUSINESS: CHANGES BETWEEN 1977-98

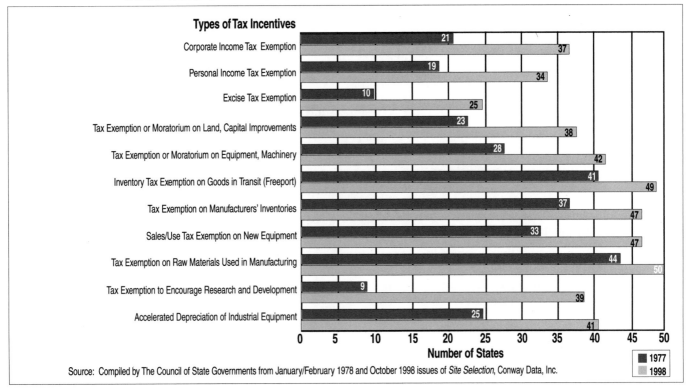

Types of Tax Incentives

Type	1977	1998
Corporate Income Tax Exemption	21	37
Personal Income Tax Exemption	19	34
Excise Tax Exemption	10	25
Tax Exemption or Moratorium on Land, Capital Improvements	23	38
Tax Exemption or Moratorium on Equipment, Machinery	28	42
Inventory Tax Exemption on Goods in Transit (Freeport)	41	49
Tax Exemption on Manufacturers' Inventories	37	47
Sales/Use Tax Exemption on New Equipment	33	47
Tax Exemption on Raw Materials Used in Manufacturing	44	50
Tax Exemption to Encourage Research and Development	9	39
Accelerated Depreciation of Industrial Equipment	25	41

Number of States (0 to 50)

■ 1977 ▨ 1998

Source: Compiled by The Council of State Governments from January/February 1978 and October 1998 issues of *Site Selection*, Conway Data, Inc.

FIGURE 2

STATE FINANCIAL INCENTIVES FOR BUSINESS: CHANGES BETWEEN 1977-98

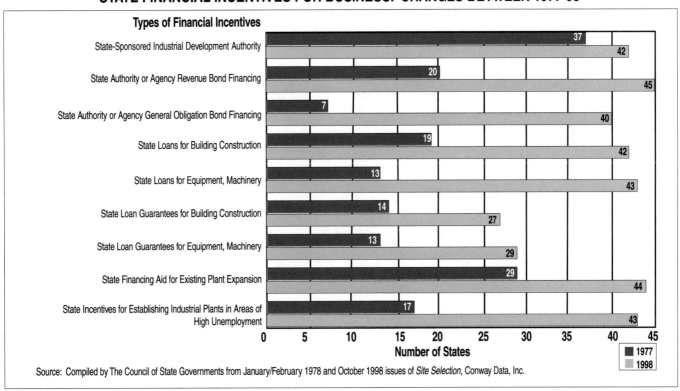

Types of Financial Incentives

Type	1977	1998
State-Sponsored Industrial Development Authority	37	42
State Authority or Agency Revenue Bond Financing	20	45
State Authority or Agency General Obligation Bond Financing	7	40
State Loans for Building Construction	19	42
State Loans for Equipment, Machinery	13	43
State Loan Guarantees for Building Construction	14	27
State Loan Guarantees for Equipment, Machinery	13	29
State Financing Aid for Existing Plant Expansion	29	44
State Incentives for Establishing Industrial Plants in Areas of High Unemployment	17	43

Number of States (0 to 45)

■ 1977 ▨ 1998

Source: Compiled by The Council of State Governments from January/February 1978 and October 1998 issues of *Site Selection*, Conway Data, Inc.

cially with the perception that everyone else is offering them.

Opponents of state business incentives argue:

• Tax and financial incentives are not the only factors considered in business-location decisions. Other components of the state business climate, such as geographical location, transportation, labor, raw materials, unions and infrastructure, are regarded as more important than business incentives. In reality, business incentives may have a minimal effect on business-location decisions.

• Incentives raise questions of inequity. For example, why should a few industries, especially manufacturing, receive preferential treatment when others, such as service industries, also need tax breaks and financial assistance from the states? Moreover, why should large firms be rewarded with more and larger incentive packages when most jobs are created by small- and medium-sized companies?

• Empirical studies show that business incentives are not cost-effective. No statistical evidence exists that incentives are effective in creating jobs. In most cases, costs of creating jobs by offering incentives are too high to justify.

• Incentives pull dollars away from the improvement of public services and infrastructure. The location or expansion of firms requires additional public services and infrastructure improvements, all of which must be paid for through the state or local governments' revenue base. Tax concessions and financial incentives can undermine state and local fiscal capacity. States and localities are better off if they instead allocate resources to improve other components of the business climate.

• Incentives create a self-defeating zero-sum game. As the use of business incentives spreads across the country, their individual effects cancel each other out. As a result, questions have been raised about the intrinsic value and usefulness of such incentives. A business incentive that is adopted by all states is equivalent to no incentive at all. And once the incentive is awarded it is extremely difficult to take away.

ISSUES AND IMPLICATIONS

The national surveys on state business incentive programs conducted by The Council of State Governments in 1994, 1996 and 1999 indicate that state policy-makers should consider adopting written guidelines and pay particular attention to information on incentive recipients' potential for job creation as well as reliable data evaluating the effectiveness of business incentives.

• *Guidelines.* Over the years, state economic development officials and legislative service agency staff have tried to develop standard guidelines to determine whether their states should offer tax and financial incentives to businesses. It appears that states have made some progress in this area. For example, in response to CSG's 1999 survey, only 24 states said they used written guidelines in deciding whether

to offer business incentives for economic development. That's up from 19 states in the 1994 survey.

• *Evaluation of costs and benefits.* In the 1999 CSG survey, 28 states indicated that they use a formal cost-benefit model to gauge the impact of tax and financial incentives. Cost-benefit analyses are needed to make informed decisions on the potential benefits or actual impacts of business incentives. In offering an incentive package to a new company, a state needs to consider the effects on a community's educational, environmental, health care, traffic, police, fire and public utility resources. State officials should regularly evaluate business incentive programs, not just when incentives are given. The agency doing the evaluation must have some political insulation. Governors and legislators should not rely solely on cost-benefit data prepared by consultants hired by the firms involved. They should seek additional information from sources having no direct interest in the case and identify those responsible for a customized incentive package so they might assess its integrity.

• *More information for decision-making.* The literature on state business incentives indicates that tax and financial incentives may be necessary and cost effective in certain targeted businesses or projects. States may offer tax and financial incentives primarily to assist existing small- and medium-sized business within the states. Most business incentive studies show that, in the past decade, eight out of 10 new jobs have been created by the expansion of existing in-state businesses, mostly small- and medium-sized firms. State policy-makers need to seek additional information when offering customized incentive packages. Some states have demonstrated the short-term success of customized incentives. Most business incentive studies, however, have concluded that tax and financial incentive packages provided to a single company have enormous opportunity costs, especially when the state is in a tight fiscal condition. Furthermore, there is no guarantee a large recipient firm will not later displace workers should the company restructure or the economy stagnate.

• *Interstate competition.* Continuous economic warfare among the states contributes little to the overall U.S. economy. State legislators and governors need to consider adopting tougher worker dislocation policies to deal with interstate competition for businesses. For example, some policy consultants argue, when a state lures a firm from another state, the "winning" state might be expected to pay the other state. This might include costs for an alternative use feasibility study of the abandoned facility, extended unemployment benefits for employees, job-training costs for employers and relocation costs for those employees desiring to relocate with the new facility.

POLICY CONSIDERATIONS

What should state policy-makers do to more effectively deal with the business-incentives issues?

• *Entrepreneurial policy with period evaluation.* State legisla-

STATE TAX INCENTIVES FOR BUSINESS, 1998

	Corporate Income Tax Exemption	Personal Income Tax Exemption	Excise Tax Exemption	Tax Exemption or Moratorium on Land, Captial Improvements	Tax Exemption or Moratorium on Equipment, Machinery	Inventory Tax Exemption on Goods in Transit (Freeport)	Tax Exemption on Manufacturers' Inventories	Sales/Use Tax Exemptions on New Equipment	Tax Exemption on Raw Materials Used in Manufacturing	Tax Incentive for Creation of Jobs	Tax Incentive for Industrial Investment	Tax Credits for Use of Specified State Products	Tax Stabilization Agreements for Specified Industries	Tax Exemption to Encourage Research and Development	Accelerated Depreciation of Industrial Equipment
ALABAMA	x	x	x	x	x	x	x	x	x	x	x				x
ALASKA		x	x	x				x	x				x		x
ARIZONA	x	x		x	x		x	x	x	x	x			x	x
ARKANSAS	x		x	x	x		x	x	x	x	x	x		x	x
CALIFORNIA		x	x	x	x	x	x	x	x	x	x			x	x
COLORADO	x		x		x	x	x	x	x	x	x				
CONNECTICUT	x			x	x	x	x	x	x	x	x			x	
DELAWARE	x	x	x	x	x	x	x	x	x	x	x			x	x
FLORIDA	x	x	x	x	x	x	x	x	x	x	x			x	x
GEORGIA				x	x	x	x	x	x	x	x				x
HAWAII	x	x	x		x	x	x	x	x	x			x	x	x
IDAHO	x				x	x	x	x	x		x			x	x
ILLINOIS	x	x	x	x	x	x	x	x	x	x	x			x	x
INDIANA	x	x		x	x	x	x	x	x	x	x			x	x
IOWA	x	x	x	x	x	x	x	x	x	x	x			x	x
KANSAS	x	x		x	x	x	x	x	x	x	x			x	x
KENTUCKY				x	x	x	x	x	x	x	x			x	x
LOUISIANA	x	x		x	x	x	x		x	x	x		x	x	x
MAINE	x	x		x	x	x	x	x	x	x	x			x	x
MARYLAND	x	x	x	x	x	x	x	x	x	x	x			x	x
MASSACHUSETTS	x	x	x	x	x	x	x	x	x	x	x		x	x	x
MICHIGAN	x	x		x	x	x	x	x	x	x	x				x
MINNESOTA			x	x	x	x	x	x	x	x			x	x	x
MISSISSIPPI	x	x		x	x	x	x	x	x	x	x			x	x
MISSOURI	x	x	x	x	x	x	x	x	x	x	x			x	x
MONTANA	x	x		x	x	x	x	x	x	x	x	x	x	x	x
NEBRASKA		x		x	x	x	x	x	x	x	x				x
NEVADA	x	x	x			x	x	x	x	x					
NEW HAMPSHIRE		x		x		x	x	x	x	x	x				x
NEW JERSEY	x	x		x	x	x	x	x	x	x	x			x	
NEW MEXICO				x	x	x	x	x	x		x			x	x
NEW YORK	x	x	x	x	x	x	x	x	x	x	x			x	
NORTH CAROLINA						x	x	x	x	x	x			x	
NORTH DAKOTA	x		x	x	x	x	x	x	x	x	x			x	
OHIO	x	x		x	x	x	x	x	x	x	x			x	x
OKLAHOMA	x	x	x	x	x	x		x	x	x	x	x	x	x	x
OREGON		x		x	x	x	x	x			x			x	x
PENNSYLVANIA	x		x	x	x	x	x	x	x	x	x	x		x	x
RHODE ISLAND		x		x	x	x	x	x	x	x	x	x	x	x	x
SOUTH CAROLINA	x			x	x	x	x	x	x	x	x			x	x
SOUTH DAKOTA	x	x	x	x		x	x		x	x	x			x	x
TENNESSEE	x	x	x	x	x	x	x	x	x		x			x	x
TEXAS	x	x		x	x	x		x	x	x	x				
UTAH					x	x	x	x	x	x					x
VERMONT			x			x	x	x	x				x		x
VIRGINIA	x	x		x	x	x	x	x	x	x	x			x	x
WASHINGTON	x	x	x			x	x	x	x	x	x			x	
WEST VIRGINIA	x	x		x		x		x	x	x	x	x	x	x	x
WISCONSIN	x	x			x	x	x	x	x	x	x			x	x
WYOMING	x	x	x			x	x			x					
STATE TOTALS	37	34	26	38	42	48	46	47	50	43	43	7	9	38	41

Source: Compiled by The Council of State Governments from October 1998 issue of *Site Selection*, Conway Data, Inc.

tors and governors may continue to use traditional economic-development programs that provide business incentives primarily to support their existing business base. They should evaluate the programs within the context of their guiding principles (see Table 5). They also need to develop a standard cost-benefit model to measure the effect of tax and financial incentives on the economy. They can measure cost-effectiveness by the ratio of benefits received by a company to the actual cost of the assistance provided by the government. The model should incorporate several factors, including the interaction of federal, state and local taxes; time flow of benefits generated by the firm; direct and secondary benefits (multipliers) and costs; time flow of costs to the state and local government; and the real value of the short- and long-term costs of incentives. One example of a cost-benefit model is the Regional Impact Model, developed by Regional Economic Modeling, Inc., to calculate financial returns of business incentives.

• *De-escalation of customized incentives in binding wars.* State policy-makers should refrain from offering large, customized incentive packages in bidding wars. In cases when customized incentives are provided, states should consider some form of controls to protect public subsidies offered to businesses. Such control measures may include "recision" (canceling a subsidy agreement), "clawbacks" (recovery of all or part of the subsidy costs), "penalties" (in case of nonperformance) and "recalibrations" (subsidy adjustments to reflect changing business conditions). Regarding interstate economic wars, state policy-makers may consider three possible approaches: laissez-faire, federal intervention or interstate cooperation.

• *Mutual cooperation between governors and corporate executives.* State leaders and corporate executives should collectively adopt and implement principles of mutual cooperation to guide them toward interstate cooperation for industrial development. Governors and legislative leaders should develop innovative solutions to interstate bidding contests. The principles of "mutual cooperation" adopted by the National Governors' Association in 1993 may be used as a starting point. Adopting a policy statement, however, may not be sufficient alone to change state and local incentive practices.

• *Improvement of the overall business climate.* State policy-makers should engage in strategic planning to improve their overall business climates. They should review regulatory barriers; business permits; workers' compensation systems; labor relations; environmental protection; transportation facilities; heath care; housing and construction, water and energy, banking and crime rates. Over the years, states' business climates have been evaluated and ranked by several private organizations, including Grant Thornton, Corporation for Economic Development and Conway Data, Inc. Each of these ranking systems is designed to assess the hospitality of the states to business.

• *Sustainable investment.* States should adopt sustainable development strategies that support human resources, infrastructure and environmental stewardship. State leaders might consider terminating or radically curtailing some monetary incentives that have not been cost-effective. States should instead improve education, job training and their infrastructure. There will be a greater demand in the future for workforce training as businesses change. Resources put into education will prepare the workforce of the future. State policy-makers also should consider ways to integrate long-term social, economic and environmental consideration into individual, business and governmental decisions. The goal should be to develop a statewide sustainable economy.

INTERSTATE COMPETITION:

Future Courses of Action

State policy-makers can consider three courses of action in dealing with interstate competition in job creation: status quo, federal intervention, and interstate and intergovernmental cooperation.

• Status Quo — This option would involve no new actions by state policy-makers, allowing the status quo to continue. The rationale behind this option is that individual states have the ultimate authority and discretion in dealing with their economic development policies, including the use of various business incentives.

Under this approach, tax and financial incentives can be offered by start-up businesses in selected industrial sectors — enterprise zones, export trade, research and development and firms hiring displaced workers under states' defense conversion projects. The best incentives are the ones that benefit entire communities, not just particular firms or certain projects.

• Federal Intervention — In the past several years, a federal approach has been proposed by some labor groups, bankers, state legislators and members of Congress. In 1993, for example, the Federation for Industrial Retention & Renewal declared that "workers and taxpayers are the losers in the 'state-eat-state' civil war over jobs." The groups called for a federal solution to "level the playing field." In its 1994 annual report, the Federal Reserve Bank of Minneapolis said, "Congress should end the economic war among the states." The report stated, "Only Congress has the power to enact legislation to prohibit and prevent the states from using subsidies and preferential taxes to compete with one another for businesses. In addition to its power under the commerce clause, Congress has the ancillary power it derives from its power to tax and appropriate money, and the power to make all laws that are needed to carry out its enumerated constitutional powers."

• Interstate Cooperation — While most states continue their existing business recruitment practices, some states have adopted a "no give-away" policy and have rejected incentive requests from businesses. Several governors have appealed to other states to agree to "non-aggression" pacts designed to de-escalate interstate competition. Even the governors and legislators in the states perceived

TABLE 4:
STATE FINANCIAL INCENTIVES FOR BUSINESS, 1998

	State-Sponsored Industrial Development Authority	Privately-Sponsored Development Credit Corporation	State Authority or Agency Revenue Bond Financing	State Authority or Agency General Obligation Bond Financing	City and/or County Revenue Bond Financing	City and/or County General Obligation Bond Financing	State Loans for Building Construction	State Loans for Equipment Machinery	City and/or County Loans for Building Construction	City and/or County Loans for Equipment, Machinery	State Loan Guarantees for Building Construction	State Loan Guarantees for Equipment, Machinery	State Financing Aid for Existing Plant Expansion	State Matching Funds for City and/or County Industrial Financing Programs	State Incentives for Establishing Industrial Plants in Areas of High Unemployment	City and/or County Incentives for Establishing Industrial Plants in Area of High Unemployment
ALABAMA	x	x	x		x	x	x	x	x	x			x	x	x	x
ALASKA	x	x	x	x	x	x	x	x	x	x	x	x	x	x	x	x
ARIZONA					x	x	x	x			x	x	x		x	x
ARKANSAS	x	x	x	x	x	x	x	x	x	x	x	x	x		x	x
CALIFORNIA	x	x	x	x		x	x	x	x	x	x	x	x		x	x
COLORADO	x	x			x			x	x	x	x	x	x	x	x	x
CONNECTICUT	x	x	x	x	x	x	x	x	x	x	x	x	x	x	x	x
DELAWARE	x	x	x		x		x	x	x	x			x	x	x	x
FLORIDA		x	x		x	x	x	x	x	x			x		x	x
GEORGIA	x	x	x		x	x				x	x				x	x
HAWAII	x		x	x	x	x		x					x		x	x
IDAHO		x			x	x			x	x						
ILLINOIS	x	x	x		x		x	x	x	x			x		x	x
INDIANA	x	x	x		x	x	x	x	x	x	x	x	x	x	x	x
IOWA	x	x	x		x	x	x	x	x	x	x	x	x	x	x	x
KANSAS		x		x	x	x			x	x		x	x		x	x
KENTUCKY	x		x	x	x	x	x	x	x	x			x	x	x	x
LOUISIANA		x	x	x	x	x	x	x	x	x	x	x	x	x	x	x
MAINE	x		x		x	x	x	x	x	x	x	x	x		x	x
MARYLAND	x	x	x	x	x	x	x	x	x	x	x	x	x	x	x	x
MASSACHUSETTS	x	x	x		x	x	x	x	x	x	x	x	x	x	x	x
MICHIGAN	x	x	x		x	x	x	x	x	x			x	x	x	x
MINNESOTA	x	x	x	x	x	x	x	x	x	x			x	x	x	
MISSISSIPPI	x	x	x	x	x	x	x	x	x	x	x	x	x		x	x
MISSOURI	x	x	x		x	x	x	x	x	x	x	x	x		x	x
MONTANA		x	x	x	x	x	x	x	x	x			x			
NEBRASKA	x	x	x	x		x	x	x	x	x	x	x	x	x	x	x
NEVADA	x	x	x	x	x				x	x					x	x
NEW HAMPSHIRE	x	x	x		x	x			x	x	x	x	x			
NEW JERSEY	x		x		x	x	x	x	x	x			x		x	x
NEW MEXICO	x	x	x	x	x	x	x	x	x	x			x		x	x
NEW YORK	x	x	x	x	x			x	x	x	x	x	x		x	x
NORTH CAROLINA	x				x	x			x	x					x	
NORTH DAKOTA		x	x	x	x	x	x	x	x	x	x	x	x		x	x
OHIO	x	x	x		x		x	x	x	x			x	x	x	x
OKLAHOMA	x	x	x	x	x	x	x	x	x	x	x	x	x	x	x	x
OREGON	x	x	x	x	x	x	x	x	x	x	x	x	x	x	x	x
PENNSYLVANIA	x	x	x	x	x	x	x	x	x	x	x	x	x	x	x	x
RHODE ISLAND	x	x	x	x	x		x	x	x	x	x	x	x	x	x	x
SOUTH CAROLINA	x	x	x		x	x		x	x	x			x		x	x
SOUTH DAKOTA	x		x	x	x	x	x	x	x	x			x	x	x	
TENNESSEE		x	x	x	x	x	x	x	x	x	x	x	x	x	x	
TEXAS	x	x	x	x	x	x	x	x	x	x	x	x	x	x	x	x
UTAH	x	x			x	x			x	x					x	
VERMONT	x	x	x		x	x	x	x	x	x	x	x	x	x	x	
VIRGINIA	x	x	x		x	x	x	x	x	x			x		x	x
WASHINGTON	x	x	x		x			x				x		x	x	x
WEST VIRGINIA	x	x	x		x		x	x	x	x	x	x	x	x		
WISCONSIN	x		x		x	x	x	x	x	x			x		x	
WYOMING	x	x	x		x	x	x	x	x	x	x	x	x	x		
STATE TOTALS	42	39	45	24	49	41	42	43	47	47	28	30	44	27	43	37

Source: Compiled by The Council of State Governments from October 1998 issue of *Site Selection*, Conway Data, Inc.

as "winners" in recent bidding wars tend to agree that states should not focus too much on monetary incentives when competing with other states for jobs. Efforts to stop the economic wars have been made by several neighboring states. But none of these efforts has been effective in de-escalating or ending the ongoing interstate bidding wars.

CONCLUSION

There are signs for change in state practices in offering business incentives. As the most recent CSG survey shows, a majority of the states are likely to maintain their business incentive activities at current levels in the next few years, rather than escalating the intensity of interstate competition. More states are enacting laws to treat new and existing firms equally in offering business incentives. Also, an increasing number of states are reforming their business regulations, including permits, environmental protection and workers' compensation laws. Finally, the past few years witnessed efforts to raise the business incentives issue to the regional and national level in search for a solution to the economic war among the states. As long as interstate competition for business and industries continues, the debate on business incentive programs is likely to continue for some time.

TABLE 5

A GUIDE FOR LEGISLATORS FOR EVALUATING JOB CREATION PROPOSALS

State legislators need to use written guidelines when considering business incentive packages. The following list of suggestions might be useful in designing state guides. Not all questions are appropriate to all programs and all states.

Evaluating Job Creation Proposals for New Businesses:

- Does the proposed job creation proposal fit within the framework of the state's economic development policy?
- Does the proposal have specific missions and goals?
- Are these goals likely to be achieved by this proposal?
- Does the proposal provide for a way to monitor its success?
- Why is the proposal being created?
- What are the projected short-term and long-term costs of the proposal?
- Is there some way to provide a service other than through a government program?
- Can a market problem be addressed by changing rules and regulations instead of creating a program?
- Does the proposal help every business or only a small number of businesses?
- If the proposal is targeted to a narrow sector of the economy, is it a sector the state wants to target?
- Will the program help diversify the state's economy?
- Is there a provision for return of the state's investment if certain criteria are not met?
- If the proposal provides direct assistance to certain companies, will a company benefiting from a state program be asked to report on its compliance with program standards?
- Does the state want to give a competitive advantage to a specific company the state provides?
- Should government provide such services as direct financing at all, or should the state provide more basic services such as job training and information?
- Is the legislature getting the right kind of data upon which to base programs and policy?

Evaluating Existing Programs:

- Is the program meeting its goals?
- Has the program outlived its usefulness?
- Has the program been monitored by the agency on a regular basis?
- Has the state development agency surveyed businesses to see if they were satisfied with the assistance they received through various state programs?
- Is the agency overstating the multiplier effect of a particular program?
- Has the agency calculated the actual costs of the program?
- Are the benefits of a program being accurately interpreted? Are the job creation figures accurate?
- Is the program meeting acceptable criteria for state investment?
- Has the program been audited?
- Does the agency have a uniform and standard policy for collecting data such as job creation figures?
- Has the agency conducted site visits to monitor its investment?
- Is the state agency's program evaluation based on verifiable data or on projections?
- Has the economic impact of a project been accurately detailed?

Source: Compiled from "Monitoring State Economic Development Programs: A Guide for Legislators," Midwestern Office, The Council of State Governments, 1991.

SAMPLE PAGE

State profiles contain the following information:

Legislative Timeline:

This section highlights major legislation on business incentives over the past 10 years (1990-1999). Information in this section was extracted from Conway Data, Inc.'s annual surveys of state economic development officials.

TAX INCENTIVES:

"Tax incentives" include any credits or abatements of corporate income, personal income, sales-and-use, property or other business taxes to create, retain or lure businesses.

FINANCIAL INCENTIVES:

"Financial incentives" include any type of direct loan, loan guarantee, grant, infrastructure development, or job training assistance offered to help create, retain or lure businesses. Since every state has state and local industrial development bond issues, this section is for non-bond, financial incentives. Also, federal financial assistance programs for businesses are not included in this section as such programs are available in every state.

OTHER INCENTIVES:

This section highlights information on state-funded programs that do not fall under the categories of typical tax or financial incentives.

Examples of other incentives include job-training, public-private partnerships, airport assistance, environmental regulation, regulatory relief, child care facilities, and research and development programs.

SUCCESSFUL INCENTIVES:

The last section in selected states highlights examples of the most successful programs. Business incentive programs summarized in this section were chosen by respondents to the 1999 survey conducted by The Council of State Governments.

CONTACT:

Name of individual who may be contacted for more information on the state's business incentives.

ALABAMA

TAX INCENTIVES:

- **Corporate income tax.** 5.0 percent.

- **Personal income tax.** 2.0 to 5.0 percent.

- **Sales and use tax.** 4.0 percent. An exemption from the sales and use tax is offered on equipment or materials purchased primarily for the control, reduction or elimination of air or water pollution.

- **Capital Investment Tax Credit Summary.** This program allows qualifying companies to claim a tax credit against their Alabama income tax liability generated by or arising out of a qualifying Alabama project in the amount of 5 percent of total capital investment each year for 20 years, beginning in the year the project is placed in service. Eligible businesses include process or treatment facilities which recycle, reclaim or convert materials to a reusable product; and corporate headquarters facilities.

- **Enterprise Zone Incentives (EZI).** The Alabama EZI is another marketing tool to help attract new businesses to Alabama. The Alabama Enterprise Zone Act was passed by the Alabama Legislature in 1987. Twenty-seven Enterprise Zones across the state encourage economic growth in areas considered to have depressed economies. Each area offers innovative packages of local tax and non-tax incentives to encourage businesses to locate in their Enterprise Zones.

- **Ad Valorem (Property) Tax.** All equipment, facilities or materials constructed or acquired primarily for the control, reduction or elimination of air or water pollution are statutorily exempt from ad valorem taxation.

- **Corporation Income Tax.** This is another deduction offered for pollution control equipment/materials. All amounts invested in pollution control equipment/materials acquired or constructed in Alabama primarily for the control, reduction or elimination of air or water pollution are deducted directly from income apportioned to Alabama.

FINANCIAL INCENTIVES:

- **Industrial Revenue Bonds (IRBs).** IRBs are financing instruments issued by designated local industrial development boards (IDBs) or other issuers authorized by state law. Since 1949, IRBs have been a preferred method of financing used by industries locating to and expanding in Alabama. Often, financial institutions and other intermediaries participate by providing letters of credit backing the bonds. Thus, the company seeking the bonds must be considered creditworthy by the financial institution.

- **Alabama Plan for Linked Deposits.** The Alabama Plan for Linked Deposits is a program operated as a division of the State Treasurer's Office. It allows the State Treasurer to make deposits in state banks on which banks pay 2 percent below the normal interest rate paid to the state for its funds. The reduction in the interest rate paid by the bank must be passed on to the borrowers on loans qualifying for this program. It amounts to a 2 percent subsidy on the borrower's interest rates for two years to help stimulate economic growth in the state.

LEGISLATIVE TIMELINE:

1990: Instituted an enterprise-zone program in economically distressed areas and offered tax credits.

1992: Passed legislation to promote research and development in the state's aerospace industry.

1993: Enacted a 1 percent or higher decrease in taxes.

1994: Created a new economic development program offering income tax incentives to eligible companies.

1995: Revised the legislature's economic development incentive program, allowing new and expanding industries to write off 5 percent of their construction costs each year for 20 years against their state income taxes.

1996: Enacted new tax exemptions for businesses that employ at least 1,200 people and make capital investments and improvements of at least $75 million within an enterprise zone.

1999: Passed legislation to create a special fund known as the Alabama 21st Century Fund, into which tobacco revenues will be deposited and the funds used for the issuance of bonds in limited amounts for purposes of economic development and industrial recruitment.

- **Revolving Loan Funds.** Revolving Loan Funds are locally controlled sources of capital which may be used to finance start-up and existing businesses whose projects will create permanent jobs. The Revolving Loan Funds are not designed to compete with the banking community but to complement it by providing gap financing between what the bank can reasonably lend on a project and what the business can provide in equity.

- **USDA Rural Development.** Efforts to strengthen the economy of rural communities include the USDA Rural Development community and business programs, which can provide guaranteed loans, direct loans and grants in qualified rural areas and towns.

- **SBA 504 Loan.** This combination-type loan package provides the small business with a better financial package than is otherwise available in the market. The private lender (bank) makes a loan of only 50 percent of the project cost and still receives first mortgage. The SBA makes a subordinated second loan of 40 percent of the project cost. The business owner is only required to provide 10 percent to 20 percent equity. The loan program is used for the purchase of land, buildings, machinery and equipment for new and expanding businesses. It is structured as a subordinated gap financing loan. Certified development corporations can package the loan and present the total project to the SBA for approval.

- **Appalachian Regional Grant.** The Appalachian Regional Commission (ARC) provides supplemental funding for economic development projects under its Area Economic and Human Resources Development Program. These funds can supplement another federal or state-administered federal fund up to a total of 80 percent federal funding in a project. Eligible activities include access roads, water and sewer system installation, rail spurs and dock facilities. No grant funds may be expended on any form of electric power transmission or land acquisition costs. A committed industry, either new or expanding, is mandatory. No speculative projects will be considered. Factors to be considered in an application include number of new jobs to be created by the project and capital investment. There are 37 counties in North Alabama that are within the ARC region.

- **Commercial Lending Sources.** Commercial lenders provide a high percentage of the capital and liquid needs for new and expanding industry. The requirements by lending institutions are basically the same and loan decisions are made quickly when a company has a well-prepared business plan and comprehensive financial information. While lenders will vary in the type of loans they extend, as well as amounts and terms under which financing may be available, the applicant has an advantage if all financial information is submitted in a well-organized format. The plan should also be realistic in the area of future growth expectations. Alabama's commercial lending institutions work well with the Alabama Economic Development Loan Program, Small Business Administration, and other government agencies which may guarantee loans in order to help businesses acquire financing which they otherwise might not be able to obtain.

- **Alabama Industrial Access Road and Bridge Program.** The Alabama Industrial Access Road & Bridge Corporation was created through legislation in May 1985, and provides funding for industrial access road and bridge construction in Alabama. The Department of Transportation (DOT) administers this program and reviews applications from an engineering standpoint. The Alabama Development Office (ADO) reviews each application to insure economic viability of projects. The results of both reviews are presented to the Industrial Access Bond Authority for consideration. The members include the DOT Director, the State Treasurer, and the State Finance Director.

- **SBA 7A Loan.** The SBA 7A Loan program can provide small businesses with long-term financing for real estate acquisition, building construction, renovation, expansion, purchase of machinery and equipment, purchase of inventory and working capital. Repayment of debt is also permitted where existing short-term credit is not meeting the financial needs of the business.

OTHER INCENTIVES:

- **International Incentives.** To facilitate foreign investment, Alabama has The Alabama Development Office (ADO) - Industrial Recruitment Division and ADO - International Trade Division. For export assistance there is the Alabama Foreign Trade Commission, the Alabama Department of Agriculture and Industries, ADO - International Trade Division, The University of Alabama-University Center for Economic Development, The Alabama State Docks, and The Alabama Forestry Commission.

- **Technology Incentives.** The Alabama Technology Network, the Alabama Commission on Aerospace, Science and Industry, and the NASA Technology Transfer Program assist in the development of new technology.

- **Public/Private Partnership.** The Retirement System of Alabama is a public/private partnership that totals $22 billion for the Public Pension Fund.

Contact:

Mr. Gene Crum
Economic Development Director
Alabama Development Office
401 Adams Ave., Suite 640
Montgomery, AL 36130
(334) 242-0474

TAX INCENTIVES:

- **Corporate income tax.** 5.0 percent.

- **Personal income tax.** None.

- **Sales and use tax.** None.

- **Depreciable Property.** Eighteen percent of the federal income tax credit for investment in specified depreciable property can be applied to Alaska state corporate income tax. Each tax year, as the property is put into use, up to $20 million of qualified investments may be claimed with the exception of the unlimited credit allowed on pollution control facilities.

- **Work Opportunity Tax Credit (WOTC).** WOTC offers employers tax credits as an incentive to hire people from seven target groups including Alaska Temporary Assistance Program (ATAP) and Aid for Families with Dependent Children (AFDC) recipients, food stamp recipients, veterans, vocational rehabilitation recipients, ex-felons and high risk youth. The credit amount is 40 percent of up to $6,000 in qualified first year wages with maximum credit of $2,400.

- **Welfare-to-Work Tax Credit (W2W).** The W2W tax credit is available for hiring long-term ATAP and AFDC clients. The W2W tax credit is 35 percent of the first $10,000 in wages paid the first year, and 50 percent of the first $10,000 paid for the second year. The maximum tax credit is $3,500 the first year and $5,000 the second year, for a total of $8,500.

- **Exploration Incentive.** Up to $20 million in qualifying costs can be credited against future state corporate income tax, mining license tax and production royalties. Geophysical and geochemical surveys, trenching, bulk sampling, drilling, metallurgical testing and underground exploration are included as qualifying costs. Unused credit can be retained for 15 years and may be assigned to successors in interest.

FINANCIAL INCENTIVES:

- **Community Development Block Grant Program.** Among other services, this program may fund special economic development activities in communities that will result in the creation of jobs for low and moderate income people. All municipal governments in Alaska with the exception of Anchorage are eligible for block grants of up to $200,000 as long as 51 percent of the people have low to moderate incomes.

- **Alaska Science and Technology Foundation Grants.** Major individual grants of over $2,000 and group grants are both available under this program. Projects that provide economic development, direct benefits and utilize end user participation are considered ideal. ASTF typically requires a financial match equal to the amount they contribute and technology projects that develop a product or process are required to repay ASTF funds through revenue, license fees or profit from sales of the product.

LEGISLATIVE TIMELINE:

1991: Repealed a unitary tax.

1992: Enacted laws providing new financing options for state businesses and expanded the state's limited business partnership law to encourage more investments from out of state.

1993: Enacted laws providing funding for road maintenance, port development and for upgrading water and sewer service in rural areas and created a Small Business Assistance Program to provide technical advice to small firms to help them comply with federal clean-air regulations.

1994: Enacted a law that provides employers immunity from civil lawsuits regarding job performance information. Enacted a law limiting pollution lawsuits by landowners against nearby companies.

1995: Enacted several new economic development laws that target oil, mining and high-tech industries.

1996: Passed a tax incentive for the mining industry; corporate income tax rebates for up to five years will help offset the cost of mineral exploration.

1997: Substantially increased taxes on products containing tobacco. Established an international trade and business endowment.

1998: Established a grant program to aid the development of new businesses in the state.

• **Power Project Fund.** This provides loans to local utilities, local governments or independent power producers for the development or upgrade of electric power facilities, including conservation bulk fuel storage and waste energy conservation, or potable water supply projects. Loan term is related to the life of the project.

• **The Polaris Fund.** The purpose of the Polaris Fund is to finance young companies with potential to achieve profitable sales by providing equity capital. Ideal companies should have an experienced management team, an innovative, distinctive product with a $100 - $500 million growing market and a well-defined channel for sales. Polaris investments are usually in the $100,000 to $500,000 range, and favor companies that align Polaris closely with management.

• **Business Incentive Program.** Under this program companies will be reimbursed (rather than paid up front) for designated portions of relocation costs, site development costs, special employee training not covered by other programs, and special analysis of sites in Alaska. The program was passed into law in April 1998 and is limited to $3 million annually.

• **Alaska Product Preference, Forest Product Preference and The Alaska Recycled Product Preference Programs.** These programs provide incentives for Alaska businesses responding to bids or proposals for state contracts by giving preferential consideration. The Alaska Product Preference program and the Alaska Forest Product Preference Program can provide a cost preference of up to 7 percent, while the Recycled Product Preference Program offers a 5 percent preference.

• **Small Business Economic Development Revolving Loan Fund.** The purpose of the program is to provide private sector employment in the areas designated by EDA. The maximum loan amount is $300,000. Applicants are required to obtain additional private, non-public financing of approximately twice the amount requested. The interest rate of prime minus 4 points is set by the Loan Administration Board consisting of three members from the existing divisional loan committee and two members from the private sector. The board is responsible for setting loan policy and for making all major loan decisions.

• **Commercial Fishing Revolving Loan Fund.** Commercial fishing loans are available for various purposes at prime plus two percent (up to a maximum of 10.5 percent) for a 15-year term. All loans must be secured by adequate collateral:

1. Section A loans ($300,000 maximum) are available to eligible commercial fishers for the purchase of Alaska Commercial Fishing Limited Entry Permits or the upgrade of an existing vessel or gear to improve the quality of Alaska seafood.

2. Section B loans ($100,000 maximum) are available to eligible individuals to purchase limited entry permits or to purchase, repair, or upgrade vessels or gear.

3. Section C loans ($300,000 maximum) are available to eligible individuals for the purchase of quota shares for halibut or sablefish fisheries.

OTHER INCENTIVES:

• **Alaska Industrial Development Export Authority (AIDEA).** AIDEA assists businesses through different programs:

1. Loan Participation – Eligible projects include commercial facilities such as office buildings, warehouses, retail establishments, hotels and manufacturing facilities. AIDEA participation may total up to 80 percent of a commercial lending institution loan with a maximum of $10 million.

2. Business and Export Assistance – This loan guarantee program provides financial institutions with up to an 80 percent guarantee on the principal of a loan.

3. Accelerated Amortization Program – Under this program, AIDEA may allow the financial institution to amortize its portion of the loan using an accelerated amortization schedule if the project can support the increased debt service, and if the shortened schedule is necessary for the bank's participation. Borrowers may obtain such financing for manufacturing facilities, real estate and equipment under the Loan Participation Program.

4. Development Finance – AIDEA may own and operate projects that provide infrastructure support for resource development and bring economic benefit to Alaska. To qualify, a project must be endorsed by the local government where the project will be sited and be economically feasible.

• **Alaska Growth Capital.** This is a commercial financial institution, licensed and regulated by the State of Alaska. It is not regulated as a bank, but rather as a Business and Industrial Development Corporation (BIDCO). BIDCOs do not accept deposits and do not do consumer lending.

Contact:

William G. Paulick
Industrial Developer
Division of Trade & Development
P.O. Box 110804
Juneau, AK 99811-0804
(907) 465-3961

ARIZONA

TAX INCENTIVES:

- **Corporate income tax.** 9.0 percent.

- **Personal income tax.** 2.9 to 5.2 percent.

- **Sales and use tax.** 5.0 percent.

- **Enterprise Zone Program**. The program has two incentive components (at least 35 percent of the workforce must be hired within the boundaries of the zone in order to qualify for either incentive): 1) Income Tax Credits are available to any non-retail business that creates net new quality jobs. A "quality job" is full-time and permanent, pays an hourly wage above a certain level and provides at least 50 percent of the health insurance costs for the employee. Businesses can receive up to $3,000 in tax credits per job retained over three years. A five-year carry forward is allowed for unused credits. 2) Property Tax Reclassification is available to manufacturing businesses that are either woman or minority owned or "independently owned and operated" and "small." These businesses must make at least a $2 million investment in fixed capital assets. All property is reclassified from a 25 percent assessment ratio to a 5 percent assessment ratio for five years.

- **Research & Development Income Tax Credit.** If the state exceeds its forecasted revenues by a certain level in either 1999 or 2000, the research and development tax credit will undergo revision. The maximum allowable limits on the credit, but reduces the credit on qualified expenses over $2.5 million to 11 percent from 20 percent. However, the first $2.5 million of qualified expenses allowable as a credit in a taxable year would remain at 20 percent. It would clarify that any unused credits from a taxable year, instead of expenses in excess of the allowable credit, can be carried forward for up to 15 years. It also extends the credit to partnerships and subchapter S corporations and makes the credit permanent by eliminating the expiration date.

- **Defense Restructuring Program.** The program is intended to maintain and attract the maximum share of available U.S. Department of Defense (DOD) contracts. The Arizona Department of Commerce is authorized to certify eligible contractors until June 30, 2001. The goals of the legislation are to: assist qualified defense contractors in maintaining and attracting available contracts with the DOD, encourage qualified defense contractors to diversify into commercial markets and consolidate facilities in Arizona, and encourage qualified defense contractors to adopt new manufacturing processes and technologies. Under current Arizona law, a "qualified defense contractor" must meet all of the following requirements: employ at least 200 full-time equivalent employee positions in Arizona working on DOD contracts, have one or more current contracts directly with the DOD that: a) total at least $5 million in sales of tangible personal property manufactured, assembled, fabricated, researched, developed or designed in Arizona and, b) do not require provision of products or services directly to a particular military base or installation.

LEGISLATIVE TIMELINE:

1990: Passed a $20 million tax increase to balance the state budget.

1991: Revised the state corporate income tax, doubling the sales portion of the formula used to compute the levy.

1992: Established property and income tax incentives for businesses locating in designated military reuse zones. Passed legislation designed to make the state more attractive to aerospace firms and established R&D tax credits.

1993: Created an Environmental Technology Manufacturing Assistance Program to provide investment tax credits and sales and use tax exemptions. Provided research grant funds for emerging Arizona-based technology companies.

1994: Reduced the state's corporate income tax rate. Established individual and corporate income tax credits for the purchase of pollution control equipment.

1995: Passed a $431.7 million tax relief package including reductions in income tax and property taxes. Provided funding for the state's European Trade Office and the state's North American Free Trade Agreement strategy.

1996: Modified the state's enterprise zone program and extended it to 2001. Enacted incentives for satellite television facilities that exclude some telecommunications services and some tangible personal property from sales and use taxes.

1999: Extended the corporate income tax credit for construction materials from December 31, 1999 to December 31, 2004 (i.e. five years).

ARIZONA

FINANCIAL INCENTIVES:

- **Revolving Energy Loans for Arizona (RELA)**. The RELA program, administered by the Arizona Department, offers financial assistance to qualified Arizona businesses for the following uses: 1) fixed asset plant expansion for manufacturers of energy conserving products, 2) energy conserving building retrofits, including the acquisition of qualified energy conserving improvements and equipment. Qualified businesses include existing for-profit businesses, nonprofit organizations and political subdivisions, existing manufacturers of renewable energy, alternative energy or energy conserving products, existing companies that are acquiring renewable energy or energy conserving products for use. Loans requests may range from $10,000 to $500,000 (up to 60 percent of total project costs). The interest rate is 5 percent APR, fixed for the loan. The 1 percent up-front origination fee may also be financed and repaid as part of the loan. Repayment terms are structured within RELA program guidelines and are tailored to the payback for the specific project.

- **Commerce and Economic Development Fund.** The Commerce and Economic Development Commission Fund provides financial assistance (loans, loan guarantees, and interest rate subsidies) to businesses locating or expanding in Arizona. Eligible applicants include businesses, universities, and nonprofit economic development organizations. Financial assistance may range from $10,000 to $1 million, or up to 50 percent of the total project financing needs, whichever is less. CEDC program funds are generally designated for financing fixed assets such as plant, machinery and equipment. Interest rates are usually fixed at a spread below the current market interest rate. Loan term usually coincide with those offered by private lenders for the project and, in most cases, correspond to the useful life of the assets. The CEDC program is not a stand-alone financing source, but rather serves to compliment and work in conjunction with other private sector financing sources.

- **The Work Force Recruitment and Job Training Program.** The Work Force Recruitment and Job Training (WFRJT) Program provides grants for short-term customized training for new employees and retraining for companies undergoing economic conversion. The training must be job and business specific. The program will be funded at $6 million in 1999 and $7 million in 2000. State law stipulates that 25 percent of the fund is dedicated for small businesses (less than 100 employees) and 25 percent is dedicated for businesses located in rural communities. The program can fund up to 75 percent of the total eligible cost with the company contributing at least 25 percent of the eligible cost. Eligible companies must have a profitable history of at least two years.

OTHER INCENTIVES:

- **International Trade & Investment.** The International Trade & Investment Division within the Arizona Department of Commerce has a dual mission of helping Arizona businesses successfully expand in foreign markets and attracting foreign investment to Arizona. This mission is accomplished through educating Arizona individuals and businesses on how to export; promoting Arizona businesses abroad and matching them with foreign buyers; promoting Arizona; and publishing documents related to international trade. Arizona has foreign trade offices in Europe, Japan, Taiwan and Mexico.

- **Research and Development.** Research and Development Tax Credit for technology sectors; Defense Restructuring for the aerospace industry; Accelerated depreciation for business property, providing tax savings to capital-intensive industries.

- **Regulatory Relief Programs.** The state has undergone a process of streamlining the regulatory appeals process for businesses. In addition, state agencies and departments have specified time limits for promulgating administrative rules affecting businesses.

- **Public/Private Partnerships.** The Governor's Strategic Partnership for Economic Development (GSPED) is a public/private partnership that enhances the competitiveness of Arizona's economy through export-driven industry clusters and linking its activities with workforce development.

Contact:

Dean Miller
Arizona Dept. of Commerce
3800 N. Central Ave., Ste. 1500
Phoenix, AZ 85012
(602) 280-1396

TAX INCENTIVES:

- **Corporate income tax.** 1.0 - 6.5 percent.

- **Personal income tax.** 1.0 - 7.0 percent.

- **Sales and use tax.** 4.265 percent. Exemptions from sales and use taxes include property that becomes a recognizable, integral part of property manufactured, compounded, processed or assembled for resale; machinery and equipment used directly in manufacturing that are purchased for a new manufacturing facility or to replace existing machinery or equipment; machinery and equipment required by Arkansas law to be purchased for air or water pollution control; and waste fuel used for manufacturing. Arkansas exempts the following agricultural items from sales and use taxes: feedstuffs for livestock, agri-chemicals, and new and used farm machinery and equipment. Catalysts, chemicals, reagents and solutions that are consumed or used in manufacturing, producing, fabricating or processing are also exempt.

- **The Arkansas Economic Investment Tax Credit Act.** This program offers a credit against state sales and use tax liability of 7 percent of the amount of the total project cost, not to exceed 50 percent of the total sales and use tax liability. To qualify for the investment sales and use tax credit, a company must be a manufacturer in SIC codes 20 through 39 in continuous operation in Arkansas for at least two years prior to the initial application; invest at least $5 million (or $6 million of projects involving multiple Arkansas locations) in a plant construction or expansion project; obtain a direct pay sales and use tax permit from the Revenue Division of the Department of Finance and Administration (DF&A); and submit a project plan to the director of the Arkansas Department of Economic Development 30 days prior to construction. To be eligible to receive the sales and use tax credits, the company must submit an application and a project plan to the department which must approve the company's application and project plan. If approved, the DF&A monitors and administers the program.

- **Arkansas Enterprise Zone Program Incentives.** The Enterprise Zone Program offers three incentives: (1) a state income tax credit for each new position or job created based on the average wage of new workers multiplied by 100 in areas with unemployment rates equal to or in excess of 50 percent of the state's average unemployment rate for the previous calendar year. The above formula used is 400 times the average hourly wage. The cap is $6000 per employee in high unemployment counties. The cap is $3000 per employee in other counties; (2) a refund of sales and use taxes on the purchase of materials used in construction of a new facility or expansion of an existing facility; and (3) a refund of sales and use taxes on machinery and equipment to be used in connection with the business. To qualify for the Arkansas Enterprise Zone Program, a company must meet job creation criteria and prove the new employees are Arkansas residents during the year in which the credits are earned.

LEGISLATIVE TIMELINE:

1991: Created a linked-deposit program to provide low-interest loans for small businesses and agricultural enterprises. Approved a one-half percent corporate income tax increase to help fund the state's vocational technical schools.

1992: Passed the Aerospace Enterprise Zone Act which offers sales and use and income tax credits to eligible companies.

1993: Passed a reform bill making workers' compensation more affordable for employers. Established a sales and use tax exemption for businesses to build and equip child-care facilities. Established a new financing program which made $36 million available for loans to businesses with above-average risk.

1995: Authorized the Arkansas Development Finance Authority to take an equity position with banks and other investors to make more venture capital available to small businesses. Amended the state's Enterprise Zone Program to include biotechnology firms. Passed a new law to provide funding assistance to Arkansas companies for upgrading worker skills.

1996: Passed a constitutional amendment to increase the state sales and use tax by one-eighth percent to fund capital improvements to Arkansas state parks and natural attractions. The change went into effect July 1, 1997.

1999: Revised existing business identities programs to include high-tech, knowledge-based industries. Reduced capital gains taxes. Created small business loan programs.

FINANCIAL INCENTIVES:

• **The Arkansas Science and Technology Authority (ASTA) Investment Fund.** The ASTA administers a special investment fund of $2.8 million which can provide seed capital for new and developing technology-based businesses through loans, royalty agreements and limited stock purchases. ASTA also administers $1 million for grants to colleges and universities for basic and applied research. The Applied Research Partnership Program requires a matching grant from a private sector sponsor. In addition, ASTA administers a program that encourages the transfer of technology from the laboratory to the manufacturing or processing plant.

OTHER INCENTIVES:

• **Foreign Investment.** The Arkansas Department of Economic Development maintains four foreign offices in Japan, Belgium, Mexico and Malaysia.

• **Trade and Export Development.** Trade and export programs are available to assist businesses in expanding and diversifying their markets. Programs range from organizing trade shows, catalog shows, and trade missions to hands-on assistance to help businesses identify and penetrate international markets and learn the mechanics of trade, including export, trade and documentation. Four international offices (located in Europe, Latin America, Japan and Southeast Asia) support this effort through research, meeting scheduling and consultation for Arkansas businesses.

• **Arkansas Biotechnology Development and Training Act of 1997 and Arkansas Emerging Energy Technology Development Act.** The purpose of these Acts is to offer several income tax credits furthering biotechnical business development and to encourage businesses to purchase or construct a facility that designs, develops or produces photovoltaics (solar cells), electric vehicle components or fuel cells.

• **Arkansas Child Care Facility Incentive Program.** Businesses can receive a sales and use tax refund on the initial cost of construction materials and furnishing purchased to build and equip an approved child care facility. Additionally, a corporate income tax credit of 3.9 percent of the total annual payroll of the workers employed exclusively to provide child care services, or a $5,000 income tax credit for the first year the business provides its employees with a child care facility is also available.

• **Public/Private Partnership.** The Arkansas Capital Corporation (ACC) is a privately owned, non-profit organization established in 1957 to serve as an alternative source of financing for businesses in Arkansas. Its main goal is to improve the economic climate in the state by providing long-term, fixed-rate loans to Arkansas businesses. As a preferred lender for the Small Business Administration, ACC makes loans to existing operations and business start-ups for everything from new construction and equipment to working capital. ACC loans may be used in combination with bank loans, municipal bond issues or other sources of financing.

Contact:

Gregory Dale
Incentives Coordinator
Arkansas Department of Economic Development
One Capital Mall
Little Rock, AR 72201
(501) 682-7310

TAX INCENTIVES:

• **Corporate income tax.** 8.84 percent.

• **Personal income tax**. 1.0 to 9.3 percent.

• **Sales and use tax**. 6.0 percent.

• **Manufacturers' Investment Credit.** A 6 percent manufacturers' investment credit for the purchase or lease of manufacturing equipment which is "depreciable" under certain federal regulations. In addition, "special purpose buildings and foundations," (i.e. clean rooms) for certain electronics manufacturers, semiconductor equipment manufacturers, commercial space satellite manufacturers, and property related to specific biopharmaceutical activity are eligible for this credit. The credit can be claimed against the bank and corporation's tax or the alternative minimum tax. Any unused credit can be carried forward for up to 8 years. Specified biopharmaceutical and biotech activities of start-up companies benefit from net operating loss carryover and enhanced carry forward of the manufacturer's investment credit. The state also provides start-up companies the option of a 5 percent partial sales or use tax exemption on all qualifying manufacturing property purchased or leased during the company's first three years of operation. Commercial parts are now exempt from sales tax. This program targets general business development.

• **Research & Development Tax Credit**. Encouragement to companies to increase their basic research and development activities in California. Allows companies to receive a credit of 11 percent for qualified research expenses (research done in-house), and 24 percent for basic research payments (payments to an outside company), making it the highest in the nation. Research must be conducted within California and must not include research for the purpose of improving a commercial product for style, taste, cosmetic or seasonal design factors.

• **Net Operating Loss Carryover**. This program provides businesses with the opportunity to carry a loss forward from one tax year to the next, in order to offset income in the following years. New businesses can carry over 100 percent of their losses over eight years if the loss is in their first year of operation, 100 percent over seven years if the loss is in their second year of operation and 100 percent over six years if the loss is in their third year of operation. Existing California business can carry over 50 percent of their losses for five years.

• **Enterprise Zones.** These provide the following various tax credits and benefits:
   1. Tax credits for sales or use taxes paid on up to $20 million of qualified machinery purchased per year.
   2. A hiring credit of $26,894 or more for each qualified employee during the employee's first 60 months on the job.
   3. A 15 year carryover of up to 100 percent of net operating losses.
   4. Expensing up to $40,000 of certain depreciable property.

LEGISLATIVE TIMELINE:

1990: Expanded the state's Enterprise Zone Program, authorizing the creation of 15 additional zones.

1991: Approved a record $6.6 billion tax increase including a boost in the sales tax. Extended the research and development tax credit through 1996.

1992: Restored net operating losses for the 1991 and 1992 tax years for enterprise zones and employment and economic incentive areas.

1993: Passed a workers' compensation reform package to reduce litigation and provide a 7 percent rate reduction for employers.

1994: Passed a 6 percent tax credit on purchases of manufacturing equipment made after Jan. 1, 1994. Passed a law making California's existing research and development tax credit permanent.

1996: Approved a 35 percent increase in research and development tax credits and a 5 percent corporate and business tax cut, which took effect Jan. 1, 1997.

1999: Passed a bill that is intended to help start a secondary market for economic development loans in order to make those loans available to small businesses.

5. Lender interest income deductions for loans made to zone businesses.
6. Preference points on state contracts.

• **Recycling Zone**. This program provides aid to communities and businesses that use recycled materials. Businesses locating within the forty zones can take advantage of low interest loan packaging, local permit streamlining, technical assistance and information sharing. Businesses using recycled materials such as paper, newsprint, plastic, tires and green-waste in the manufacture of goods are eligible.

• **Local Agency Military Base Recovery Area (LAMBRA).** Designations similar to Enterprise Zones that allow communities to extend tax credits to companies locating in a LAMBRA Zone. This program targets areas experiencing military base downsizing and closure. Local incentives may also be available including the reduction or elimination of permit and construction-related fees, expedieted processing plants and permits, reduced utility rates and low interest revolving loans. As with Enterprise Zone communities, LAMBRA communities have community incentives as a part of the business attraction package. There are currently three military designations under the state's LAMBRA program including Mare Island Naval Shipyard in Vallejo, Castle Air Force Base in Merced and George Air Force Base in Victorville. Alameda Naval Air Station in Alameda and the Tustin Marine Corps Air Station in Tustin were conditionally designated in 1997.

FINANCIAL INCENTIVES:

• **Industrial Development Bonds.** Low interest financing through the use of tax-exempt industrial revenue bonds. An eligible bond project can be the construction of a new plant, expansion of an existing plant or replacement of all or part of an existing plant. To qualify for tax-exempt industrial development bonds, the borrower needs to meet certain eligibility criteria:
1. The firm must be engaged in manufacturing, processing or value-added industry.
2. The total project cost should be at least $1 million and may not exceed $10 million.
3. The borrower must secure a standby letter of credit for 100 percent of the issue value from a bank with a substantial credit base.
4. The capital expansion must provide a public benefit such as creating new jobs, and
5. The project must have city or county support.

• **Small Business Loan Guarantee.** This provides loan guarantees for small business entrepreneurs, particularly among minorities, women and disabled persons. All loan proceeds must be used in California and the proceeds cannot be used for entertainment enterprises or speculative purposes. To qualify, a borrower must be unable to obtain credit based solely on his or her own financial condition, but must demonstrate reasonable capacity to repay the loan. The maximum guarantee is 90 percent of the loan value, not to exceed $350,000 and the maturity of the guarantee is not to exceed seven years. Interest rate and loan origination fees are negotiated by the borrower and the lender.

• **SBA Loans**. SBA Loans are marketed, processed, closed and serviced by California Development Corporations (CDC) throughout California. CDC's provide 90 percent of the real estate financing. The company should create one full time equivalent job with two years of project funding. Individual job goals can be somewhat compromised if the CDC's overall portfolio meets these requirements. This program focuses on rural and distressed urban areas.

• **Sudden Severe Economic Dislocation Loan Program.** This program provides business loans in areas of the state affected by plant and military base closures, defense downsizing, industry layoffs and President-declared disasters. Below market-rate loans of up to $500,000 are available for land, buildings, machinery and equipment and working capital for projects which would not normally qualify for conventional financing.

• **Technology Investment Partnership.** Matching grants and technical assistance for projects qualifying for federal funds through cost-share technology-based applications from a variety of agencies. An application/proposal must be submitted to the appropriate Regional Technology Alliance (RTA). Proposals are evaluated based on immediate ability to create jobs, clearly identified product line and market, inclusion of a training component for workers associated with the project, demonstrated links with other applicable programs, and whether the proposers and partners are small businesses. This program targets new, globally competitive technology-based commercial products.

• **Old Growth and Diversification Revolving Loan Program.** Capital leading to the creation and retention of jobs in areas of California affected by timber harvest and sawmill and related plant closure. A minimum of 25 percent of the total project financing must come from either equity contributed by the applicant or other nonfederal funding sources. Preference is given to those projects which employ displaced timber workers.

OTHER INCENTIVES:

• **Foreign Trade Zones.** The trade zone provides the following: secured areas legally outside the U.S. Customs territory usually located in or near customs points of entry; entry of foreign or domestic merchandise without formal customs entry or government excise taxes; a site where merchandise can be sorted, tested, sampled, relabeled, repackaged, displayed, repaired, manipulated, mixed, cleaned, assembled, manufactured, salvaged, destroyed or processed; for products imported into or exported out of the foreign trade zone, exclusion from customs duty and excise taxes until the time of transfer from the foreign trade zone. The project must be located in one of California's foreign trade zones which are located in San Francisco, San Jose, Long Beach, Oakland, West Sacramento, San Diego, Bakersfield, Palmdale, Los Angeles and Port Hueneme.

• **California Export Finance Loan Guarantee.** This program provides working capital loan guarantees to financial institutions to help small and medium-sized California companies finance their export sales. The California Export Finance Office's (CEFO) guarantees cover up to 90 percent of an export loan, allowing for a maximum guarantee of $750,000 and a loan of $833,000. CEFO offers three types of guarantees: Pre-Shipment Working Capital Guarantee, Post-Shipment Receivable Guarantee and a Combination Guarantee. CEFO guarantees support for: short-term (up to 18 months) transaction-specific working capital loans, single or multiple transactions (revolving line of credit), and cash loans or the issuance of standby letters of credit. This program targets general business development for small and medium-sized business.

• **Joint Strike Fighter Program Credits**. California recently created two entirely new income tax credits for businesses involved in the Joint Strike Fighter program. They are: 1) a hiring wage and 2) a property credit. These credits apply to taxpayers under initial contract or subcontract to manufacture property for ultimate use in the Joint Strike Fighter. The credits are available for taxable years beginning on or after January 1, 2001, and before January 6, 2006.

• **Child Care Tax Credits**. This provides a tax credit for employers who pay or incur costs for the start-up of a child care program or construction of an on-site child care facility. The state's child care tax credits include a credit against state income tax equal to 30 percent of its cost, up to a maximum of $50,000 in one year. Excess credits may be carried over to succeeding years.

• **Regulatory Relief.** The Office of Permit Assistance (OPA) within the California Trade and Commerce Agency assists individuals and corporations in identifying all of the permits needed for development projects and responds to questions about the permitting process. OPA helps businesses identify applicable permits, permit requirements and timetables associated with permits. OPA monitors the progress of permit applications, plans and schedules for permit review and arranges meetings when necessary to assist in the permit process. The Regulation and Review Unit (RRU), within the California Trade and Commerce Agency, evaluates the economic and business impacts of proposed regulations prepared by state government. RRU maintains an inventory of regulations reviewed, provides general information on regulatory impacts and works to improve the quality of proposed regulations.

• **California Capital Access Program**. This provides loans to "near-bankable" small businesses. A business's primary location must be in California. Businesses must have fewer than 50 employees working California and have at least 25 percent of their sales derived from a CalCAP-eligible industry. This program targets small businesses with higher than conventional risk.

Contact:

Dave Snyder
Acting Director
Office of Major Corporate Projects
The California Trade and Commerce Agency
801 K Street, # 1700
Sacramento, CA 95814
(916) 327-0027

COLORADO

1990: Approved a bill requiring out-of-state mail-order firms to collect state and local sales and use taxes on sales in Colorado.

1991: Passed a measure authorizing sales and use tax exemptions for aircraft maintenance facilities locating in approved enterprise zones. Approved $150 million in state incentives in an effort to lure a 10,000-employee United Airlines' maintenance facility to Colorado.

1992: Passed an economic development bill to allow sales tax exemptions for railroad equipment and a bill to grant employers new immunity protection from civil suits for disclosing information about a former employee.

1993: Passed a law that provides proceeds from tire-recycling fees to fund direct loans to recycling companies.

1994: Passed a law expanding enterprise zone tax credits to trucking companies and a consumer credit law designed to attract the consumer credit-card industry.

1995: Created a loan pool for recycling companies, funded by a $1 per tire waste disposal fee. Established enterprise zone credits to encourage economic development in disadvantaged areas of the state. Approved a bill that opens a local telephone exchanges to competition by July 1, 1996.

1996: Modified the sales and use tax credit for machinery and machine tools used in manufacturing. Provided a new credit of 10 percent for qualified job training and school-to-work programs in enterprise zones, and increased the limit and time for investment tax credits. Reduced the tax credit rate on contributions to enterprise zone projects from 50 percent to 25 percent.

1997: House Bill 97-1152 allows an income tax credit equal to 10 percent of the total qualified investments in a school-to-career program.

1998: Created an income tax credit for alternative fueling facilities.

1999: Created an exemption of farm equipment from the state sale and use tax.

TAX INCENTIVES:

- **Corporate income tax.** 5.0 percent.

- **Personal income tax.** 5.0 percent.

- **Sales and use tax.** Three percent on goods purchased by a business that are not intended for resale; services are not taxed, only sales of nonfood items. Exemptions include manufacturing equipment and machine tools costing more than $500, component parts, fuels and electricity, ink and newsprint and packaging material. Counties and municipalities and a few special districts may collect additional sales tax. The combined state and local sales tax averages 6.2 percent statewide.

Enterprise Zone Credits.

1. Three percent investment tax credit: Businesses making investments in equipment used exclusively in an enterprise zone which would have qualified for the pre-1986 federal investment tax credit may claim a credit against their Colorado income taxes equal to 3 percent of the amount of the investment, subject to limitations on the amount which can be claimed in any one year. Investment which results from an in-state relocation is not eligible for the credit unless the new location qualifies as an expansion. Excess credits may be carried back three years and forward twelve.

2. $500 job tax credit: Businesses hiring new employees in connection with a "new business facility" located in an enterprise zone may claim a tax credit against state income taxes of $500 for each such employee. An expansion of an existing facility may be considered a "new business facility" if the expansion adds at least 10 employees or a 10 percent increase over the previous annual average, if it is at least $1 million in investment, or, if less, at least doubles the original investment in the facility. The credit may be taken in subsequent years of the enterprise zone for each additional employee above the maximum number employed in any prior tax year. Excess credits may be carried forward five years (applies to 3 and 4 below).

3. Double job tax credit for agricultural processing: An additional credit of $500 per new business facility employee may be claimed by businesses which add value to agricultural commodities through manufacturing or processing.

4. $200 job tax credit for employer health insurance: In order to encourage employer-sponsored health insurance plans, a taxpayer with a qualifying new business facility is allowed a two-year $200 tax credit for each new business facility employee who is insured under a qualifying employer-sponsored health insurance program.

5. R&D tax credit: Taxpayers who make private expenditures on research and experimental activities (as defined in federal tax law) conducted

in an enterprise zone qualify for an income tax credit. This credit equals 3 percent of the amount of the increase in the taxpayer's R&D expenditures within the zone for the current tax year above the average of R&D expenditures within the zone area in the previous two years. No more than one-fourth of the allowable credit may be taken in any one tax year.

6. Credit to rehabilitate vacant buildings: Owners or tenants of commercial buildings in an enterprise zone which are at least 20 years old and which have been vacant for at least 2 years may claim a credit of 25 percent of the cost of rehabilitating each building. The credit is limited to $50,000.

7. Credit for contributions to zones: A taxpayer who makes a contribution to a local zone administrator for enterprise zone development projects, for assisting job training and placement for the homeless, or for promoting child care in zones may claim a tax credit. The amount of the credit is 25 percent of the value of the contribution, up to $100,000. (A higher percentage may apply in some cases.)

8. Ten percent job training credit: Beginning with the 1997 tax year, employers who carry out a qualified job training program for their enterprise zone employees may claim an income tax credit of 10 percent of their eligible training costs.

9. Exemption from state sales and use tax for manufacturing and mining equipment: Purchases of manufacturing machinery, machine tools, and parts thereof are exempt from the 3 percent state sales and use tax statewide. In addition, when used solely within an enterprise zone this exemption may be claimed for purchases of: (a) mining equipment; (b) materials used to make eligible machinery. Eligible purchases used in an enterprise zone are exempt whether the purchases are capitalized or expensed for accounting purposes.

10. Local government tax incentives: Any city or county within an enterprise zone is authorized to negotiate with individual taxpayers who have qualifying new business facilities: (a) an incentive payment equal to not more than the amount of the increase in property tax liability over pre-enterprise zone levels; and (b) a refund of local sales taxes on purchases of equipment, machinery, machine tools or supplies used in the taxpayer's business in the enterprise zone.

• **Sales and Use Tax Exemptions.** The state of Colorado collects a 3 percent sales or use tax on goods purchased or used in Colorado that are not intended for resale. Colorado's state sales tax rate is tied for the lowest rate among the 45 states that collect sales tax. Major exemptions include:

1. Manufacturing equipment or machine tools over $500 purchased in one calendar year

2. Component parts

3. Fuels and electricity

4. Packaging materials

5. Aircraft parts used in general maintenance

6. Interstate long distance telephone charges

7. Ink and newsprint

FINANCIAL INCENTIVES:

• **Customized Job Training.** These programs are intended to provide customized job training assistance for new and expanding companies throughout the State of Colorado, thereby upgrading the skills of the labor force and the competitiveness of Colorado companies. These training programs were created legislatively to encourage quality economic development by providing job training assistance to new and expanding companies within the state, and to companies with existing employees affected by major technological changes or for employee retention efforts.

• **Community Development Block Grant Revolving Loan Fund Program.** A significant portion of the State of Colorado's annual allocation of federal Community Development Block Grant funds is set aside for economic development within the state's "non-entitlement" (primarily rural) areas. These funds are used to capitalize its fifteen Regional Revolving Loan Funds which have service areas covering the majority of the rural areas of the state. These funds have local boards of directors, and make decisions on loans under $100,000. Loans over $100,000 must be approved by a Financial Review Committee with state approval.

• **Community Development Block Grant Funds Infrastructure Program.** Another important use of federal CDBG funds for rural economic development in Colorado is the awarding of infrastructure grants to support economic development projects. This program is designed to create new permanent jobs and retain existing jobs, primarily for low and moderate income persons. Grants may be provided to construct and/or improve water and wastewater facilities, sewer and water projects, roadways, utility lines, railroad spurs and similar projects. The grants are made to the local governments in which the economic development projects will be located. The Office of Business Development also may make loans to businesses to finance machinery and equipment, or to purchase land, finance new construction, and other eligible uses. As with the infrastructure component, this financing must go through an eligible local government.

• **Colorado Economic Development Commission.** This commission was legislatively created by the General Assembly in 1987 to encourage, promote and stimulate economic development throughout the state through the use of incentive and marketing funds. The commission receives an annual General Fund appropriation which is used in incentive packages to support economic development projects, as well as for marketing programs and special projects. Incentive funds are typically used to support business expansions and relocations which have the potential to generate a significant number of jobs. Marketing dollars generally support programs such as the state's designated Enterprise Zones and marketing activities conducted by the Department of Agriculture, the Office of Economic Development and the Motion Picture and Television Commission.

OTHER INCENTIVES:

• **Foreign Trade.** Colorado trade representatives are in Japan, Mexico and the U.K. The state hosts visits from foreign companies, provides business development assistance and participates in reverse investment. Seminars, trade missions, and technical assistance to foreign companies are also provided.

• **Regulatory Relief Programs.** Environmental self-monitoring (Colorado Department of Public Health and Environment).

Contact:

David Solin
Director
Office of Economic Development
1625 Broadway, Suite 1710
Denver, CO 80202
(303) 892-3840

CONNECTICUT

TAX INCENTIVES:

- **Corporate income tax.** 7.5 percent.

- **Personal income tax.** 3.0 to 4.5 percent.

- **Sales and use tax.** 6 percent on retail sales of most tangible personal property and certain services.

- **New Facilities Credit.** Financial institutions constructing new facilities and adding new employees can receive a credit of as much as 50 percent for up to 10 years based on size of the facility and levels of employment. May be extended for an additional 5 years.

- **Capital Investment**. 4 percent annual credit increasing to 5 percent after 1999 for fixed capital investment in regional infrastructure projects and tangible personal property.

- **Human Capital Credit.** 4 percent annual credit increasing to 5 percent after 1999 for investments in human capital: employee training, child care and donations to higher education for technology training.

- **Machinery and Equipment Credit.** 10 percent credit for increased investment in machinery and equipment for companies with 250 or fewer full-time permanent employees. 5 percent credit for companies with 251 to 800 full-time permanent employees.

- **Research and Development Credit.** For income years beginning on or after January 1, 2000, a credit of 6 percent will be available for research and development expenses incurred by a qualified small business. A qualified small business is defined as a company that has gross income the previous income year that does not exceed $600 million and has not met the gross income test through trancactions with a related person. Qualified small business credits may be carried forward to each successive income year until such credits are fully taken.

- **Hardware and Software Credit.** 100 percent credit for property taxes paid on data processing hardware, peripheral equipment and software. Credit may be applied against certain other Connecticut corporate taxes.

- **Technology R&D Credit.** 25 percent credit for any increase in grants to institutions of higher learning for R&D related to technology advancement over the average grants provided during the preceding 3 years.

- **Insurance Fund Credit.** 100 percent credit for investment over 10 years in an investment fund creating insurance-related facilities and jobs.

- **Other Tax Credits.** Other credits available for a) low-income housing, b) contributions to neighborhood assistance programs, or c) alternative employee transportation.

LEGISLATIVE TIMELINE:

1990: Enacted a capital-gains tax on nonresidents' sales of real property.

1991: Enacted for the first time in Connecticut's history a personal income tax.

1992: Broadened sales and property tax by expanding the definitions of manufacturing, machinery and equipment. Created corporate tax credits for experimental research and development.

1993: Created a $60 million fund for new loan program for small businesses with fewer than 100 employees. Approved a $32 million incentive package to help save 2,300 jobs at jet engine maker Pratt & Whitney.

1994: Levied $300 million in new taxes on hospitals and other new taxes on dry-cleaning establishments.

1995: Enacted legislation to remove environmental compliance barriers to the development of former manufacturing sites. Increased the number of enterprise zones and enacted new tax incentives related to computer and data processing equipment.

1996: Voted to phase out the "S" corporation tax over the next five years. Small businesses received a 10 percent tax break in 1997 and the tax will be eliminated entirely in 2001.

1998: The legislature provided funds for remediating "Brownfield" sites and enacted laws limiting the liability of developers who remediate these sites up to specified standards.

1999: Expanded the Department of Labor's job-training program and the Connecticut Development Authority's job-training financing program to include businesses involved in certain kinds of manufacturing and R&D.

• **Corporate Income Tax Exemptions.** This exemption applies to all insurance companies, Connecticut incorporated and non-Connecticut incorporated, as well as to passive investment companies that hold loans secured by real property. Financial services companies are allowed a single factor apportionment method based on customer location. There are exemptions from all corporate income, insurance premiums and sales tax and state regulation for certain banks, insurers and investment companies locating in the Hartford Financial Services Export Zone that conduct all business with non-U.S. persons.

• **Corporate Property Tax Exemptions.** 100 percent for 5 years on newly acquired and installed machinery and equipment eligible for 5-7 year depreciation. 100 percent for inventories. 30-100 percent for the increased assessment for personal property for manufacturers, and 20-50 percent for eligible real property improvements can be offered by towns for 2 to 7 years, depending on the investment amount. 100 percent for unbundled software. 100 percent for 5 years on new commercial motor vehicles for hire rated over 26,000 pounds.

• **Corporate Sales Tax Exemptions.** 100 percent on machinery, raw materials, tools and fuel used in the manufacture or fabrication of finished products or in the biotechnology industry. 50 percent on machinery, tools, fuels and equipment that may not meet the requirements for the 100 percent exemption. 100 percent on computer and data processing services beginning July 2002. Declining 1 percent annually from current 4 percent. 100 percent on repair, replacement component parts manufacturing machinery. 100 percent on fuel or electric power used in manufacturing or to heat a manufacturing facility. 100 percent of the cost of services related to creating and maintaining a Web site. 100 percent of the cost of aircraft, repairs, parts and services on aircraft exceeding 6,000 lbs. 100 percent on goods purchased inside or outside Connecticut for use outside Connecticut.

• **Targeted Investment Community (TIC) Benefits.** (For any community with an Enterprise Zone): 80 percent for 5-year real property and personal property tax exemptions for manufacturers. 40-80 percent for 5-year real property and personal property exemptions for service facilities, depending on amount invested. 50-80 percent for 5-year tax exemption for personal property when part of a process technology upgrade, depending on the asset acquired. Manufacturers or firms conducting research & development related to manufacturing and newly constructed distribution facilities may be eligible to receive a state corporate business tax credit of 25 percent for 10 years. Corporate business tax credits ranging from 15 percent to 50 percent for 10 years are available to certain selected service facilities based upon the number of jobs created.

• **Additional TIC Benefits.** Within Enterprise Zones or within areas of certain non-TIC municipalities designated for Enterprise Zone Benefits, manufacturers and certain service firms may obtain a 50 percent corporate business tax credit for 10 years. Must meet specific hiring thresholds and investment requirements. A $750 or $2,250 grant for each new, full-time position created as a direct result of plant expansion or renovation by an eligible company. Must meet specific hiring thresholds for $2,250 grant. 100 percent for 3-year corporate tax credit followed by a 50 percent, 7-year credit for businesses created after January 1, 1997. Must employ: a) 375 or more with 40 percent residing in targeted community, or b) fewer than 375 with 150 residing in targeted community.

• **Enterprise Corridor Zone Benefits.** Selected communities bordering Route 8 and I-395 are eligible for full Enterprise Zone Level benefits.

FINANCIAL INCENTIVES:

Connecticut provides direct loans and investments and guaranteed loans to encourage job creation and business expansion.

• **Inducement Financing.** Below-market rate loans are available from the Connecticut Development Authority and the Department of Economic and Community Development for targeted companies relocating to the state or planning significant in-state expansion that offers strong economic development potential. Tax Incremental Financing provides capital contributions for large-scale economic development projects through the Connecticut Development Authority in concert with towns and municipalities, when the future incremental revenues from sales tax or real and personal property taxes service the debt on the respective long-term bonds.

• **Business Financing.** Loan guarantees and enhancements are provided by the Connecticut Development Authority through participating lenders when the business' financing needs exceed the lenders' credit policy or capacity or the business has strong economic development potential. Direct loans of up to $5 million are offered to businesses by the Connecticut Development Authority – often in concert with private lenders – when the business' financing needs exceed the lenders' credit policy or capacity or the business has strong economic development potential. Risk capital and business development funding for proprietary and prototype technology is available through Connecticut Innovations. Investments may be in the form of equity, convertible debt, warrants or based on future royalties. Assistance with the assessment, remediation and redevelopment of contaminated properties is available from state organizations working in partnership with private businesses and municipalities.

• **Utilities.** Customized programs targeted at job creation and business expansion are available to promote economic development and competitiveness from Connecticut's telecommunications, electric, gas and water companies. Electric deregulation will save businesses millions of dollars annually as the industry is restructured and competition encouraged.

OTHER INCENTIVES:

Employment & Training

• **Training Expense Reimbursement.** Training grants up to $25,000 per year are available from the Connecticut Development Authority for manufacturing and related R&D, and for most high technology, telecommunications, information systems, agriculture, aquaculture and other manufacturing-related industries. A portion of training expenses incurred by small- and mid-sized manufacturers experiencing growth and change may be reimbursable by the Connecticut Department of Labor. Assistance in identifying public and private training and funding resources is available through the Connecticut Department of Economic and Community Development.

• **Tax Credits For Employment & Training.** Up to $4,800 for each qualified apprenticeship-training program in the plastics-related and manufacturing trades. Up to $1,000 for each qualified apprenticeship training program in the construction trades. Certification for federal tax credits for hiring: a) individuals from target groups – up to $2,400; b) long-term temporary family assistance recipients – up to $8,500. Up to $1,500 for each qualified temporary family assistance recipient hired.

Contact:

Mark Prisloe
Associate Economist
Dept. of Economic and Community Dev.
505 Hudson St.
Hartford, CT 06106
(860) 270-8166

DELAWARE

LEGISLATIVE TIMELINE:

1990: Enhanced the state's Small Business Revolving Loan Fund to provide credit enhancements that banks can access as collateral in making loans.

1991: Passed the Greer Industry Initiative making certain recycling companies eligible for technical and financial assistance. Authorized banks and trust companies to engage in the insurance business.

1992: Created tax credits for job creation and job training assistance. Passed legislation supporting small businesses by offering a 15 percent personal income tax credit to individuals investing in qualified state companies.

1993: Approved the Delaware Access Program, an initiative to encourage banks to make business loans that typically are turned down because of high risk.

1994: Doubled to $10 million the budget of the Delaware Strategic Fund, the state's primary tool for economic development financing, and increased the budget of the Delaware Development Office by 20 percent. Cut the public utility tax to 2.25 percent from 4.5 percent.

1995: Reduced personal tax rates. Cut the public utility tax by more than half for Delaware businesses.

1996: Lowered the top personal income tax rate from 7.1 percent to 6.9 percent and cut all levels by 3 percent. Reduced the tax rate on gross receipts by 4 percent across the board.

1999: Passed an Act that will reduce the gross receipts tax rate on manufacturing activities by 25 percent.

TAX INCENTIVES:

- **Corporate income tax.** 8.7 percent.

- **Personal income tax.** 3.1 - 6.9 percent.

- **Sales and use tax.** None.

- **Targeted Industry Tax Incentives.** The corporate income tax credits that this program provides are $400 for each new qualified employee and $400 for each $100,000 investment. During the ten-year life of credits, credits may not exceed 50 percent of the company's pre-credit tax liability in any one year. Unused credits may be carried forward. The Blue Collar Jobs Act requires that the credits will be available to: (a) manufacturers; (b) wholesalers; (c) laboratories or similar facilities used for scientific, agricultural or industrial research, development or testing; (d) computer processors; (e) engineering firms; (f) consumer credit reporting services; (g) aviation services (special rules apply); (h) public utility telecommunication providers (special rules apply); (i) wholesalers of computer software; (j) businesses involved in any combination of these activities, who invest a minimum of $200,000 in a new or expanded facility and hire a minimum of five new employees.

Qualifying aviation services must be located at a publicly-owned or operated airport and employ a minimum of 100 employees. Telecommunication firms must invest at least $750,000 in qualified investment and employ at least 50 new employees. Qualifying employees are those new employees for which at least $15,000 in new investment has been made. In addition to corporate income tax credits, firms that meet Blue Collar Jobs Act requirements may be eligible to reduce gross receipts taxes.

- **Targeted Area Tax Credits.** Firms which qualify as a Targeted Industry and locate in one of the targeted areas qualify for corporate income tax credits of $650 for each new employee and $650 for each new $100,000 investment. Firms qualifying for both Area and Targeted Industry credits will also not be subject to gross receipts taxes for five years and will then have these gross receipts taxes reduced on a declining scale for a period of ten years as indicated in the section on Targeted Industry Gross Receipts Tax Reduction. Targeted areas are defined as: (a) real property that is owned by any level of government or any of their agencies, (b) real property owned by a nonprofit organization which is organized and operated solely for the purpose of fostering economic development, (c) real property which has been approved as a Delaware Foreign Trade Zone, and (d) 30 low-income Census Tracts throughout the State. Maps of the Targeted Census Tracts are available from the Delaware Economic Development Office.

- **Delaware Research and Development Tax Credits.** The Delaware Research and Development Tax Credit is adapted from similar federal tax credits but with respect to qualified research conducted within Delaware to be applied against corporate income tax or, where applicable, against personal income tax. The statewide cap on such credits is $5 million per year, to be granted first in December 2001, with regard to tax year 2000 expenses. Whenever statewide applications exceed $5 million, receipts are to be allowed pro rata according to the approved amount so that the total approved credits do not exceed $5 million. The act sunsets with regard to tax year 2005. Unused credits may not be carried back, but may be carried forward fifteen years.

- **Commercial and Retail Business Tax Incentives.** Selected commercial and retail businesses which locate in a targeted area and meet the Blue Collar Jobs Act criteria qualify for corporate income tax credits of $400 per new qualified employee and $400 for each $100,000 investment. These businesses also qualify for the ten-year reduction in gross receipts taxes.

- **Retention and Expansion Tax Credits.** Corporate income tax credits are available to qualifying manufacturers and wholesalers planning new facilities or large expansions. Such companies investing a minimum of $1 million or 15 percent of unadjusted basis in the facility are eligible to receive 75 percent of Blue Collar Tax Credits (75 percent of $400 = $300). Wages cannot fall below 85 percent of the total wages for the period 12 months prior to the opening of a new facility. Maximum annual credit cannot exceed $500,000. Gross receipts tax credits are also available with a maximum total credit of $500,000.

- **Public Utility Tax Rebates for Industrial Users.** Industrial firms meeting the criteria for the targeted industries tax credits are eligible for a rebate of 50 percent of the Public Utilities Tax imposed on new or increased consumption of gas and electricity for five years.

- **Investor Tax Credits.** Personal income tax credits are available to individuals who invest in approved Delaware small businesses. Tax credits of 15 percent are applicable to no more than $100,000 of investment per investor in any one company. Tax credits can be spread over five years.

FINANCIAL INCENTIVES:

- **Industrial Revenue Bond Financing.** The Delaware Economic Development Authority provides statewide financial assistance to new or expanding business through the issuance of Industrial Revenue Bonds (IRBs). IRBs are purchased by investors at low interest rates, since interest from the bonds is exempt from federal income taxes and State income taxes for Delaware residents. The business person benefits by obtaining long-term financing at interest rates below the prime rate. IRBs can be especially cost-effective for projects involving over $750,000 in fixed assets. Delaware enjoys a competitive advantage over most states by virtue of the comparatively large amount of IRB dollars per resident that can be issued. The maximum for IRBs issued annually in Delaware is $150 million.

Projects are approved on their own merits and are funded on a first-come, first-served basis under the State's allocation.

- **SBIR Bridge Grant Assistance.** The purpose of this program is to encourage Delaware businesses to participate in the Federal Small Business Innovation Research (SBIR) grant program. The SBIR program requires that 1.25 percent of all federal research dollars be made available to small businesses.

- **Delaware Innovation Fund.** The purpose of the Delaware Innovation Fund is to assist in the initial capitalization of pre-seed and seed stage enterprise within the State of Delaware. The Fund provides financial and technical assistance to Delaware-based businesses which have the potential to launch innovative products and processes into national markets, to create new jobs, and to make a significant contribution to the economic diversity of the technology base of Delaware's communities.

- **Venture Capital.** Venture Capital, which is high-risk equity capital, is often necessary to enable start-up companies to commercialize new technologies and create jobs. Recognizing this, the State is a limited partner in three institutional venture capital funds. These funds – Anthem Capital, Blue Rock Capital and Triad Investors Corporation – have the ability to invest in a variety of seed, early and later stage companies in both technology-related and non-technology fields. The investment focus of each fund varies, but all are focused on the Mid-Atlantic region and investments can range from $150,000 for seed stage companies up to $2,000,000 or more for later stage companies. Anthem Capital and Blue Rock are also licensed Small Business Investment Companies (SBICs) by the U.S. Small Business Administration.

- **Export-Import Bank Financing.** Delaware is a part of the cooperative efforts by banks in the state and region which can assist exporters in submitting applications for export working capital financing through the Export-Import Bank of the United States (EximBank). This enables EximBank to respond to financing requests more promptly. These organizations can also help facilitate processing of applications for other EximBank programs, e.g., direct and intermediary loans and loan guarantees.

- **Economic Development Loan Program.** The purpose of this program is to assist Delaware businesses in financing projects when 100 percent financing cannot be obtained through a bank. Financing can be provided for fixed assets as well as working capital. Funds are not available for debt consolidation or debt repayments. The program does not require 70 percent bank financing. The remaining 30 percent is financed through the program up to a maximum of $450,000. In most cases, the interest rate for monies loaned through the Economic Development Loan Program is 60 percent of the prime lending interest rate. To be eligible for a loan, a project should serve a public purpose by maintaining or expanding employment in the state, by maintaining or diversifying business and industry in the state, and/or by maintaining or increasing its tax base.

- **Small Business Administration Assistance.** The Delaware Economic Development Office assists small businesses in seeking loans guaranteed by the U.S. Small Business Administration (SBA) under the 7(a) business loan program. The SBA generally guarantees 90 percent of the loan from a local financial institution with a maximum guarantee of $750,000. Guaranteed loans are utilized by firms with loan needs that exceed the usual banking criteria. Financing can be obtained for both working capital and fixed assets. The SBA may require up to one-third equity when evaluating loan applications from new companies. Equity requirements for ongoing businesses vary. Financial institutions tend to restrict the financing to projects exceeding $50,000, and the interest rate and term is negotiated between the borrower and the lender within limits prescribed by the SBA.

- **Delaware Development Corporation Loans.** This program offers long-term, fixed asset financing at fixed rates to the growing small firm. In addition to land, buildings and equipment, many of the costs associated with construction (interim financing costs, architectural drawings, etc.) that are usually "out-of-pocket" expenses may be included in the 504 loan package. To be eligible, a small business must be a "for-profit enterprise" with a net worth of less than $6 million and average net profits of less than $2 million for the past two years. In addition, the project must create one new job for approximately every $35,000 of SBA funding.

- **Delaware ACCESS Program.** The Delaware Access Program is designed to give banks a flexible and extremely non-bureaucratic tool to make business loans that are somewhat riskier than a conventional bank loan, in a manner consistent with safety and soundness. It is designed to use a small amount of public resources to generate a large amount of private bank financing, thus providing access to bank financing for many Delaware businesses that might otherwise not be able to obtain access.

OTHER INCENTIVES:

- **Foreign Investment**. The Delaware Economic Development Office (DEDO) staff meet with individuals from international firms and initiate contacts with businesses which seek to locate in Delaware. Delaware's strategic location permits easy access to the United States marketplace, the largest in the world. International business can easily incorporate in the state through the Department of State, Division of Corporations. DEDO is responsible for the administration and promotion of the Foreign

Trade Zone. Delaware also includes numerous subzones.

- **Export Assistance.** The International Trade Section is a one-stop resource for international trade information and exporter assistance. Experienced staff provide in-house and on-site counseling to small and medium-sized businesses wishing to export for the first time or to expand their current export sales.

- **Company Target Incentives.** The DEDO focuses on attracting companies associated with bio-life sciences, high technology firms, semiconductors and advanced materials. The Delaware general economic climate contains a number of benefits that act as incentives for companies in these areas.

- **Regulatory Relief Programs**. The Delaware Economic Development Office works closely with businesses to ensure expedited and prompt review of regulatory matters; not only those of State Government, but also those involving Federal, county and municipal government. In addition, regarding environmental matters, Delaware has a Clean Air Act Ombudsman. The Ombudsman acts as an advocate for small business within the Department of Natural Resources and Environmental Control concerning issues related to regulation and compliance with the Clean Air Act.

SUCCESSFUL INCENTIVES:

- **AstraZeneca Incentive Package**. In April of 1999, Delaware Governor Thomas R. Carper welcomed AstraZeneca — the third largest pharmaceutical company in the world — to Delaware. Delaware's quality of life, business climate and cost of doing business all contributed to AstraZeneca's decision to build its North American headquarters there. The total incentive package was equal to $18.7 million. AstraZeneca may also be eligible for tax credits of $30 million based on employment and infrastructure investments. It is estimated that the combined company, at full employment, will generate over $50 million per year in taxes. The number of jobs associated with this merger currently totals almost 4,000 but is estimated to grow to close to 6,500 over the following few years.

Contact:

Rob Skomorucha
Director of Business Research
Delaware Economic Development Office
99 Kings Highway
Dover, DE 19901
(302) 739-4271

TAX INCENTIVES:

- **Corporate income tax**. 5.5 percent. An exemption of $5,000 is allowed. Investment tax credit of up to 5 percent a year for 20 years on certain investments.

- **Personal income tax**. None.

- **Sales and use tax**. 5.0 percent. Goods manufactured or produced in the state for export outside the state, electrical energy used in manufacturing, and the purchase of certain manufacturing machinery and equipment are exempt from the state sales and use tax.

- **Qualified Target Industry Tax Refund Program**. The Qualified Target Industry Tax Refund Program (QTI) is an economic development tool designed to create high value-added jobs and encourage the growth of corporate headquarters and other targeted high value-added industries. The program provides for a tax refund of up to $3,000 per new job created ($6,000 for projects locating in an enterprise zone) in Florida through the expansion of existing Florida businesses or businesses relocating in Florida. There is a tax refund for wages in excess of 150 percent of the area average and additional refund if over 200 percent. There is a cap of $5 million per single qualified applicant in all years, and no more than 25 percent of the total refund approved may be taken in any single fiscal year. To participate in the program, a company must create at least 10 new jobs in Florida in a target industry business, increase employment by at least 10 percent, and pay an average annual wage that is at least 115 percent of local area wages.

- **Qualified Defense Contractor Tax Refund Program**. The Qualified Defense Contractor Tax Refund Program is designed to minimize the negative economic impacts of defense downsizing in Florida. The program provides for a tax refund of up to $5,000 per job created or saved in Florida through the conversion of defense jobs to civilian production, the acquisition of a new defense contract, the consolidation of a defense contract that results in at least a 25 percent increase in employment, or the reuse of certain defense facilities at one of Florida's ports. There is a cap of $7.5 million per single defense contractor in all years, and no more than 25 percent of the total refund approved or $2.5 million may be taken in any single fiscal year. To participate in the program a company must pay an average annual wage that is at least 115 percent of local area wages; have in the last year derived at least 70 percent of its Florida gross receipts from Department of Defense contracts and not less than 80 percent over the preceding five years; create at least a 25 percent increase in employment or 80 new jobs if it is a consolidation project; and, for a reuse project, have a contract with at least two years duration for the reuse of a port facility that has, within the last year, been occupied by a business that held a Department of Defense contract.

- **Florida Enterprise Zone Program**. The Florida Enterprise Zone Program provides a credit against either its sales or corporate income tax to a business located within or hiring from within the zones. There are also credits for building materials used in the zone and other activities in the zone.

LEGISLATIVE TIMELINE:

1991: Approved a $3 billion, 10-year program to protect the state's natural spaces from unrestrained development.

1992: Created the Enterprise Florida program to leverage both public and private resources to attract and retain industry.

1993: Enacted a law to streamline environmental permitting. Created Quick Response Training. Created Technology and Innovation Partnerships to encourage cooperative R&D between universities and industry, and the Florida Technology Research Investment Fund to provide capital for technology development projects.

1994: Created the Qualified Target Industry Tax Refund Program, and the Qualified Defense Contractor Tax Refund Program. Created a performance-based worker training program.

1995: Created the First Florida-Based Business Bond Pool for large investment projects. Passed a new telecommunications law to open up local markets to competition.

1996: Reorganized the Department of Commerce and replaced it with a public/private agency that is the primary economic development organization.

1997: Created the High Impact Performance Incentive (HIPI), to provide large incentives for major investments in certain high impact sectors. Exempted electrical energy used in manufacturing from the sales and use tax.

1998: Created as an investment tax credit on Florida's corporate income tax of up to 5 percent of an investment over $50 million for up to 20 years for industries in designated HIPI sectors. Exempted accounts receivable and certain other business assets from the intangibles tax.

1999: Streamlined and refocused Enterprise Florida, Inc. Created Front Porch Florida neighborhood revitalization program. Simplified the Qualified Target Industry Tax Refund program.

- **Shared Foreign Sales Corporation**. This aids smaller firms in taking advantage of federal and state tax exclusions developed as export incentives. Depending on a firm's profit margin, the income exemption can allow for a tax savings of 15 to 30 percent.

FINANCIAL INCENTIVES:

- **Florida Economic Development Transportation Fund**. This fund is available to local governments in need of financial assistance for transportation projects to facilitate economic development. The local government must apply on behalf of a company that is considering an expansion or relocation of facilities and that has an existing or anticipated transportation problem. A transportation fund award must be an inducement to the company to locate, remain and/or expand in the local government's jurisdiction. Up to $2 million may be provided to a local government to implement the improvements.

- **Florida Development Finance Corporation**. The Corporation pools small bond issues to reduce costs for small businesses.

- **Community Development Corporation Support and Assistance Program**. This program provides funds to local communities which in turn make loans to businesses to facilitate the establishment of new business or to purchase equity interests in business.

- **Florida Energy Loan Program**. The Florida Energy Loan Program provides low-interest loans to small businesses for the purchase and installation of energy-efficient equipment and improvements to the energy efficiency of structures.

- **The Rural Revolving Loan Fund**. This Fund makes loans of up to $500,000 available to local governments to complete funding for projects that result in improvements for business development and job growth.

OTHER INCENTIVES:

- **The Quick Response Training Program**. Provides rapid, effective start-up training tailored to benefit specific companies. Quick Response is administered by the Department of Commerce, in cooperation with community colleges, vocational-technical centers, state universities and private institutions. Eligible projects are new or expanding Florida businesses that produce exportable goods or services, create new jobs and employ Florida workers who require customized entry-level skills training. Special consideration will be given to applicants who fit the following criteria: training for high-quality jobs that pay an average annual wage of at least 115 percent of the local or state private-sector wage, whichever is lower; location of the business in a distressed urban or rural area or enterprise zone; are important to the economic base of the community; and provide in-kind or cash matches.

- **The Seaport Employment Training Grant Program**. Funds job skills training programs designed to improve the movement of cargo or passengers.

- **Enterprise Florida Innovation Public/Private Partnership**. The Innovation Partnership is a nonprofit corporation that centers on the creation and expansion of innovative, technology-based firms in the state such as biochemical, computer, micro-electronics and software development. The partnership provides seed capital, expertise and direct production problem assistance. The partnership created Innovation and Commercialization Corporations (ICCs), which provide management, financial and marketing services for the commercialization of technologies developed at universities, federal laboratories and private firms. The Technology Research Investment Fund co-invests with Florida companies to develop new products or processes for the marketplace. Repayment through royalties is required. Florida Manufacturing Technology Centers, consisting of six regional field engineers, assist small- to mid-size manufacturers in overcoming problems and improvements in the manufacturing process.

- **Enterprise Florida Jobs and Education Partnership**. This program is an incentive-based funding system that compensates educational organizations for graduating and placing students in targeted occupations. This process has resulted in a statewide workforce training program that is more responsive to the needs of business.

- **Expedited Permit Review Process**. This allows significant economic development projects to obtain expedited review of all needed state and regional permit applications and, at the option of a participating local government, local development permits or orders and comprehensive plan amendments.

SUCCESSFUL INCENTIVES:

- **The Qualified Target Industry Tax Refund Program.** The program has been widely used throughout the state and has encouraged the creation of over 33,000 direct, high wage jobs over the last four years.

Contact:

Wynnelle Wilson
Executive Office of the Governor
Tallahassee, FL 32399
(850) 487-2568

TAX INCENTIVES:

- **Corporate income tax**. 6.0 percent.

- **Personal income tax.** 1.0 to 6.0 percent.

- **Sales and use tax.** 4.0 percent.

- **Job Tax Credit.** Provides a statewide job tax credit for any business or headquarters of any such business engaged in manufacturing, warehousing and distribution, processing, telecommunications, tourism, and research and development industries, but does not include retail businesses. Effective January 1, 1999, job tax credits are available to businesses of any nature, including retail businesses, in counties recognized and designated as the 40 least developed counties.

Counties and certain census tracts in the state are ranked and placed in economic tiers using the following factors:
   1. Highest unemployment,
   2. Lowest per capita income,
   3. Highest percentage of residents whose incomes are below the poverty level, and
   4. Average weekly manufacturing wage.

   - Tier 1 counties are ranked 1st through 53rd and represent the state's least developed counties. Companies creating 5 or more new jobs in a Tier 1 county may receive a $2,500 tax credit.
   - Tier 2 counties are ranked 54th through 106th. Companies creating 15 or more new jobs in a Tier 2 county may receive a $1,500 tax credit.
   - Tier 3 counties are ranked 107th through 159th. Companies creating 25 or more new jobs in a Tier 3 county may receive a $500 tax credit.

Credits are allowed for each full-time employee job for five years beginning with years two through six after the creation of the job. The total credit amount cannot be more than 50 percent of the taxpayer's state income tax liability for a taxable year. A credit claimed but not used in any taxable year may be carried forward for 10 years from the close of the taxable year in which the qualified jobs were established.

- **Jobs Tax Credit for Joint Development Authoritie**s. Provides for an additional $500 job tax credit per job for a business locating within the jurisdiction of a joint authority of two or more contiguous counties.

- **Investment Tax Credit.** This program is based on the same tiers as the Job Tax Credit program. It allows a taxpayer who has operated an existing manufacturing or telecommunications facility or support facility in the state for the previous three years to obtain a credit against income tax liability.

LEGISLATIVE TIMELINE:

1990: Georgia's Trade Secrets Law was strengthened to protect companies against the loss of proprietary information when key employees leave.

1991: Approved a bill granting employers a $150 income tax credit for each employee successfully completing an employer-provided basic skills education program.

1992: Approved changes in Quick Start, the state's workforce training program, to include worker retraining.

1993: Enacted changes to the state's Job Tax Credit Program allowing businesses locating in designated distressed urban areas to receive an annual $2,000 tax credit for each job created.

1994: Approved the Georgia Business Expansion and Support Act.

1995: Agreed to shift $12.5 million to a new grant program designed to make communities more attractive to new business. Expanded the eligibility for investment and job tax credits.

1996: Passed a measure that made job tax credits more easily available to businesses that relocate or expand in Georgia.

1999: Created the Senate Small Business Jobs Creation and Training Study Committee.

- Companies expanding in Tier 1 counties must invest $50,000 to receive a 5 percent credit. That credit increases to 8 percent for recycling, pollution control and defense conversion activities.
- Companies expanding in Tier 2 counties must invest $50,000 to receive a 3 percent credit. That credit increases to 5 percent for recycling, pollution control and defense conversion activities.
- Companies expanding in Tier 3 counties must invest $50,000 to receive a 1 percent credit. That credit increases to 3 percent for recycling, pollution control and defense conversion activities.

The credit is a percentage of the total value of all qualified investment property and cannot be more than 50 percent of the taxpayer's total state income tax liability for that taxable year. Any credit claimed but not used in any taxable year may be carried forward for ten years from the close of the taxable year in which the qualified investment was acquired.

• **Optional Investment Tax Credit.** Taxpayers qualifying for the investment tax credit may choose an optional investment tax credit with the following threshold criteria:

Designated Area	Minimum Investment	Tax Credit
Tier 1	$ 5 million	10%
Tier 2	$10 million	8%
Tier 3	$20 million	6%

The credit may be claimed for 10 years, provided the qualifying property remains in service throughout that period. A taxpayer must choose either the regular or optional investment tax credit. Once this election is made, it is irrevocable.

• **Retraining Tax Credit.** Employers who provide retraining for employees are eligible for a tax credit equal to 50 percent of the costs of retraining each full-time employee up to $500. The training must:
1. Enhance the skills of employees otherwise unable to function effectively on new equipment;
2. Be approved by the Department of Technical and Adult Education; and
3. Be provided at no cost to the employee.

The credit cannot be more than 50 percent of the taxpayer's total state income tax liability for that taxable year. Any credit claimed for any taxable year beginning on or after January 1, 1998 but not used in any such taxable year may be carried forward for ten years from the close of the taxable year in which the tax credit was granted.

• **Research and Development Tax Credit.** A tax credit is allowed for research expenses for research conducted within Georgia for any business or headquarters of any such business engaged in manufacturing, warehousing and distribution, processing, telecommunications, tourism, and research and development industries. The credit shall be 10 percent of the additional research expense over the "base amount," provided that the business enterprise for the same taxable year claims and is allowed a research credit under Section 41 of the Internal Revenue Code of 1986. The tax credit may be carried forward ten years but may not exceed 50 percent of the business' net tax liability in any one year.

• **Small Business Growth Companies Tax Credit.** A tax credit is granted for any business or headquarters of any such business engaged in manufacturing, warehousing and distribution, processing, telecommunications, tourism, and research and development industries having a state net taxable income which is 20 percent or more above that of the previous year if its net taxable income in each of the two preceding years was also 20 percent or more. The credit shall be the excess over 20 percent of the percentage growth and shall not exceed 50 percent of the business' Georgia net income tax liability. The credit is available to companies whose total tax liability does not exceed $1.5 million.

• **Ports Activity Job Tax and Investment Tax Credits.** Companies that increase their port traffic tonnage – net tons, containers, or 20-foot equivalent units (TEUs) – through Georgia ports by more that 10 percent over 1997 base year port traffic, or 75 net tons, 5 containers, or 10 TEUs, whichever is greater, during the previous 12 month period, and meet Business Expansion and Support Act (BEST) criteria for the county in which they are located, are qualified for increased job tax credits and investment tax credits. (Base year port traffic must be at least 75 net tons, five containers, or 10 TEUs). The Job Tax and Investment Tax Credits are as follows:
- Tier 1 companies: $3,500 per job, 5 percent investment tax credit, and 10 percent optional investment tax credit.
- Tier 2 companies: $3,000 per job, 5 percent investment tax credit, and 10 percent optional investment tax credit.
- Tier 3 companies: $2,500 per job, 5 percent investment tax credit, and 10 percent optional investment tax credit.

Companies that create 400 or more new jobs, invest $20 million or more in new and expanded facilities, and increase the port traffic by more than 20 percent above base year port traffic may take both job tax credits and investment tax credits. (Effective January 1, 1998 – July 1, 2002.)

• **Manufacturing Machinery Sales Tax Exemption.** Provides an exemption from the sales and use tax for:

1. Machinery used directly in the manufacturing of tangible personal property when the machinery is bought to replace or upgrade machinery in a manufacturing plant presently existing in the state.
2. Machinery used directly in the manufacture of tangible personal property when the machinery is incorporated as additional machinery for the first time into a manufacturing plant existing in the state.
3. Machinery used directly in the manufacture of aircraft engines, parts and components.
4. Tangible personal property consumed in the performance of a contract between the U.S. Government and a contractor employing 500 or more full-time employees engaged in manufacturing. This exemption was phased in at a 25 percent increment rate each year from January 1, 1997 to January 1, 2000.

- **Primary Material Handling Sales Tax Exemption.** Provides an exemption from the sales and use tax on purchases of primary material handling equipment which is used directly for the storage, handling, and movement of tangible personal property in a new or expanding warehouse or distribution facility when such new facility or expansion is valued at $5 million or more and does not engage in direct retail sales.

- **Electricity Exemption.** Electricity purchased that interacts directly with a product being manufactured is exempt from sales taxes when the total cost of the electricity exceeds 50 percent of the cost of all materials, including electricity, used in making the product. This exemption was phased in over five years beginning in 1995. It allowed 20-40-60-80-100 percent exemptions on the sales tax and was available for new and existing firms. By 1999, electricity used in this manner was completely exempt.

FINANCIAL INCENTIVES:

- **Regional Revolving Loan Funds.** Regional Revolving Loan Funds have been established in seven of Georgia's Regional Development Centers. Businesses may use loans for land acquisition, fixed assets, construction, renovation and working capital. Terms vary, with interest rates normally at or below prevailing levels. Loan amounts are generally between $25,000 and $500,000, with collateral required.

- **Agribusiness Loan Program.** The Georgia Development Authority's Agribusiness Loan Program makes available low-interest loans under its tax-free revenue note program. Limited to $1 million, loans carry the provision that no more that 25 percent or $150,000 may be used to purchase land.

- **Child Care Credit.** Employers who provide or sponsor child care for employees are eligible for a tax credit of up to 75 percent of the employer's direct cost. The credit cannot be more than 50 percent of the employer's total state income tax liability for that taxable year. Any credit claimed but not used in any taxable year may be carried forward for five years from the close of the taxable year in which the cost of the operation was incurred. In addition, employers that construct child care centers can deduct the total cost of building the facility at 10 percent per year for ten years.

Contact:

Thomas G. Roche
Research Unit Supervisor
Strategic Planning and Research Division
Georgia Department of Industry, Trade and Tourism
285 Peachtree Center Avenue
Atlanta, GA 30303-1230

HAWAII

LEGISLATIVE TIMELINE:

1990: Established the Hawaii Community Based Development Loan and Grant program and revolving fund for small business.

1991: Passed a measure to allow the state's high-technology development organization to make loans up to $1 million, a bill to provide matching grant funds for rural-area development projects and a measure to permit greater funding flexibility in the state's financing programs.

1992: Passed new legislation which allows the High Technology Development Corp. to provide grants of up to 50 percent of the federal government grant (up to $25,000) to firms receiving a federal Small Business Innovation Research Phase I award. Appropriated $200,000 to the Department of Business, Economic Development and Tourism to attract international technologies and businesses.

1994: Approved a privatization law that prohibits state government agencies from implementing new programs until the agency demonstrates that it is an appropriate function of government.

1995: Eliminated $65 million in annual tax credits as part of its fiscal legislation to balance the budget.

1996: Enacted a regulatory relief bill that seeks to identify troublesome state administrative rules and regulations that are obstacles to business.

1998: Passed Regulatory Flexibility Act that requires review and reduction of regulatory impact in rules and waiver/reduction in penalties.

1999: Act 105: Authorized issuance of revenue bonds to assist high tech industry.

TAX INCENTIVES:

- **Corporate income tax.** 4.4 to 6.4 percent.

- **Personal income tax.** 1.6 to 8.75 percent.

- **Sales and use tax.** 4.0 percent. Exemptions include pollution control facilities, certain scientific contracts with the United States, ships used in international trade and commerce, sugar and pineapple manufacturers and sales of tangible personal property to the federal government. A use tax is imposed upon tangible personal property, imported or purchased from unlicensed out-of-state sellers for use or for resale in Hawaii, at a rate of 0.5 percent, if the property is intended for resale at retail. Vessels engaged in intrastate transportation are exempt from the use tax.

- **Tax Incentives.** Hawaii has only two levels of government taxation: state and local. There is no personal property tax, no unincorporated business tax and no state tax on goods manufactured for export (Manufactured products or those produced for export are exempt from the GET, including custom computer software). No tax on inventories, furniture, equipment or machinery. Businesses are allowed a credit against taxes paid on the purchase of capital goods and machinery. Banks and financial institutions pay only one business tax.

FINANCIAL INCENTIVES:

- **Hawaii Capital Loan Program.** This program makes loans to small businesses in amounts up to $1,000,000. Preferences are made to businesses: with job creating potential, that use local resources or by-products, that displace imports, that create export opportunities, in the commecial or service sector, in research and development, and involved in Pacific Basin Activities.

- **Employment and Training Fund (ETF).** The fund was created to improve long term employability of Hawaii's people.

- **Hawaii Strategic Development Corporation.** Giving priority to high-tech business, this invests public funds in return for equity or ownership positions in private businesses to stimulate capital formation.

- **Hawaii's Foreign Trade Zone Program.** Hawaii's Foreign Trade Zone (FTZ) lies outside U.S. customs territory for tax, duty, and quota purposes, helping companies engaged in international trade significantly reduce their operating costs.

- **Hawaii Small Business Innovation Research (SBIR) Grant Program.** The participating federal agencies in the SBIR program provide grants equaling 50 percent of a company's total Phase I funding. The maximum grant is $25,000 and companies must be incorporated and operate in Hawaii. Loans are administered by the High Technology Development Corporation.

- **Enterprise Zones Program.** Established to increase business activity and create jobs in areas with above normal unemployment and/or below average income levels.

OTHER INCENTIVES:

- **Immigrant Investor Attraction Program.** The Immigrant Investor Attraction Program offers a federal "green card" for investment over $500,000 and 10 jobs.

- **High-Tech Incentive.** High-Tech firms doing IRC HI type work and all software development companies' investors get 10 percent income tax credit. They receive a larger credit if Research and Development is increased.

- **Public/Private Partnership.** The Hawaii Strategic Development Corporation provides equity funding to private limited partnership venture capitalists who, in turn, invest in Hawaii companies.

SUCCESSFUL INCENTIVES:

- **General Excise Tax/Use Tax Abatement.** This abatement plus exclusion of GET on construction was a major factor in attracting a new regional wide-body aircraft maintenance facility in Honolulu. The General Excise Tax (sales tax) and Hotel Boom Tax credits for film/video production in Hawaii have resulted in a record number of film/video projects in Hawaii.

Contact:

Thomas J. Smyth
Administrator, Business Support Division
Department of Business, Economic Development and Tourism
250 S. Hotel St. #500
Honolulu, HI 96813
(808) 586-2591

IDAHO

1991: Increased motor-fuel tax by 3 cents to build, repair and maintain state roads.

1993: Appropriated $150,000 to fund worker training for a furniture manufacturer relocating to Idaho.

1995: Reduced property taxes.

1996: Established a workforce training fund to assist new, expanding or threatened businesses. Repealed the income-tax credit for hiring new employees. Granted a tax break for manufacturers of products made from post-consumer or post-industrial wastes.

1999: Appropriated an additional $122,300 to the Department of Commerce for fiscal year 1999, totaling $24 million for 1999.

TAX INCENTIVES:

• **Corporate income tax.** 8.0 percent.

• **Personal income tax.** 2.0 to 8.2 percent.

• **Sales and use tax.** Businesses are required to collect and/or remit a 5 percent tax on retail sales and on the use, consumption or storage of tangible personal property. The tax also applies to certain rentals, leases and services based on the sales price.

• **Investment Tax Credit.** A provision adopted by the 1982 Legislature allows a 3 percent credit for new investments made in the state, not to exceed 45 percent of the tax liability for the year. The credit may be carried forward up to seven years.

• **Clean room tax exemption.** Provides an exemption from the sales tax for any sale at retail, storage, use or other consumption of tangible personal property which is exclusively used in, to maintain the environment of, or is or becomes a component part of a clean room (effective 2/1/2000).

FINANCIAL INCENTIVES:

• **Energy Conservation Loan Program.** Projects must show an estimated payback period of 10 years or less from the energy savings (e.g., a $1,500 project must save at least $150 in energy costs per year to be eligible). Loan amounts range from $1,000 to $100,000 for commercial and industrial applications, and carry a 4 percent interest rate. Eligible projects include insulation, energy-efficient lighting, energy-efficient windows and doors, heating, ventilation, and air conditioning systems including pumps and motors.

OTHER INCENTIVES:

• **International Assistance.** International Business Development Division provides export assistance to Idaho businesses.

Contact:

Jay Engstrom, Administrator
Economic Development Division
Idaho Department of Commerce
P.O. Box 83720
700 West State Street
Boise, ID 83720-0093
(208) 334-2470

TAX INCENTIVES:

• **Corporate income tax.** 7.3 percent. Includes the 4.8 percent corporate income tax and the 2.5 percent corporate personal property replacement tax. The corporate personal property replacement tax, a tax on corporate income, was enacted when Illinois abolished the property tax on personal property of corporations. The 2.5 percent replacement tax generates a credit equivalent to deducting the replacement before paying the corporate income tax.

• **Personal income tax.** 3.0 percent. The rate is the second lowest of all the states having a personal income tax.

• **Sales and use tax.** General sales tax rate is 6.25 percent, telephone 7.0 percent, electricity 5.0 percent, and natural gas is 5.0 percent. The sales tax is collected on retail sales of tangible personal property; services are not taxed.

• **Economic Development Through A Growing Economy (EDGE).** EDGE will provide tax credits to new and expanding businesses in Illinois. Companies investing $5 million and creating at least 25 jobs may qualify for credits for up to 10 years limited by their employees' personal income tax paid, the corporation's income tax due and the corporation's investment.

• **Corporate Income Enterprise Zone Incentives.** These incentives include a 0.5 percent investment tax credit; a $500 per job, jobs tax credit; a deduction for dividends paid by a corporation operating in an Illinois enterprise zone; and a deduction for interest paid on loans to businesses operating in an Illinois enterprise zone. The jobs tax credit requires that a minimum of five workers be hired and that the workers be dislocated or disadvantaged (There are no local corporate income taxes in Illinois).

• **Sales Tax Exemptions.** These exemptions include: manufacturing machinery, replacement parts for manufacturing machinery, computers used to control manufacturing machinery, pollution controls, custom software, farm machinery, farm chemicals and water delivered through mains.

• **Sales Tax Enterprise Zone Incentives.** These exemptions include: a sales tax exemption for building materials to be used in an enterprise zone if bought in the municipality or county which created the zone; a sales tax exemption for materials consumed in a manufacturing process (contingent on a business making a $5 million investment and creating 200 jobs, or a $40 million investment which retains 2,000 jobs, or a $40 million investment which causes the retention of 90 percent of the existing jobs); a utility tax exemption on gas, electricity and telephone (contingent upon a business making a $5 million investment and creating 200 jobs, or investing $175 million and creating 150 jobs, or investing $20 million and retaining 2,000 jobs).

• **Property Taxes.** Real property only, land and buildings, is subject to the property tax in Illinois; therefore machinery, equipment, inventories, in-

LEGISLATIVE TIMELINE:

1990: Passed the Technology Advancement and Development Act to directly fund research in Illinois universities and nonprofit research laboratories.

1991: Authorized the addition of six new enterprise zones, bringing the total to 88.

1993: Authorized corporate income tax credits of up to 20 percent of the cost of providing cooperative youth vocational education programs and up to 5 percent of the cost of providing on-site day-care programs. Authorized increased sales tax credits for manufacturers to offset the cost of machinery and other purchases.

1994: Extended the research and development tax credit to Dec. 31, 1999, and provided additional funding for the state's Industrial Training Program.

1995: Increased the state's manufacturing machinery purchaser's credit from 15 to 25 percent.

1996: Extended the Illinois Replacement Investment Tax Credit for seven years from 1996. Increased annual funding for the Industrial Training Program by $2.75 million to total $15 million.

1997: Enterprise zone tax break was passed that enables municipalities to make certain tax exemptions.

1998: Made Economic Development Grants available to local governments and nonprofit organizations to promote Illinois localities as business sites.

1999: Passed the Micro-Enterprise and Self-Employment Assistance Act.

tangibles and all other categories of personal property are exempt from the property tax. Nor is there any other property-tax-like tax on any of those categories of personal property. Property is generally assessed at 33.4 percent for property tax purposes, and the statewide property tax rate, which is applied to assessed value, is 8.86 percent.

- **High Impact Business.** This program allows any business which invests $12 million and creates 500 jobs or invests $30 million and retains 1,500 jobs to qualify for the benefits available in Illinois enterprise zones.

FINANCIAL INCENTIVES:

- **Build Illinois Small Business Development Loan Program (SBDP).** Through the SBDP, the Department can provide term, fixed-rate loans, at a negotiable interest rate, in cooperation with private sector lenders and investors. Principal and interest payments from the loans return to the Department and are used to maintain a state revolving loan fund for use by other eligible small businesses. The Department awards financing to companies using specific funding criteria. Staff conducts a technical and financial review of each complete application. Financing is provided to those companies which best address the program's objectives. The ultimate purpose of the program is to provide employment opportunities for Illinois citizens, either through job creation and retention or to modernize or improve the competitiveness of the firm.

- **Minority, Women, and Disabled Business Loan Program (MWDBLP).** The MWDBLP can provide term fixed-rate, low-interest loans to Illinois' minority, women, and disabled-owned small businesses in cooperation with private sector lenders and investors. Principal and interest payments from the loans revert to the Department and are used to maintain a state revolving loan fund for use by other eligible small businesses. The Department awards financing to companies using specific funding criteria. The staff conducts a technical and financial review of each complete application. Financing is provided to those companies which best address the program's objectives. The purpose of the program is to help minority, women, and disabled-owned businesses obtain access to capital and provide employment opportunities for Illinois citizens, either through job creation and retention or to modernize or improve the competitiveness of the firm.

- **Participation Loan Program.** Through the Participation Loan Program, the Department will purchase participation interests in loans extended to small businesses for business start-up, expansion, modernization and competitiveness improvement. The purpose of the program is to help small businesses that otherwise would not receive loans to obtain access to capital in order to create or retain substantial employment in Illinois or to modernize or improve the competitiveness of the borrower.

- **Community Development Corporation Participation Loan Program.** Through this program the Department will purchase participation interests in loans extended to small businesses for business start-up, expansion, modernization and competitiveness improvement. The purpose of the program is to help small businesses that otherwise would not receive loans to obtain access to capital in order to create or retain substantial employment in Illinois or to modernize or improve the competitiveness of the borrower.

- **Enterprise Zone Participation Loan Program.** Through this program the Department will purchase participation interests in loans extended to small businesses for business start-up, expansion, modernization and competitiveness improvement. The purpose of the program is to help small business that otherwise would not receive loans to obtain access to capital in order to create or retain substantial employment in Illinois or to modernize or improve the competitiveness of the borrower.

- **Capital Access Program (CAP).** This program is designed to encourage lending institutions to make loans to new and small businesses that do not qualify for conventional financing. CAP is based on a portfolio insurance concept where the borrower and the Illinois Department of Commerce and Community Affairs (DCCA) each contribute a percentage of the loan amount into a reserve fund located at the lender's bank. This reserve fund enables the financial institution to make loans beyond its conventional risk threshold and is available to draw upon to recover losses on loans made under the program.

- **Development Corporation Program.** Through the Development Corporation Program the Department can provide qualified investments, loans or grants to public or private development corporations, financial intermediaries or other entities whose purpose is to enhance local or regional economic development. Development corporations are most often public and bank sponsored and funded financial institutions. Development corporations must be organized (by charter or bylaws) at least in part, to finance, promote or encourage commercialization, adoption or implementation of advanced technologies, processes or products.

- **Surety Bond Guaranty Program.** This program provides Illinois' small, minority and women contractors with technical assistance and outreach services, helps them receive experience in the industry and assists them in obtaining bid, performance and payment bonds for government, public utility and private contracts.

- **Technology Venture Investment Program.** Through this

program, the Illinois Department of Commerce and Community Affairs (DCCA) will provide investment capital for young or growing Illinois businesses in cooperation with private investment companies or investors. The co-investors must assume at least 50 percent of the equity financing of the business project for commercializing advanced technologies. Program investments will be used for businesses seeking funding for any new process, technique, product or technical device commercially exploitable by Illinois businesses in fields such as health care and biomedical products, information and telecommunications, computing and electronic equipment, manufacturing technology, materials, transportation and aerospace, geoscience, financial and service industries, agriculture and biotechnology.

OTHER INCENTIVES:

• **Foreign Investment.** One half of the job of Illinois' six foreign offices is to promote foreign direct investment in Illinois. 1999's budget provided the money needed to add two additional foreign offices.

• **Export Assistance.** The second half of Illinois' six foreign offices is for export assistance. The Illinois International Business office conducts numerous foreign trade shows each year; there are also five international trade centers in Illinois to help businesses begin exporting. The Illinois Export Finance Partnership Program helps small and medium sized businesses finance exports.

• **Regulatory Relief Programs.** The First Stop Business Information Center of Illinois helps entrepreneurs and small businesses cut through bureaucratic red tape with information about permits, licenses and other requirements. The center operates the Regulatory Flexibility Program. It reviews every proposed rule, publishes a weekly regulatory alert to businesses and analyzes impacts of proposed rules. In an effort to reduce or eliminate unnecessary regulations, the center submits its analyses to the Joint Committee on Administrative Rules and the state agency making the rule.

• **Incentives For Specific Busines Sectors.** Illinois has manufacturing modernization programs, coal development programs, programs to develop and market tourism attractions, and recycling programs.

SUCCESSFUL INCENTIVES:

• **Capital Access Program.** The Capital Access Program brought home the top prize in winning the Program Excellence Award from the Council of Development Finance Agencies (CDFA), a nationwide organization. In selecting CAP for the honor, CDFA noted the effective manner in which the program has assisted so many new and

expanding businesses in Illinois, specifically pointing out the more than 200 small businesses that would not have received the financing necessary to start or expand without the program. Program evaluation methodology included in CAP contributed to its selection for the award.

Contact:

Gregg Fahey
Department of Commerce and Community Affairs
100 West Randolph, Suite 3-400
Chicago, IL 60601
(312) 814-7168

LEGISLATIVE TIMELINE:

1990: Implemented the Indiana Strategic Development Fund, designed to provide matching state funds to industry groups to promote technology development.

1991: Established a new program to provide loans to state businesses for the purpose of improving technological capacity or productivity.

1992: Established Training 2000, a new workforce training program and fund to develop basic workforce skills. Passed legislation providing that no new enterprise zones or tax-increment financing districts be established after Dec. 31, 1995.

1993: Expanded the income tax credit for investing in economically disadvantaged areas to include small businesses. Passed legislation allowing small businesses to organize as limited-liability companies.

1994: Approved the Economic Development for a Growing Economy (EDGE) tax credit program to assist companies that create jobs by locating or expanding in the state. Increased funding for processing business permits to expedite and ease the permitting process for new and expanding firms.

1995: Passed measures granting the Indiana Development Finance Authority permission to guarantee revenue bonds to finance clean coal technology and to abate taxes in economic revitalization zones until 2005.

1996: Passed Indiana's Tort Reform Act. The new law provides greater protection for manufacturers, significantly revises Indiana's product liability and comparative fault statutes and limits the recovery of punitive damages.

1997: Passed a Brownfield Revitalization Zone tax abatement.

1999: Created incentives for high growth companies with high skilled jobs, information and high technology infrastructure.

TAX INCENTIVES:

- **Corporate income tax.** 7.9 percent, consisting of 3.4 percent on income from sources within the state plus a 4.5percent supplemental income tax.

- **Personal income tax.** 3.4 percent.

- **Sales and use tax.** 5 percent.

- **Payroll-Based Tax Credits.** The Economic Development for a Growing Economy (EDGE) tax credits are based on the added payroll for Indiana jobs created as a result of a project. The payroll taxes withheld from those new employees, effectively 3.1 percent in Indiana, are the basis for the credits. Tax credits can be awarded up to that amount, i.e. up to 3.1 percent of gross payroll, for a period not to exceed ten years. The credits awarded are first applied against any Indiana corporate income tax liability, and any excess amount earned is refunded directly to the company. Eligible projects are those with a competitive disparity in project costs, including incentives, between an Indiana location and a competing state. The project must also receive significant community support and compare favorably with county wage levels. The program requires minimal paperwork. The amount of the credit is negotiated with the Indiana Department of Commerce, to be approved by a governing board. All terms and conditions for receipt of the credits are by agreement between the State of Indiana and the participating company. EDGE does require a company commitment to maintain operation of the project for a period two times as long as the tax credit term. Annual verification of the amount of individual income taxes withheld will trigger release of the credits.

FINANCIAL INCENTIVES:

- **Skilled Workforce Investment Program.** Indiana's Training 2000 Program is designed to provide financial assistance to new and expanding industries committed to training their workforce. Companies can receive reimbursement not to exceed $200,000 for retraining existing workers. Reimbursement for training new hires will be evaluated on a case-by-case basis. The following types of companies are eligible for receiving financial grant assistance from the Training 2000 Fund: a) manufacturing companies; b) distribution centers; c) regional headquarters or back offices may also receive assistance under certain circumstances. In such cases, the company must demonstrate that a significant portion of its business involves transactions with out-of-state entities. The following types of entities will not receive financial grant assistance from Training 2000 Fund: a) retail firms; b) service business; c) housing development and real estate companies; d) professional and personal services; e) not-for-profit organizations; f) educational institutions; g) start-up companies.

    Training activities eligible for reimbursement under the guidelines include: *Instruction costs* – wages for company trainers, wages for company training coordinator(s), Indiana public and/or private school tuition, contracts for vendor trainers, and training seminars; *Travel costs* - travel for trainers and training coordinators (company and other), travel for trainees;

Materials and supplies costs – training texts (books/manuals), audio/visual materials. Costs that are not eligible for reimbursement are: trainee wages, fringe benefits, tangible property (e.g. calculators, furniture, classroom fixtures), out-of-state publicly supported schools, employee handbooks, scrap produced during training, management, safety, sales, driving, health and wellness.

Eligible training activities include: *Basic skills* – reading, writing, and math; *Transferable skills* – skills that will enhance an employee's general knowledge, employability and flexibility in the workplace (welding, computer skills, blueprint reading, problem solving, team participation, etc.); *Company-Specific skills* – skills that are unique to an individual company's workplace, equipment and/or capital investment; *Quality-assurance skills* – skills that are intended to increase the quality of the company's product [Statistical Process Control (SPC), Total Quality Management (TQM), ISO 9000 and QS 9000].

Completed applications for Indiana's Training 2000 Fund will be evaluated in accordance with the following criteria: a) quality of jobs, including skill and wage levels; b) quality of the training program and the company's past commitment to training; c) number of workers to be trained; d) capital dollar investment being made by the company; e) importance of the project to Indiana's strategic future; f) financial strength of the company; g) economic need of the affected community.

• **The Industrial Development Grant Fund (IDGF).** IDGF awards grants to eligible units of government to help them meet the infrastructure needs of new or expanding facilities in Indiana. The project must be related to economic development efforts and must have job-creation potential. The eligibility requirements are: *Eligible activities* – water lines, sewer lines, drainage facilities, road improvements and rail spurs; *Eligible applicants* – cities, towns, counties, special taxing districts, water corporations, regional water, sewer and solid waste districts, and conservancy districts. The proposals will be evaluated in accordance with the following criteria: quality of jobs to be created, including skill and wage levels; number of jobs to be created; capital dollar investment being made by the company; importance of the project to Indiana's strategic future; financial strength of the company; economic need of the affected community. IDGF grants are awarded to communities and other eligible applicants. The applicant must have commitment letter from responsible representatives of the affected industry/industries indicating their plans to locate or expand a facility at the project site. The grant award is based on new job creation. All funds are available on a reimbursement basis only.

OTHER INCENTIVES:

• **Export assistance programs.** Financial: Trade show assistance grants are available to offset booth costs at select foreign trade shows. All other "export assistance" comes in the form of counseling, referrals, research, etc.

• **Strategic Development Fund.** Strategic Development Fund (SDF) grants are available to nonprofit corporations for programs that benefit two or more companies and whose purpose is to promote industrial/business development. Community Focus Fund (CFF) is a federally funded grant program administered by the IDOC that is available to small cities towns and counties for construction projects to benefit low-to-moderate income individuals to eliminate blight in communities.

• **Regulatory Relief Program.** IDOC's ombudsman works with incoming and expanding business to make sure all necessary permits are expedited and received.

• **Public/Private partnerships.** The IDOC partners with public utilities to promote economic development.

SUCCESSFUL INCENTIVES:

• **Successful Customized Business Incentive.** All of IDOC's programs are customized to each individual situation due to their adaptability and flexibility.

Contact:

Karen Northup
Indiana Dept. of Commerce
One North Capital Ave., Suite 700
Indianapolis, IN 46204
(317) 232-0160

IOWA

LEGISLATIVE TIMELINE:

1990: Established a 10 percent income tax credit for investment by an individual or firm in a qualified corporation or seed-capital fund.

1991: Established the Voluntary Shared Work Program for businesses contemplating layoffs during an economic downturn.

1992: Created a $4.1 million Strategic Investment Fund. Appropriated $1 million for workforce retraining programs. Created a statewide manufacturing technology program to provide technical assistance to industries.

1993: Eliminated the property tax on new manufacturing machinery used for recycling waste plastic and wastepaper products.

1994: Enacted the New Jobs and Income Program, which provides expanded tax credits and exemptions to companies creating at least 50 high-paying jobs with a minimal capital investment of $10 million. Boosted funding for worker retraining, making manufacturers eligible to receive a grant of up to $50,000 from their area technical schools to retrain existing workers in new manufacturing skills.

1995: Established a Loan Loss Reserve Program, which guarantees loans to private businesses that invest in employee training. Created a Workforce Investment Program to provide training to groups that have historically faced barriers to employment.

1996: Made the New Jobs and Income Program (NJIP) available to companies investing $3 million and creating 15 new jobs. Passed a measure to make more training funds available to companies that pay a target wage level.

1997: Enterprise Zones: Authorized a county to designate up to 1 percent of its total area as an enterprise zone for a period of 10 years.

1998: Recognized that an Iowa agricultural industry finance corporation is a private business corporation and not a public corporation or instrument of the state.

1999: Approved an act that provides that a community college may enter into an agreement with certain employers in the community college's merged area to establish an Accelerated Career Education (ACE) Program.

TAX INCENTIVES:

• **Corporate income tax.** 6.0 to 12.0 percent.

• **Personal income tax.** 0.36 to 8.98 percent.

• **Sales and use tax.** 5 percent sales tax on transactions involving the transfer, exchange or barter of tangible personal property on certain enumerated services and gross receipts from the sale of optional service of warranty contracts; communities may impose a local-option sales tax. Use tax of 5 percent.

• **New Jobs and Income Program.** The Iowa New Jobs and Income Program (NJIP) provides a package of tax credits and exemptions to businesses making a capital investment of at least $10.38 million and creating 50 or more jobs meeting wage and benefit targets. Qualifying businesses participating in NJIP receive substantial benefits, including:

1) A 3 percent withholding tax credit applied to the company's job training fund, essentially doubling the training funds otherwise available.

2) An investment tax credit of up to 10 percent for use against Iowa's corporate income tax. The credit, based on machinery, equipment, buildings and improvements, can be carried forward for seven years.

3) A 13 percent research and development activity corporate tax credit may be carried forward or refunded.

4) A refund will be paid for Iowa sales, service or use taxes paid to contractors or subcontractors during the construction phase of the project.

5) Foreign-owned companies may receive exemptions from land ownership restrictions.

6) The local government involved may elect to exempt from property tax the improvements to land and buildings for a period not to exceed 20 years. These exemptions can cover all or a portion of the value added by the improvements.

When good cause is shown, a community may request a waiver of the $10.38 million capital expenditure requirement and/or a waiver of the 50-new-jobs-created requirement. In order to be considered for a waiver, the eligible business must, at a minimum, agree to the following: the business must make a minimum capital investment of $3 million and the business must create at least 15 full-time production positions at a facility which has located or expanded in Iowa.

• **Enterprise Zones.** Manufacturers and other businesses expanding or locating in new or existing facilities and creating new jobs in economically distressed areas of Iowa have a new incentive to do so. Enterprise Zone legislation to promote business investments in these areas was passed by the Iowa legislature and signed by the Governor in May of 1997. Revisions to the law became effective July 1, 1998. Eligible businesses locating or expanding in an Enterprise Zone area may receive property tax exemptions and expanded state tax credits. Twenty-eight counties and eighteen cities qualify for the program under the 1997 law's provisions by having areas which meet legislative definitions of economic distress. Businesses expanding or locating in an Enterprise Zone can receive the following benefits:

1) Property tax exemptions on all or part of the costs of improvements to land and buildings for up to 10 years.
2) An investment tax credit of up to 10 percent on corporate income taxes for investments on machinery and equipment, new buildings and improvements to existing buildings.
3) Refunds of sales, services or use taxes paid to contractors or subcontractors during construction.
4) A 13 percent research and development activities credit (refundable) on corporate income taxes.
5) Supplemental new jobs training withholding credit of $1\frac{1}{2}$ percent of the gross wages. This credit is in addition to, and not in lieu of, the withholding credit of $1\frac{1}{2}$ percent authorized for the Iowa New Jobs Training Program.

To receive benefits, businesses expanding or locating in Enterprise Zones must: create at least 10 full-time, project-related jobs and maintain them for at least ten years; pay 80 percent of a standard employee medical and dental insurance plan or equivalent; pay 90 percent of the average regional or county wage, whichever is lower ($7.50 per hour minimum); make capital investments of at least $500,000; and not be a retail establishment.

Effective July 1, 1998, eligibility for Enterprise Zone Program benefits was expanded to include Alternative Eligible Businesses that might expand or locate in Iowa cities with populations of 8,000-24,000 based on 1995 census estimates. To be eligible, these cities must have geographic areas that meet two of the five distress criteria listed above for cities under the original 1997 legislation. While Alternative Eligible Businesses in this category of cities may receive the same Enterprise Zone benefits as described earlier, there are a number of differences for this "new" category of qualifying cities:

1. The Alternative Eligible Business location must be within 35 miles of an existing Iowa Enterprise Zone or an adjacent state's enterprise zone.
2. Alternative Eligible Businesses must meet the higher wage requirements of the New Jobs and Income Program (NJIP) – a median wage of $11.42 per hour or 130 percent of the average county wage, whichever is higher (check with IDED for local NJIP wage standards). No Enterprise Zone Commission is required for this category of cities; they only need a City Council resolution of approval.

FINANCIAL INCENTIVES:

- **Community Economic Betterment Account (CEBA).** The CEBA program provides financial assistance to companies that create new employment opportunities and/or retain existing jobs and make new capital investment in Iowa. The amount of funding is based, in part, on the number of jobs to be created/retained. Funds are provided in the form of loans and forgivable loans. Projects eligible for CEBA funding include, but are not limited to, the following: building construction or reconstruction; land or building acquisition; equipment purchases; operating and maintenance expenses; site development – clearance, demolition and building removal; and working capital.

CEBA investments should not be considered a sole funding source. The program leverages other financial support such as bank financing and private investment. The CEBA program also contains a "Venture Project" component specifically designed for early-stage and start-up businesses. Financial assistance is provided in forms conducive to the company's stage of maturity. The "Venture Project" component allows for longer-term job creation and investment performance periods than otherwise offered through CEBA. The CEBA program can provide assistance up to $1 million. As an alternative, nontraditional, short-term float loans or interim loans greater than $1 million may be available. The funding level for start-up companies varied depending upon employee wage rates. Assistance through CEBA's "Venture Project" component is provided as an "equity-like" investment, with a maximum award of $100,000.

- **Economic Development Set-Aside Program (EDSA).** The EDSA program provides financial assistance to companies that create new employment opportunities and/or retain existing jobs and make new capital investment in Iowa. The amount of funding is based, in part, on the number of jobs to be created/retained. Funds are provided in the form of loans and forgivable loans. Projects eligible for EDSA funding include, but are not limited to, the following: building construction or reconstruction; land or building acquisition; equipment purchases; operating and maintenance expenses; site development – clearance, demolition and building removal; and working capital.

EDSA investments should not be considered a sole funding source. The program leverages other financial support such as bank financing and private investment. The EDSA program assistance is targeted toward business projects located in communities of under 50,000 population. At least 51 percent of the created/retained employment opportunities must be made available to individuals presently earning wages defined as low-and-moderate income. The EDSA program can provide assistance up to $500,000.

- **Rail Economic Development Program.** The Iowa Department of Transportation provides funds for construction or rehabilitation of rail spurs to serve new or existing industries. The rail project must be a key to the creation or retention of jobs.

• **Revitalize Iowa's Sound Economy (RISE).** This program is administered by the Iowa Department of Transportation for expenditures on city, county and state highways to help attract new development or to support growth with existing developments. Projects are evaluated on economic potential and impact. Funding may be used in conjunction with other sources of federal, state, local and private financing for the purpose of improving area highways and specific access to roads.

• **Public Facilities Set-Aside Program.** The program, administered by the Iowa Department of Economic Development, provides financial assistance to cities and counties to provide infrastructure improvements for businesses which require such improvements in order to create new job opportunities. The form of assistance is limited to grants to cities of population under 50,000 and counties for the provision of or improvements to sanitary sewer systems, water systems, streets and roads, storm sewers, rail lines and airports. Assistance is limited to two-thirds of the total cost of the improvements needed. The emphasis of this program is to increase the productive capacity of the state. Priority will be given to projects that will create manufacturing jobs, add value to Iowa resources and/or export out-of-state.

OTHER INCENTIVES:

• **Export Trade Assistance Program (ETAP).** The State of Iowa offers financial assistance to Iowa companies who wish to take advantage of international trade shows and trade missions to enter new markets. Through ETAP, the International Division of the Iowa Department of Economic Development will reimburse 75 percent of a company's direct expenses up to $4,000 per pre-approved event.

• **Value Added Products and Processes Financial Assistance Program (VAPPFAP).** The VAPPFAP seeks to increase the innovative utilization of Iowa's agricultural commodities. It accomplishes this by investing in the development of new agri-products and new processing technologies. The program includes two components. Innovative Products and Processes encourages the processing of agricultural commodities into higher-value products not commonly produced in Iowa, or the utilization of a process not commonly used in Iowa to produce new and innovative products from agricultural commodities. Renewable Fuels and Co-Products encourages the production of renewable fuels, such as soy diesel and ethanol, and co-products for livestock feed.

Program Eligibility Requirements are as follows: the proposed project must be located in Iowa; the business must have a business plan demonstrating a viable market and managerial and technical experience; the business should also have completed a feasibility study documenting the viability of the proposed start-up business; the degree to which the facility will increase the utilization of agricultural commodities produced in the state; the proportion of local match to be contributed to the project; the level of need of the region where the existing facility is, or the proposed facility is to be located; and the degree to which the facility produces a co-product that is marketed in the same locality as the facility.

• **The Iowa Department of Economic Development Regulatory Assistance.** This team, a partnership between IDED and the Iowa Department of Natural Resources, works to streamline the environmental permitting process for industrial expansion.

SUCCESSFUL INCENTIVES:

• **New Jobs and Income Program (NJIP).** Since 1994, NJIP has been a pivotal factor in the decisions of 32 companies to bring new technologies and research and development processes to Iowa. Planned investments using NJIP total $2.4 billion. The projects will create 2,721 jobs with extensive employee benefit packages. The average wage of the projects is $14.86 per hour. Fifty-nine percent of the new jobs are from expansions of existing facilities; 41 percent of the jobs are at new facilities.

• **Investment Tax Credit of the New Jobs and Income Program and Enterprise Zones.** In 1999, the General Assembly and Governor approved legislation expanding these programs. The investment tax credit (10 percent of investment with 7 year carry forward for unused portion) now includes the cost of land and existing buildings for qualifying projects in addition to facilities construction and renovation and purchases of machinery, equipment and computers used in processing.

Contact:

Bob Henningsen
Administrator, Division of Business Development
Iowa Department of Economic Development
200 East Grand Ave.
Des Moines, IA 50309
(515) 242-4707

TAX INCENTIVES:

- **Corporate income tax.** 4.0 percent, plus a surtax of 3.35 percent taxable in excess of $50,000.

- **Personal income tax.** 3.5 to 7.75 percent.

- **Sales and use tax.** 4.9 percent.

- **Enterprise Zone Incentives**. Enterprise zone incentives are available to qualifying businesses throughout the state, based on the location of the facility, the type of facility (manufacturing, nonmanufacturing or retail), the capital investment and the number of jobs created. A sales tax exemption is available on the materials, equipment and services purchased when building, expanding or renovating a business facility. State income tax credits are available for job creation and capital investment. The job creation tax credit is $1,500 per net new job (enhanced incentive for designated nonmetropolitan regions - $2,500 per net new job). The investment tax credit is $1000 to $100,000 of qualified business investment or major portion thereof. Earned credits may be used to offset up to 50 percent of the business's annual state income tax liability. Unused credits may be carried forward indefinitely and applied in subsequent tax years until the credits are exhausted. Manufacturing and nonmanufacturing businesses are eligible for all enterprise zone incentives. The sole enterprise zone incentive for retail businesses is the sales tax exemption, available only in communities with a population less than 2,500.

- **Job Expansion and Investment Tax Credits**. Job Expansion and Investment Tax Credits are available to all eligible businesses that are not eligible for enterprise zone credits and that create at least two net jobs. These 10-year credits are determined by the amount of qualified business investment made in the company and the number of net jobs created. The job creation tax credit of $100 per net new job. The investment tax credit is $100 to $100,000 of qualified business investment or major portion thereof. Earned credits may be used to offset up to 50 percent of the business's annual state income tax liability. Business may defer credits up to three years. Unused credits may not be carried forward.

- **High-Performance Incentive Program**. This 1993 incentive program was designed to retain Kansas' existing high-performance businesses, encourage investment by existing companies in worker training and education and spur the attraction of new, high-quality firms to the state. The incentives offered under the program are limited to manufacturers, certain business service firms, corporate headquarters and back-office operations of national or multinational corporations. These firms pay above average wages for their industry in the county where they are located and invest either two percent of their payroll on training or participate in one of Kansas' workforce training programs. Specific incentives extended to firms meeting the qualifications include the following: a sales tax exemption, a 10 percent investment tax credit against corporate income tax on capital investment exceeding $50,000, a workforce training tax credit of up to $50,000 per annum on training expenditures above 2 percent of total company payroll, potential matching funds for approved private consulting fees and priority consideration for other state business assistance programs.

LEGISLATIVE TIMELINE:

1990: Established the Community Strategic Planning Assistance program to award grants for the development of countywide economic development strategy plans.

1991: Approved the Kansas Investments in Lifelong Learning Program, under which eligible businesses may receive finding for job training, adult basic education, vocational and skill assessment services and testing and other program services for employees in new jobs.

1992: Increased the state's sales and use tax and repealed several sales tax exemptions. Reduced the state's corporate income tax rate and increased the surtax (effective at a taxable income level of $50,000). Eliminated existing enterprise zones and made the tax benefits of the program available to qualified businesses throughout the state.

1993: Authorized tax incentives to manufacturers investing in facilities, equipment or employees. The incentives are tied to the amount of the investment rather than the number of jobs created.

1994: Authorized economic development incentives for specific types of service firms (e.g. back-office operations and regional headquarters). Allowed Certified Kansas Venture Capital Companies to invest in similar non-manufacturing businesses and maintain their ability to offer tax credits to potential investors.

1995: Established a new high-tech venture capital fund, expanded eligibility for the High Performance Incentive Program, set aside money for the Microloan Program and for Mainstreet Development Grants.

1996: Approved legislation to extend a two-year moratorium on the unemployment tax for a third year.

1997: Amended the law governing the High Performance Incentive Program making more options for eligibility.

1998: Abolished the privilege tax on Kansas insurance companies and expanded the magnitude of the premium tax.

1999: Expanded the type of businesses that may qualify for tax incentives associated with the High Performance Firms Incentives Program.

- **Tax Credit for Research.** To encourage research and development activities within the state, the state gives tax credits to taxpayers who invest in research and development. The maximum credit is 6.5 percent of an enterprise's annual qualified research and development expenditures. However, only 25 percent of the allowable annual credit may be claimed in any one year. Any remaining credit may be used in 25 percent increments against future income tax obligation, until the credit is exhausted.

- **Tax Credit for Day Care Facilities.** Tax credits are offered against Kansas income tax liability for businesses providing child day care services to employees. These credits apply to taxpayers who pay for or provide child day care services for their employees or provide facilities and necessary equipment for child day care services. The credit is equal to 30 percent, up to $30,000, of the amount spent in Kansas during the tax year for child day care services purchased for dependent children of the taxpayer's employees. Employers wishing to establish a child day care facility primarily for the employees' dependent children can claim a credit of up to 50 percent of the amount spent in the establishment of a day care facility, up to $45,000 per taxpayer, during the first year. In the taxable years after the year of establishment, the annual credit available to the taxpayer would be 30 percent of the amount expended for the annual operation of the facility, less the amounts received by the taxpayer as payment for use of the child day care services, not to exceed $30,000 for any tax year.

- **Venture Capital Tax Credit.** This tax credit is designed to encourage cash investments in certified Kansas venture capital companies. The tax credit equals 25 percent of the taxpayer's cash investment in a venture capital firm in the year in which the investment is made. The entire amount of the credit allowable for deduction may be claimed in one year. If the amount of the credit claimed annually exceeds the taxpayer's liability in any year, the amount in excess may be carried forward until the credit is used.

- **Local Seed Capital Pool Tax.** This tax credit is designed to encourage cash investments in certified local seed-capital pools. The tax credit is equal to 25 percent of the taxpayer's cash investment. The entire amount of the credit allowable for deduction may be claimed in one year. If the amount of the credit claimed annually exceeds the taxpayer's liability in any year, the amount in excess may be carried forward.

FINANCIAL INCENTIVES:

- **Kansas Development Finance Authority.** The Kansas Development Finance Authority (KDFA) is a state body performing public financial functions. The authority, governed by a five-member board, issues bonds to finance capital improvements, industrial enterprises, agricultural business enterprises, educational facilities, health-care facilities and housing development, or any combination mortgage on such facilities.

OTHER INCENTIVE PROGRAMS:

- **Job Training.** Kansas offers funding for customized training and retraining of employees of new an expanding businesses through three programs.

- **Kansas Industrial Training (KIT).** Provides pre-employment training for new and expanding businesses creating at least five jobs.

- **Kansas Industrial Retraining (KIR).** Provides on-the-job training for restructuring companies whose employees are likely to be displaced due to obsolete or inadequate job skills. This program requires matching funds from the company.

- **State of Kansas Investments in Lifelong Learning (SKILL).** Provides pre-employment training for new and expanding businesses, or consortiums of business, that are creating large number of new jobs or new jobs paying above average wages. This program allows up to 50 percent of funds to be used to lease or purchase training equipment for local educational institutions. Up to 10 percent of the funds may be used to cover the administrative costs of the school.

- **Public/Private Partnership - Kansas Venture Capital, Inc. (KVCI).** The KVCI is a state-wide risk capital system designed to meet the special needs of business throughout Kansas. The system seeks to create private risk capital for investment in smaller Kansas businesses. All funds invested by KVCI must be invested in Kansas businesses solely for the purpose of enhancing productive capacity within the state, or for the purpose of adding value to goods or services produced or processed within the state. Most corporate businesses that meet the Small Business Administration's definition of a small business qualify for KVCI assistance. Any type of business can apply to the KVCI for assistance.

- **Day Care Assistance.** The credit to employers during the first year is 50 percent of their expenditures to provide services. In subsequent years, the allowed credit is 30 percent. Maximum annual credit: first year = $445,000; after first year = $30,000.

Contact:

Mark Barcellina
Research Analyst
Kansas Department of Commerce and Housing
700 SW Harrison Street, #1300
Topeka, KS 66603-3712
(785)296-3481

TAX INCENTIVES:

- **Corporate income tax.** 4.0 to 8.25 percent.

- **Personal income tax**. 2.0 to 6.0 percent.

- **Sales and use tax.** 6 percent state tax; no local sales taxes.

- **Kentucky Jobs Development Act (KJDA).** Service and technology related companies that invest in new and expended non-manufacturing, non-retail projects that provide at least 75 percent of their services to users located outside of Kentucky, and that create new jobs for at least 25 full-time Kentucky residents may qualify for tax credits. Projects approved under KJDA may receive state income tax credits and job assessment fees for up to 50 percent of project startup costs and 50 percent of annual facility rental costs or rental value for up to 10 years. Maximum approved start-up costs are $10,000 per new full-time job for Kentucky residents subject to Kentucky income taxes. The company receives a 100 percent credit against the state income tax arising from the project and may collect a job assessment fee up to 5.0 percent of the gross wages of each employee whose job is created by the project and who is subject to Kentucky income taxes. Job assessment fee is limited to 4.0 percent if the local jurisdiction does not assess a local occupational license fee. Unused credits may be carried forward for the term of the agreement. The employee receives credits for the fee against state income taxes and local occupational taxes.

- **Kentucky Industrial Development Act (KIDA).** Investments in new and expanding manufacturing projects may qualify for tax credits. Companies that create at least 15 new full-time jobs and invest at least $100,000 in projects approved under KIDA may receive state income tax credits for up to 100 percent of annual debt service costs (principal and interest) for up to 10 years on land, buildings, site development, building fixtures and equipment used in a project, or the company may collect a job assessment fee of 2 percent of the gross wages of each employee whose job is created by the approved project and who is subject to Kentucky income taxes. Ground leases having a term of 60 years or more are considered acquisition of real estate, but lease payments are not eligible for tax credit recovery. Eligible equipment costs are limited to $10,000 per new full-time job. Financing may be provided by any source except debt service paid in connection with other state grant programs. Unused credits may be carried forward for the term of the agreement.

- **Kentucky Rural Economic Development Act (KREDA).** Larger tax credits are available for new and expanding manufacturing projects that create at least 15 new first-time jobs in counties with (1) unemployment rates higher than the state average in each of the five preceding calendar years, or (2) average unemployment rates higher than the state average by at least 200 percent in the most recent twelve consecutive months. The project must be at least $100,000. Once a company is operating under a KREDA agreement, the company maintains KREDA benefits, even if the county

LEGISLATIVE TIMELINE:

1990: Passed a sweeping education-reform bill to completely restructure the school system.

1991: Approved a corporate tax incentive to help land a major United Airlines facility.

1992: Established the Kentucky Economic Development Partnership, a quasi-independent corporation headed by the secretary of economic development, to lead the state's economic development efforts. Created the Kentucky Jobs Development Authority to provide income tax incentives to new non-manufacturing firms. Created the Kentucky Industrial Revitalization Authority, which can provide income tax credits to existing manufacturing companies faced with an imminent closure.

1993: Ford Motor Co., International Paper, and Canadian steel manufacturers Dofasco and Co-Steel tapped the new tax incentive programs and located or expanded in Kentucky.

1994: Established a low-interest loan pool from the state's unclaimed and abandoned property program for agricultural and small business development. Created the Kentucky Research and Technologies Infrastructure, which will consist of research centers to provide research, development and technology transfer to businesses on a fee-for-service basis.

1996: Passed a law to allow tax credits for private investment in tourism projects. Set up a new exemption to the sales tax for manufacturing processors that only complete part of the manufacturing.

1998: Created the Kentucky Investment Fund Program to assist investment fund managers.

loses KREDA status.

- **Kentucky Industrial Revitalization Act (KIRA).** Investments in the rehabilitation of manufacturing operations that are in imminent danger of permanently closing or that have closed temporarily may qualify for tax credits. Companies that save or create 25 jobs in projects approved under KIRA may receive state income tax credits and job assessment fees for up to 10 years limited to 50 percent of the costs of the rehabilitation or construction of buildings and the reoutfitting or purchasing of machinery and equipment. When approved by a majority vote of employees at the plan, and with the consent of the local taxing jurisdiction, the approved company can levy a job assessment fee of up to 6.0 percent of the gross wages of each employee subject to Kentucky individual income tax whose job is preserved or created by the approved project. The employee receives credits for the fee against state income taxes and local occupational taxes; however, the employee must give up that portion of the assessment fee equal to 1.0 percent of gross wages.

- **Other Income Tax Credits.** A credit of $100 is allowed for each unemployed person hired for at least 180 consecutive days. To qualify for the credit the company must hire a worker who has been unemployed for at least 60 days. Credits cannot be claimed for close relatives, dependents, or persons for whom the company receives federal payments for on-the-job training. Credits are allowed for up to 50 percent of the installed costs of equipment used exclusively to recycle or compost business or consumer wastes (excluding secondary and demolition wastes) and machinery used exclusively to manufacture products composed substantially from business or consumer waste materials. During the year that the equipment is purchased, credits are limited to 10 percent of total credits allowed and 25 percent of the taxpayer's state income tax liability. The unused portion of the total allowable credits can be carried forward to succeeding tax years, with the credit claimed during any tax year limited to 25 percent of the taxpayer's state income tax liability. A credit is allowed for up to 4.5 percent of the value of Kentucky coal (excluding transportation costs) used for industrial heating or processing. The credit is allowed for 10 years following either the installation or conversion to coal burning units. The credit in any year cannot exceed the corporation's tax liability, minus other credits. Unused credits cannot be carried forward.

- **Order of Use of Credits.** State statutes specify the order in which Kentucky income tax credits must be taken when a taxpayer is entitled to more than one tax credit for a tax year (KRS 141.0205):

  1. Economic development credits for KIDA, KREDA, KJDA or Skills Training
  2. Credits for hiring unemployed persons
  3. Recycling equipment credits
  4. Coal conversion credits
  5. Credits for enterprise zone businesses that hire unemployed persons.

- **Kentucky Enterprise Zone Program (EZP).** State and local tax incentives are offered to businesses located or locating in zones, and some regulations are eased to make development in the area more attractive. A zone remains in effect for 20 years after the date of designation. To qualify, businesses must meet the following criteria: 50 percent of their employees must perform substantially all of their services within the enterprise zone; and to apply as a NEW business (companies which began operations in the enterprise zone after the date the zone was designated), 25 percent of the company's total full-time workforce must meet the targeted criteria as long as the business is enterprise zone certified. To apply as an existing business (companies which were in operation in the enterprise zone prior to the designation of the zone) the company has the option of (a) a 20 percent increase in capital investment; or (b) a 20 percent increase in total workforce – 25 percent of these new employees must meet the targeted workforce criteria. Targeted workforce – Kentucky residents who (a) reside within the enterprise zone, or (b) were unemployed 90 days prior to being hired, or (c) were receiving public assistance benefits for at least 90 days prior to employment with a qualified business.

FINANCIAL INCENTIVES:

- **Kentucky Economic Development Finance Authority (KEDFA).** KEDFA encourages economic development, business expansion and job creation by providing business loans to supplement other financing. KEDFA provides loan funds at below market interest rates. The loans are available for fixed asset financing (land, buildings and equipment) for business startup, locations, and expansions that create new jobs in Kentucky or have a significant impact on the economic growth of a community. The loans must be used to finance projects in agribusiness, tourism, industrial ventures or the service industry. No retail projects are eligible.

- **Commonwealth Small Business Development Corporation (CSBDC).** The CSBDC is an economic development entity created under the auspices of the Small Business Administration (SBA) to foster development. The CSBDC is certified to make SBA 504 loans anywhere in the Commonwealth of Kentucky. The CSBDC works with state and local economic development organizations, banks and the SBA to achieve community economic development through job creation and retention by providing long-term fixed asset financing to small business concerns. The CSBDC can lend a maximum of 40 percent of project cost or $750,000 per project (in certain circumstances $1 million). The maximum loan term is 20 years for land and buildings and 10 years for equipment.

- **Community Development Block Grant (CDBG) Loans.** Businesses in Kentucky can obtain low-interest loans through the federally-funded CDBG system. Cities and counties lend the grant funds to businesses for the creation or retention of jobs. The preferred use of the loan funds is for fixed asset financing.

- **Linked Deposit Program.** Provides loans up to $100,000 for small business and agribusiness. Credit decisions are the responsibility of the lender making the loan. The state will purchase certificates of deposit from participating lenders through the State Investment Commission, at the New York Prime interest rate less four percent, but never less than 2 percent. Loans will be made by lenders to eligible companies at a rate equal to New York Prime and never greater than 5 percent. Loan terms are for up to 7 years. Loans will be reviewed by the Department of Agriculture (for agribusiness loans) and the Cabinet for Economic Development (for small business loans) to assure loans comply with the statute.

- **Industrial Revenue Bonds.** IRBs issued by state and local governments in Kentucky can be used to finance manufacturing projects and their warehousing areas, major transportation and communication facilities, most health care facilities, and mineral extraction and processing projects. Bonds issued under U.S. Internal Revenue Code (I.R.C) are more restrictive than Kentucky statutes. Bond funds may be used to finance the total project costs including engineering, site preparation, land, buildings, machinery and equipment, and bond issuance costs.

- **Bluegrass State Skills Corporation (BSSC).** BSSC, an independent *de jure* corporation within the Cabinet for Economic Development, provides grants for customized skills training of workers for new, expanding and existing businesses and industries in Kentucky. Matching grants are awarded for portions of an employer's eligible costs for training Kentucky residents in job skills ranging from entry level to advanced, including retraining, occupational upgrading and skills upgrading of existing employees. The BSSC works with other employment, job training resources and financial incentive agencies to design a training program customized to meet the specific needs of a company. Approved training can be provided by an educational institution, training consultants or the company's own trainers. BSSC funds can be used for curriculum development and customization, instructor fees, instructional materials and the purchase of training equipment.

- **Kentucky Investment Fund (Venture Capital).** The Kentucky Investment Fund encourages venture capital investment by certifying privately operated venture funds, thereby entitling their investors to tax credits equal to 40 percent of their capital contributions to the fund, not to exceed 25 percent in any one year. Criteria for certification include an evaluation of the business plan, analysis of the investment strategy and past experience of the fund manager. Separate requirements exist for initial fund capitalization, as well as ceilings on cash contributions and total credits authorized. Total qualified investments made by each fund in any single small business may not exceed 25 percent of that fund. The qualifications for a small business are a net worth of less than $3 million, and 100 or fewer employees. More than 50 percent of its assets, operations and employees must be located in Kentucky.

- **Job Development Incentive Grant Program.** Job Development Incentive Grants are made to eligible counties from their coal severance accounts for the purpose of encouraging job development. Projects are administered through the Kentucky Economic Development Finance Authority (KEDFA), with the requirement that at least 25 new full-time jobs, with a minimum wage of at least 130 percent of the federal minimum wage, be created. The grant amount cannot exceed $5,000 per job created. Employees at the project site must be paid an average of at least 150 percent of the federal minimum wage, and there must be an investment of at least $10,000 per new job created.

OTHER INCENTIVES:

- **Export Assistance Program.** The Division of International Trade provides opportunities for increased export sales of Kentucky-produced goods and services by Kentucky businesses that are either (1) potential exporters willing to make a commitment to export sales to areas outside of the U.S., or (2) existing exporters with the potential for increased sales in existing or new foreign markets.

SUCCESSFUL INCENTIVES:

- **Kentucky Tourism Development Act.** Provides sales tax credit for qualifying tourism attractions. A new aquarium was built and a motor race track is being built in Kentucky as a result of the program.

Contact:

Renée F. True
Director of Research
Kentucky Cabinet for Economic Development
500 Mero St.
Frankfort, KY 40601
(502) 564-4886 ext. 4316

LOUISIANA

1990: Approved $300 million in sales taxes, including a 3 percent tax on food, utilities and other traditionally exempt items.

1991: Passed a development incentives law that provides a tax credit for employment of previously unemployed persons in newly created fulltime jobs.

1992: Created a program designed to lure aerospace companies to Louisiana. Created the Louisiana Airport Authority, charged with financing a new international airport between Baton Rouge and New Orleans.

1994: Suspended the sales tax exemption for food and other goods, raising an estimated $410 million for the state.

1995: Enacted the Quality Jobs Program, a rebate to companies based on their net worth to the state. Expanded enterprise zone coverage, created a small business incubator program and established a fund for customized workforce training.

1996: Approved tax credits for eligible companies that participate in the Louisiana Quality Jobs Program. Created the Louisiana Economic Development Council and mandated that a strategic plan be devised.

1997: Created the Tri-State Delta Economic Compact to be composed of Louisiana, Arkansas and Mississippi for the purpose of promoting the economy of the delta region by providing job opportunities.

1999: Provides that a cooperative economic development project may be undertaken by the state or any agency or corporation acting on behalf of the state, with prior written approval of the commissioner of administration.

TAX INCENTIVES:

- **Corporate income tax.** 4.0 to 8.0 percent.

- **Personal income tax.** 2.0 to 6.0 percent.

- **Sales and use tax.** 4 percent levied on the sale of tangible personal property at retail, as well as the use, consumption, distribution or storage of tangible personal property and the sale of services in the state; 1 percent to 5 percent local rate.

- **Industrial Property Tax Exemption.** The Industrial Property Tax Exemption abates, up to ten years, local property taxes (ad valorem) on a manufacturer's new investment and annual capitalized additions. This abatement applies to all improvements to the land, buildings, machinery, equipment, and any other property that is part of the manufacturing process. Granting this incentive must be considered to be in the best interest of the State of Louisiana by the Board of Commerce and Industry. Tax exempt property must remain on the plant site at all times. The land itself is not tax exemptable.

- **Enterprise Zones.** Qualified businesses locating or expanding in Louisiana enterprise zones are eligible for a one-time tax credit of $2,500 for each net new employee added to the payroll. The credit may be used to satisfy state income and corporate franchise tax obligations. If the entire credit cannot be used in the year claimed, the remainder may be applied against the income tax or franchise tax for the succeeding 10 taxable years, or until the entire credit is used, whichever occurs first. Aviation and aerospace industries are eligible for a one-time tax credit of $5,000 per new employee hired. In addition, the qualified company would receive a refund of 4 percent of state sales and use taxes on materials used to construct or improve a building to house a business operation, and machinery and equipment used in the business. Unencumbered local sales/use taxes are rebateable through an Endorsement Resolution of that government body. Local sales taxes that are encumbered toward payment of bond indebtedness or school taxes are not eligible for a refund.

- **Restoration Tax Abatement.** The Restoration Tax Abatement (RTA) Program is a tax incentive created by the state for use by municipalities and local governments to encourage the expansion, restoration, improvement and development of existing commercial structures and owner-occupied residences in Downtown Development Districts, Economic Development Districts or Historic Districts. The RTA program does not exempt the acquisition cost of the structure. In addition, only equipment which becomes an integral part of that structure can qualify for this exemption (not machinery and equipment used in the business, i.e.: retail gondolas or movable property such as furniture and fixtures, etc.)

- **Quality Jobs Incentive Program.** This program provides a refundable tax credit as an incentive to encourage certain businesses to locate in Louisiana. Manufacturers and certain other businesses that locate in Louisiana and have at least one million dollars in net new annual payroll, to employees that reside within the state, can get an annual refundable tax credit equal to a maximum of 5 percent of the annual new payroll for up to ten years. The company must pay at least half of a basic health care premium for all new employees who average at least 25 hours per week. Additionally, at least 80 percent of the new direct jobs must work an average of 25 hours per week.

• **Biomedical Research and Development Parks.** Qualified medical concerns locating in a research and development park may be granted exemptions from state corporate income and franchise taxes. Such credits, which may be carried forward up to five years, cannot exceed the cost of purchase of machinery and scientific equipment. Qualified medical firms also may be granted tax exemptions for state and/or local sales and use taxes on machinery and equipment used by the company on materials and building supplies to be used in the repair, reconstruction or construction of facilities and on materials and supplies used in the production of the company's product. The same benefits apply to all companies located in university research and development parks.

• **Corporate Jobs Tax Credit.** Companies may take a one-time tax credit ranging from $100 to $225 for each net new job created as the result of the start-up of a new business or the expansion of an existing one. The credits can be used to satisfy state corporate income tax obligations. Manufacturing companies can elect to take this credit in lieu of the Industrial Ad Valorem Tax Exemption Program or the benefits of the Enterprise Zone Program.

FINANCIAL INCENTIVES:

• **Small Business Loan Program.** The Louisiana Economic Development Corporation (LEDC) provides loans and loan guarantees to small businesses as defined by the Small Business Administration (SBA). LEDC can participate up to a maximum of 40 percent of the total loan requested, and up to 50 percent for businesses owned by women, minorities or disabled persons. Loan guarantees are limited to 75 percent of the loan amount, except for businesses owned by women, minorities or disabled persons, which are guaranteed up to 90 percent of the loan. In all cases, LEDC's participation cannot exceed $700,000. Loan proceeds may be used for the purchase of fixed assets, including buildings, machinery and equipment, inventory, working capital and, with restrictions, debt restructuring.

• **Micro Loan Program.** Qualified small businesses are eligible to apply for the Micro Loan participation program or guarantee program administered by the LEDC. LEDC can participate up to 50 percent of the total loan request,

or a maximum of $25,000. LEDC can guarantee up to 80 percent of the loan, or a maximum of $50,000. For business owned by women, minorities or disabled persons, LEDC can guarantee up to 90 percent or $50,000. Loan proceeds may be used for purchasing fixed assets, including buildings, machinery and equipment, inventory and, with restrictions, debt restructuring.

Contact:

Ed Baker
Supervisor, Business Inc. Div.
Louisiana Department of Economic Development
P.O. Box 945185
Baton Rouge, LA 70804
(225)342-5402

MAINE

LEGISLATIVE TIMELINE:

1991: Passed a tax-increment financing law under which municipalities can receive up to 25 percent of both state sales and income tax revenues generated by designated businesses within a tax-increment financing district.

1993: Approved a research expense tax credit, tied to the federal tax credit for research expenses. Expanded the Maine Seed Capital Investment Tax Credit and created the Maine Technology Investment Fund.

1996: Passed a measure that provides for $11 million in proposed bonds to be used to provide financing to small businesses. Changed the state's tax increment financing program to allow businesses that create 15 or more jobs over two years to get a tax break.

1997: Passed an act to encourage the development of high-technology industry in the state.

1998: Passed an act to reduce income and property taxes.

TAX INCENTIVES:

• **Corporate income tax.** 3.5 to 8.93 percent.

• **Personal income tax.** 2.0 to 8.5 percent.

• **Sales and use tax.** 5.5 percent (certain exemptions apply).

• **Business Equipment Property Tax Reimbursement (BETR) Program.** Any business (except public utilities, radio paging services, mobile communications, cable television, satellite-based direct television broadcast, multichannel and multipoint television distribution services, certain energy facilities, most natural gas pipelines, and property used to produce or transmit energy primarily for resale) that pays property taxes on qualified business property is eligible. The program reimburses, for up to 12 years (less any number of years for which an Investment Tax Credit was claimed), all local property taxes paid on eligible business property. Once the business pays its taxes, it has 60 days in which to file for BETR. Once Maine Revenue Services receives the BETR form, a check will be issued within 180 days. The definition of eligible business property is defined by law, but generally means personal property first placed in service in Maine after April 1, 1995. Eligible property includes certain property affixed or attached to a building or other real estate if it is used to further a particular trade or business on that site and so may include property which would be classified as real property for other purposes. Starting with property tax year April 1, 1997, office furniture, lamps and lighting fixtures are not eligible for reimbursement and are excluded from the program.

• **Employer Provided Long-term Care Benefits Credit.** Employers that provide long-term care policy coverage as part of a benefits package are eligible. Long-term care is defined by Title 24-A, Section 5051. It does not include regular health insurance coverage. The program provides an income tax credit equal to the lesser of $5,000, 20 percent of the cost incurred or $100 per employee covered. Application of this credit is limited to the tax otherwise due. The unused portion of the credit may be carried forward up to 15 years.

• **Employment Tax Increment Financing (ETIF).** Any business that hires a minimum of 15 net new employees within a two year period is eligible, where those employees are: 1) paid an income that exceeds the average per capita income in the county of employment, 2) provided with group health insurance, and 3) provided with an ERISA qualified retirement program. The business must also be able to demonstrate that its expansion project will not go forward without ETIF funds. ETIF is available to assist in the financing of business investment projects that create at least 15 net new, high quality jobs in Maine. An ETIF-approved business would receive either 30, 50 or 75 percent of the state income tax withholdings paid by qualified employees for up to ten years. (Qualifying jobs created in a labor market area where unemployment is at or below the state average earn a 30 percent reimbursement, while those with higher than average unemployment earn 50 percent. In areas where unemployment exceeds 150 percent of the state average, the reimbursement is 75 percent.) The percentage of reimbursement is established for a five-year period based upon the unemployment rate at the time of initial application, and again at the beginning of the sixth year. The amount of annual payment is based upon the actual number of qualified employees above the company's base level of employment. The company may not accrue ETIF benefits for any period of time wherein employment, wages and/or employee benefits fail to meet the minimum qualification criteria. (The ETIF cannot be taken concurrently with the Jobs and Investment Tax Credit).

• **Jobs and Investment Tax Credit.** Any business, other than a public utility, that invests at least $5 million in a taxable year in most types of personal property in Maine and creates 100 new jobs over the ensuing two-year period is eligible. This program provides a credit against Maine income taxes equal to 10 percent of investment in most types of personal property. The investment must total at least $5 million in a taxable year and generate at least 100 new qualifying jobs within two years of the date the investment is placed in service. Qualifying jobs must provide wages greater than the average per capita income in the labor market area where the jobs are located, and be covered by retirement and group health insurance programs.

• **Research Expense Credit.** Any business that engages in research and development activities in Maine that meet the definition in Section 41 of the Internal Revenue code is eligible. Such expenses include certain in-house and contract research expenses if they relate to discovering information that is technological in nature and intended for use in developing a new or improved business component. The program provides an income tax credit to companies that incur qualifying research expenses in Maine in excess of the base period amount. The base amount is the average research incurred over the prior three years.

• **Super R&D Credit.** Business that qualify for the research expense credit and are those whose qualified research expenses conducted in Maine for the taxable year exceed 150 percent of the average research expenses for the three taxable years prior to September 1997. The credit is equal to the amount of qualified research expenses conducted in Maine for the taxable year that exceed 150 percent of the average research expenses for the three taxable years prior to September 1997. The credit is limited to 50 percent of the net tax due (tax due after the allowance of all other credits) and cannot reduce the taxpayer's tax due to less than the net tax due in the preceding taxable year. Any unused portion of the credit may be carried forward up to five years.

• **Customer Computer Programming Sales Tax Exemption.** Any business that purchases custom computer programming qualifies for this program. This program exempts from sales tax the purchase of custom computer programming effective October 1, 1997. If a standard program is purchased then customized, the cost of the standard program would be taxable and the customizing, if separately stated, would be nontaxable.

• **Biotechnology Sales Tax Exemption.** Any biotechnology company qualifies. Sales of machinery, equipment, instruments and supplies used by the purchaser directly and primarily in a biotechnology application are eligible for a sales tax exemption.

• **Manufacturing Sales Tax Exemptions.** Any manufacturing company qualifies. Sales of machinery and equipment used by the purchaser directly and primarily in the production of tangible personal property are eligible for a sales tax exemption. In addition, items consumed or destroyed directly or primarily in production, and repair and replacement parts for qualified production equipment are exempt from sale tax.

• **Partial Clean Fuel Vehicle Sales Tax Exemption.** Businesses that sell clean fuel vehicles to the general public qualify. Clean fuels include any product or energy source, other than conventional gasoline, diesel or reformulated gasoline, that lowers emissions of certain pollutants. Clean fuel includes but is not limited to compressed natural gas, liquefied natural gas, liquefied petroleum gas, hydrogen, hythane (a combination of compressed natural gas and hydrogen), dynamic flywheels, solar energy, alcohol fuels containing at least 85 percent alcohol by volume and electricity. Clean fuel vehicles are vehicles that may be propelled by a clean fuel or a fuel-cell electric vehicle that uses any fuel. The exemption amount is based on a portion of the sale or lease price of a clean fuel vehicle. The exemption is that portion of the sale or lease price of a clean fuel vehicle sold by an original equipment manufacturer that exceeds the price of an identical vehicle powered by gasoline. When there is no identical vehicle powered by gasoline the exemption equals 30 percent of the sale or lease price of an internal combustion engine clean fuel vehicle or 50 percent of the sale or lease price of a clean fuel vehicle either fully or partly powered by electricity stored batteries, generated by dynamic flywheel or generated by a fuel cell on board the vehicle.

• **Research and Development Sales Tax Exemption.** Any business engaged in Research and Development qualifies. Sales of machinery and equipment used by the purchaser directly and exclusively in research and development are eligible for a sales tax exemption.

• **Fuel and Electricity Sales Tax Exemption.** This program exempts from sales tax 95 percent of the sales price of all fuel and electricity purchased for use at the manufacturing facility.

FINANCIAL INCENTIVES:

• **Tax-Exempt Bond.** Any person or business proposing to use loan proceeds for a hard asset manufacturing function is eligible. Borrowers must be able to demonstrate commercial viability with bond financing in place, exhibit a debt to net worth leverage of no greater than 3:1, provide debt service coverage of 1.25x, and demonstrate a current ratio of no less than 1.25x coverage and must meet a combination of the Internal Revenue Code criteria. The program provides Bond Financing that may be used to purchase and/or construct a manufacturing facility and/or purchase new machinery and equipment. Fifteen percent of the building-related purchase price must be put back into the "four wall" renovation of an existing structure, and at least 75 percent of the building must be used for the prime manufacturing function. Bonds may be structured to finance up to 90 percent of an eligible loan based on collateral value. The maximum bond amount is $10 million. The maximum bond amount with a FAME Credit Enhancement is $7 million.

• **Taxable Bond (SMART).** Any person or business proposing to use loan proceeds for a hard asset manufacturing function is eligible. Borrowers must be able to demonstrate commercial viability with bond financing in place, exhibit a debt to net worth leverage of no greater than 3:1, provide debt service coverage of 1.25x, and demonstrate a current ratio of no less than 1.24x coverage and must meet a combination of the Internal Revenue Code. Program provides credit-enhanced taxable bond financing for the construction or acquisition of real estate and the purchase of new or existing machinery and equipment. The assets do not need to be related to a manufacturing function. The maximum bond amount is $7 million.

• **Commercial Loan Insurance** Businesses that meet the general lending criteria of the institution seeking an Authority guaranty are eligible. A borrower must exhibit the ability to repay debt out of normal cash flow from business operations. Borrowers that do not qualify for one of the Authority bond programs may qualify for loan insurance. Program provides a business borrower the opportunity to secure credit for an eligible project by providing a commercial lender with loan insurance. The Authority may offer up to 90 percent insurance on an eligible loan for real estate and machinery and equipment. The maximum insurance varies by the loan application. The maximum bond amount is $7 million.

• **Major Business Expansion Program.** Any business proposing to expand or locate in Maine and whose borrowing needs fall in the $5,000,000 to $25,000,000 range is eligible. A borrower must commit to retaining or creating at least 100 jobs. The program provides tax-exempt or taxable bond financing for up to 100 percent of a project's cost. Bonds may be issued as either tax exempt (subject to the limits of the Internal Revenue Code) or taxable. Business borrowers must use bond proceeds to permanently fund the construction, acquisition or renovation of a facility used in the borrower's operation, or to acquire machinery and equipment. The bond proceeds may also be used for the take out financing of hard assets. The financing is structured to match the useful life of the assets being financed.

• **Economic Recovery Loan Program.** Small Maine businesses seeking last-resort financial assistance qualify. Business must show that all other financial options have been denied or exhausted. Borrowers must demonstrate that the loan will be repaid. The Economic Recovery Loan Program is a lending program designed as a supplemental financial resource to help Maine small businesses access the capital required to become more productive and more competitive. The maximum request for funding is $200,000. In cases where there exists substantial public benefit, larger loans may be considered.

• **Agricultural Marketing Loan Fund Program.** Any person or organization in the business of growing or harvesting of plants, raising animals, growing or obtaining plant or animal byproducts, aquacultrue or the producing, processing, storing, packaging or marketing of a product from such businesses is eligible. This program helps natural-resource-based industries by providing a source of subordinated debt for eligible projects and borrowers. The maximum loan size under this program is $250,000. Proceeds may be used for the design, construction or improvement of commodity and storage buildings and packing and marketing facilities, or for the construction, renovation or acquisition of land, buildings, equipment, docks, wharves, piers or vessels located in the State of Maine and used in connection with an agriculture enterprise. AMLF does not finance the construction phase of any project; usually the lead lender provides the construction loan. Funds are targeted at projects which improve productivity through state-of-the-art technology or innovative processes.

• **Small Enterprise Growth Program.** Businesses with a distinct competitive advantage in a strong marketplace qualify. The business must employ 25 or fewer or have gross sales of $2,000,000 or less within the past 12 months. Borrower must be engaged or involved in at least one of the following: marine science, biotechnology, manufacturing, exporting, software development, environmental sciences, value added natural resources and/or other enterprises that the Board determines will further the purposes and intent of the program. This program provides financing for small Maine companies that demonstrate a potential for high growth and public benefit. The program will seek adequate risk-adjusted returns on investment. Financing is limited to a maximum of $150,000 per loan and must be matched with other financing sources. The SEGP may also charge the borrower for its out-of-pocket expenses associated with closing and administering this loan in excess of $1,500.

- **Maine Technology Investment Fund.** A Maine business with fewer than 50 employees and less than $5 million in revenues in the prior year, in a target industry identified in the state's overall Economic Development Strategic Plan and the State's Science and Technology Plan, is eligible, i.e., biotechnology, composite materials, environmental sciences and technology, software and telecommunications, marine science, and precision manufacturing. Investment in a Maine business with technology that can lead to product or process innovation. Investments will target funding for the next step required to bring a promising idea from "the bench" to commercialization. This early step in the funding life cycle of a company is designed to feed later state funding opportunities such as seed capital. An application package can be obtained at http://www.mstf.org www.mstf.org.

OTHER INCENTIVES:

- **Foreign investment and export assistance programs.** The Maine International Trade Center is charged with this function.

- **High Technology Investment Tax Credit.** Businesses primarily engaged in high-tech activities that purchase and use eligible equipment qualify. Businesses that lease eligible equipment to lessees that are primarily engaged in high-tech activities and the lessee waives its entitlement to the credit. Lessees of eligible equipment primarily engaged in high-tech activities. High-tech activities include the design, creation and production of computer software, computer equipment, supporting communications components and other accessories that are directly associated with computer software and equipment. It also includes the provision of internet or electronic communications access services or the support of access to electronic media, data and associated communications support or certain advanced telecommunications capabilities. Eligible equipment can include computer equipment, electronics components and accessories, certain communications equipment, and computer software placed in service in the state during the tax year that the credit is being claimed.

- **Employee – Assisted Day Care Credit.** Employers that on behalf of their employees provide day care services through direct capital and personnel expenditures or subsidizing a licensed day care center qualify. The program provides an income tax credit of up to $5,000. The credit is limited to the lesser of $5,000, 20 percent of the cost incurred or $100 for each child of an employee enrolled on a full-time basis or for each full-time equivalent throughout the tax year. The usable credit cannot be greater than the income tax otherwise due in any tax year. The credit may be carried forward 15 years or back 3 years. For the first year the taxpayer provides day care services, enrollment is determined as of the last day of the year.

- **The State's Small Business Advocate.** Helps small businesses resolve problems they may be experiencing with state regulatory agencies. Also, the Small Business Technical Assistance Program helps businesses comply with environmental regulations through education, on-site assistance and pollution prevention techniques.

- **Public/Private partnership.** Maine & Company, a private non-profit corporation dedicated to attracting new businesses into the state, oversees the Maine Investment Exchange (MIX). MIX is a joint venture project created by private businesses from throughout Maine. Their mission is to provide a regularly scheduled forum to bring together providers of risk capital with qualified entrepreneurs seeking capital. The monthly forum provides for prospective investors to hear several presentations given by qualified entrepreneurs seeking investment capital. Investors includes personal investors, personal advisor, venture capital firms, corporations and banks.

SUCCESSFUL INCENTIVES:

- **Tax Increment Financing.** A TIF District is an area within a municipality that is designated as a development district to allow the municipality to financially support a business's development project using the revenue stream of new property taxes that will result from improvements made to the property. Employment Tax Increment Financing: ETIF is available to assist in the financing of business investment projects that create at least 15 net new high quality jobs in Maine. An ETIF approved business would receive 30, 50 or 70 percent of the State income tax withholdings paid by qualified employees for up to 10 years.

Contact:

James Nimon, Program Manager
Dept. of Economic & Community Development
59 State House Station
Augusta, ME 04333-0059
(207) 287-2686

MARYLAND

1990: Created the Maryland Venture Capital Trust to stimulate research and development.

1991: Approved $1.5 million in general obligation bond financing for the construction of a new marine research and exploration complex.

1992: Passed legislation that permits the state's Small Business Development Financing Authority to provide equity participation financing to technology-based companies

1993: Broadened the current sales and use tax exemption for research and development materials by deleting the requirement that materials be tested to destruction.

1994: Created a Defense Adjustment Loan program that will be used to make low-interest loans to new or existing companies in communities suffering dislocation due to defense downsizing.

1995: Reorganized the Department of Business and Economic Development to focus on job creation. Created the Maryland Economic Development Commission. Repealed the prohibition on interstate banking and branching for Maryland-based banks.

1996: Enacted the Job Creation Tax Credit Act.

1997: Enacted a 10 percent personal income tax reduction and an expansion of the sales tax exemption for manufacturing property purchases.

1998: Enacted an enhancement of the property tax exemption for biotechnology and computer software used in manufacturing.

1999: Enacted the One Maryland Economic Development Program for Distressed Counties creating a loan program for distressed counties.

TAX INCENTIVES:

- **Corporate income tax.** 7.0 percent.

- **Personal income tax.** 2.0 to 4.9 percent.

- **Sales and use tax.** A 5 percent tax is levied on the sale or use of personal property within the state, including the rental or leasing of such property. Local jurisdications do not impose a sales tax. Exemptions available.

- **Job Creation Tax Credit (Income Tax Credit).** Since 1996, Maryland has granted tax credits to businesses primarily engaged in manufacturing; mining; transportation; communications; agriculture, forestry or fishing; warehousing; research, development or testing; biotechnology; computer programming, data processing or other computer related services; central financial, real estate or insurance services; the operation of central administrative offices or a company headquarters; or a public utility. Business services firms also qualify if the facility is in a designated priority funding area. Priority funding areas include state enterprise zones, federal empowerment zones, state designated revitalization areas, incorporated municipalities, areas inside the I-495 and I-695 beltways, or a growth area designated by each county for the purpose of this credit. The business must create at least 60 new permanent jobs in a twenty-four month period. In designated priority funding areas, the minimum is only 25.

- **Other Income Tax Credits.** Additional employment-based income tax credits in Maryland include:

  Employment Opportunity Tax Credit - Includes credits for wages and child care or transportation expenses for qualifying employees who are recipients of state benefits from the "Aid to Families with Dependent Children" program immediately prior to employment.

  Employment of Individuals with Disabilities Tax Credit – Includes tax credits for wages paid and for child care or transportation expenses for qualifying individuals with disabilities.

  Neighborhood and Community Assistance Program Tax Credit – Provides tax credits for business contributions to approved nonprofit Neighborhood and Community Assistance Programs.

  Businesses That Create New Jobs Tax Credit – Certain businesses located in Maryland that create new positions or establish or expand business facilities in the state are entitled to a credit against state income tax if a property tax credit is granted by the local jurisdiction. The credit is based on a percentage of the property tax credit.

  Clean-Fuel Vehicle Tax Credit – Certain taxpayers who purchase alternative-fuel and electric vehicles and for certain property installed on a vehicle to permit the vehicle to be propelled by certain alternative fuels may be eligible for a tax credit based on the cost of placing these vehicles in service during the taxable year.

Telecommunications Property Tax Credit - A credit based on property tax of operating real property in Maryland that is used in the telecommunications business.

• **Enterprise Zone Tax Credits (Property and Income Tax Credits).** Advantages of a Maryland enterprise zone location include:

Property tax credits – Ten-year credit against local property taxes on a portion of real property improvements. Credit is 80 percent the first five years and decreases 10 percent annually thereafter to 30 percent in the tenth and last year.

Income tax credits – One- to three-year credits for wages paid to new employees in the zone. The general credit is a one-time $500 credit per new worker. For economically disadvantaged employees, the credit increases to a total of $3,000 per worker distributed over three years.

Priority access to Maryland's financing programs – There are thirty-five Maryland enterprise zones.

• **Enterprise Zone "Focus Area" Tax Credits.** The Maryland General Assembly has passed legislation to create "focus areas" within enterprise zones. This legislation was effective October 1, 1999. "Focus areas" are especially distressed portions of enterprise zones. Businesses in these "focus areas" will receive new and enhanced tax credits that include:

Property tax credits – Ten-year credit against local property taxes on a portion of real property improvements. Credit is 80 percent for ten years.

Income tax credits – Enterprise income tax credits for creating new jobs are doubled in the focus area portions of enterprise zones.

Personal property tax credits – Ten-year credit against local property taxes on increased assessments for personal property. Credit is 80 percent for ten years.

• **Property Tax Credit (Brownfields Tax Incentives).** Recently enacted legislation encouraging the voluntary cleanup and revitalization of brownfields allows local taxing jurisdictions to grant property tax credits. The counties, Baltimore City or incorporated municipalities may elect to grant a five-year credit equal to 50 percent of real property taxes attributable to the increase in the assessment resulting from cleanup and improvement of a qualified brownfields site.

• **Other Property Tax Exemptions and Credits.** Maryland does not impose a personal property tax on business. In addition, Frederick, Kent, Queen Anne's and Talbot

Counties do not tax business personal property. For those jurisdictions that do tax personal property, exemptions and credits available include the following:

— Machinery, equipment, materials and supplies used in manufacturing are totally exempt in most counties and the City of Baltimore.

— Machinery, equipment, materials and supplies used primarily in research and development are totally exempt in most counties and the City of Baltimore.

— Manufacturing inventory is exempt in all counties and the City of Baltimore.

— Commercial inventory for warehousing and distribution is totally exempt in all major jurisdictions except Wicomico County, which offers a partial exemption.

— Through their discretionary authority, local jurisdictions may grant tax credits to eligible new or expanding manufacturing, fabricating or assembling facilities.

— Non "off-the-shelf" computer software is exempt. Local jurisdictions may grant a tax credit for "off-the-shelf" computer software.

• **Sales and Use Tax Exemptions.** The following are major business-oriented exemptions from the Maryland Sales and Use Tax. Local jurisdictions do not impose a sales tax.

— Sales of capital manufacturing machinery and equipment.

— Sales of noncapitalized manufacturing machinery and equipment.

— Sales of tangible personal property consumed directly in manufacturing.

— Sales of fuels used in manufacturing.

— Sales for resale and sales of tangible personal property to be incorporated in other tangible personal property manufactured for resale.

— Sales of customized computer software.

— Sales of equipment and materials used or consumed in research and development, to include testing of finished products.

— Sales of aircraft, vessels, railroad rolling stock and

motor vehicles used principally in the movement of passengers or freight in interstate and foreign commerce.

– Sales of certain end-item testing equipment used to perform a contract for the U.S. Department of Defense and transferred to the federal government.

FINANCIAL INCENTIVES:

- **Maryland Industrial Development Financing Authority (MIDFA).** MIDFA has several programs to provide financing assistance for capital assets and working capital to small and mid-sized businesses that demonstrate a significant economic impact.

  Conventional Financing Program – insures loans made by financial institutions thus reducing credit risks and encouraging more flexible terms. Insurance is limited to the lesser of $1 million or 80 percent of the obligation.

  Taxable Bond Financing – provides access to long term capital markets at generally favorable interest rates. Bonds can be issued to an amount and/or insured up to 100 percent of the obligation, not to exceed $5 million.

  Tax-exempt Bond Financing – as restricted by the Federal tax law, can finance 501c(3) nonprofit organizations and manufacturing facilities. Bonds can be issued up to $10 million and/or insured up to 100 percent of the obligation, not to exceed $5 million.

- **Maryland Seafood and Aquaculture Loan Program.** The Seafood and Aquaculture Loan Fund provides direct secured loans at below market interest rates to finance real property and equipment. The loans are limited to the lesser of $250,000 or 80 percent of the total investment.

- **Maryland Energy Financing Administration.** The Maryland Energy Financing Administration provides assistance to businesses for projects involving energy conservation and certain forms of energy generation.

- **Maryland Small Business Development Financing Authority (MSBDFA).** The MSBDFA provides assistance to small businesses through the following programs:

  Contract Financing – through its revolving loan fund, MSBDFA makes loan guarantees and direct working capital and equipment loans (up to $500,000) to socially or economically disadvantaged businesspersons who have been awarded contracts mainly funded by government agencies and/or public utilities.

  Equity Financing – the Equity Participation Investment

Program (EPIP) provides direct loans, equity investments and loan guarantees to socially or economically disadvantaged-owned businesses in franchising, in technology-based industries, and for the acquisition of profitable businesses. EPIP funds (up to $500,000) can be used for practically any business purpose.

Loan Guarantees – the Long-Term Guaranty Program assists eligible firms through guarantees and interest rate subsidies for loans to be used for working capital, the acquisition of machinery or equipment, and acquisition and improvements to real property to be used by the applicant's business. Loan guarantees may not exceed the lesser of 80 percent of the loan or $600,000. The minimum loan is $5,000 for a period not to exceed 10 years, with a maximum interest rate of prime plus 2 percent.

Surety Bonding – the Maryland Small Business Surety Bond Program assists small contractors in obtaining bonding for primarily funded government or public utility contracts that require bid, performance and payment bonds. MSBDFA may guarantee up to 90 percent reimbursement to a surety for losses with a total exposure not to exceed $900,000. The program can issue bid, performance and payment bonds of up to $750,000 to eligible small contractors with government or public utility-funded projects.

- **Investment Financing Programs.** Maryland's Department of Business and Economic Development (DBED) provides financing for technology-based businesses using two investment vehicles: the Challenge Investment Program, and the Enterprise Investment Fund. Both programs provide equity capital to emerging technology businesses, and address a continuum of financing needs for technology companies.

- **Economic Development Opportunities Program Fund (Sunny Day Fund).** The Economic Development Opportunities Program Fund was created to enable Maryland to act on extraordinary economic development proposals that require financial assistance beyond the capabilities of existing state and local financing programs. The Sunny Day Fund provides funding to assist in the retention and expansion of existing businesses and/or the establishment or attraction of new businesses.

- **Enterprise Incentive Deposit Fund.** Businesses located in certain rural areas with high unemployment may qualify for a 3 percent interest rate subsidy on bank loans covering fixed assets including land, buildings, machinery and equipment.

- **Neighborhood Business Development Program (NBDP).**

The NBDP, administered by the Maryland Department of Housing and Community Development, provides flexible gap financing to small businesses locating or expanding in areas targeted for revitalization by local governments. Loans are made to Maryland-based small businesses. Loans and grants are made to nonprofit organizations whose activities contribute to a broader revitalization effort. Financing cannot exceed 50 percent of project cost, and must be the least amount necessary to make the project financially feasible.

• **Brownfields Revitalization Incentive Program.** Recently enacted legislation encouraging the voluntary cleanup and revitalization of brownfields establishes a Brownfields Revitalization Incentive Fund. This special fund may make available low-interest loans or grants for redevelopment of qualifying brownfields sites.

• **Maryland Industrial Training Program (MITP).** MITP provides incentive grants for the development and training of new employees in firms locating or expanding their workforce in Maryland. MITP reimburses companies for up to 100 percent of the direct costs associated with training programs customized to the work process. The level of funding provided is negotiated between the company and the Department of Business and Economic Development, with specific cost sharing items spelled out in a training grant agreement.

• **Partnership for Workforce Quality (PWQ).** The rapid rate of technological change and increasing domestic and international competition demand a skilled workforce. PWQ targets training grants and technical assistance to resident Maryland manufacturing and technology companies to upgrade the skills of the existing workforce. The objectives of the program are: to improve business competitiveness and worker productivity; to upgrade employee skills for new technologies and production processes; and to promote employment stability. Through the Partnership, companies undertake a guided self-assessment of business strengths and needs, then work with Regional Managers of the Maryland Department of Business and Economic Development to integrate training with other vital services that support business and economic growth.

OTHER INCENTIVES:

• **Trade Financing Program (TFP).** Provides assistance to industrial or commercial businesses which are engaged in the export and import of goods through Maryland ports and airport facilities. This program is also available to service providers to the overseas market. Normal program range is between $50,000 to $5 million. The program's maximum participation provides for credit enhancement to institutional lenders up to the lower of 90 percent or $1 million for exporters; and up to 80 percent or $1 million for all others.

• **Supplementary Export Financing Assistance.** The Trade Financing Program (TFP) can also arrange specialized financing for exports through the Export-Import Bank of the U.S. (Ex-Im Bank). The Ex-Im Bank is the government agency responsible for assisting in the export financing of U.S. goods and services through a variety of loan, guarantee and foreign credit insurance programs. TFP has a special cooperative agreement with Ex-Im Bank to package and coordinate applications.

• **Trade Development Program.** In the Maryland Office of International Business (OIB) Trade Specialists develop long-term client relationships with Maryland small and medium-sized firms enabling them to penetrate new foreign markets or expand sales in existing markets. OIB staff coordinate the participation of Maryland firms in foreign trade shows, assist companies in developing international business plans and provide transactional counseling.

• **Export MD Program.** Maryland companies that qualify for membership in the Program may receive up to $4,000 in foreign office assistance and $3,000 in grant funding for costs associated with entering a new foreign market. Trade specialists will work with member firms to devise an export strategy, develop a marketing plan, identify distributors or sales agents in a foreign market, identify appropriate trade shows and prepare their product.

• **Maryland Export Assistance Network.** The Network, an alliance of international business assistance centers, was developed by the OIB to facilitate the transition of small and medium-sized companies to the global marketplace. It provides Maryland businesses with convenient, regional access to foreign market reports, profiles of top industries for export, trade leads and contacts, travel information, trade statistics and a variety of other information needed for entering the global market. The centers are located in Baltimore, Salisbury, La Plata, Rockville and Cumberland.

• **EuroRep Service.** Offered by OIB, the EuroRep Service provides Maryland companies with a low-cost, low-risk method of building a continuous marketing and sales presence in Europe. Working with a European Export Representative housed within the state's office in the Netherlands, the Maryland Business Center Europe (MBCE), the service provides a Maryland exporter with a continuous and proactive multi-lingual sales and marketing presence in Europe, helping the company to develop a quality image in its target markets.

• **Technology Industry Business Incentives.** Mentioned earlier, the Challenge Investment Program Enterprise Investment Fund of the Investment Financing Programs target high technology companies. The Technology Component of the Maryland Small Business Development Financing Authority's Equity Participation Investment Program is targeted to technology-based businesses.

- **Energy Production and Recycling Businesses.** In addition to businesses seeking to conserve and co-generate energy, the Maryland Energy Financing Administration (MEFA) targets companies that produce fuels or other energy sources as well as recyclers.

- **Maryland Health Care Product Development Corporation.** The Maryland Health Care Product Development Corporation (MHCPDC) is a nonprofit corporation and is the operating entity of a Federal/State partnership principally funded by the DOD Technology Reinvestment Program. MHCPDC invests in Maryland organizations with potential for biomedical product sales and job creation in the state. Organizations with defense-related or federal-supported technologies with near-term commercial application in the biomedical field are eligible to apply for funding assistance. Investments range from $400,000 to $600,000, with matching funds sourced from commercial venture capital and other non-governmental entities. Each transaction is structured to provide reasonable financial returns to the investing parties.

- **MdBio, Inc..** MdBio, Inc., a private, nonprofit organization whose mission is to advance the commercial development of bioscience in Maryland, has several programs to provide bioscience companies in the state with a financial boost in the later stages of product development or manufacturing scale-up. Funds can also be used by companies to upgrade their capabilities to provide services to their clients. Because MdBio assumes some of the risk associated with each project, it shares in each company's success through equity positions and/or royalty payments. These returns increase MdBio's ability to fund additional investments and other industry support projects.

- **The Day Care Facilities Loan Guarantee Fund.** This fund can be used to guarantee loans for construction, renovation, purchase of equipment and supplies, and working capital. The scope of the program includes expansion and development of day care facilities for infants, pre-school-aged children, children in need of before and after school care, the elderly and persons with disabilities of all ages throughout Maryland.

- **The Child Care Facilities Direct Loan Fund.** This fund is used for construction, renovation or acquisition of real property, fixtures or equipment related to child care facilities. The Fund can also finance lease hold improvements in child care facilities located in leased premises, provided the lease is for a minimum of 10 years.

- **The Child Care Special Loan Fund.** This fund makes loans to child care providers for a variety of specific uses, excluding the purchase or construction of real property or buildings or major improvements to real property. Loans range from $1,000 to $10,000.

- **Regulatory Relief Programs.** The Office of Business Advocacy assists Maryland business in navigating through the processes and regulations of local, state and federal government. The Office provides ombudsman service to businesses and acts as an information source and liaison on behalf of the business community. Resources include the new Maryland Business Licensing System (BLIS) which offers on-line permitting information to Maryland companies. Recent legislation has set the stage for streamlining and improving the licensing and permitting process through the Maryland Department of the Environment (MDE). MDE publishes expected review times for each licensing and permitting program, and offers assistance and information to businesses in completing the permitting process.

SUCCESSFUL INCENTIVES:

- **The Maryland Job Creation Tax Credit Program.** Established in 1996, the prooogram provides income tax credits to new or expanding businesses that create full-time jobs meeting specified criteria, including wage minimums, and threshold levels. The credits are available for businesses in industry growth sectors targeted by the state. In keeping with the state's innovative "Smart Growth" policy, the credit is increased and job creation minimums are reduced for facilities located in specified areas. "Priority funding areas," for which the job creation minimum is reduced, include state enterprise zones, federal empowerment zones, state-designated neighborhood revitalization areas, incorporated municipalities, areas inside the I-495 and I-695 beltways and county-designated growth areas.

Contact:

Jerry Wade
Job Creation Tax Credit Program Administrator
Maryland Department of Business and Economic
   Development
217 E. Redwood Street
Baltimore, MD 21202
(410) 767-6438

TAX INCENTIVES:

- **Corporate income tax**. 9.5 percent.

- **Personal income tax**. 5.95 percent; a 12.0 percent tax rate applies to interest, dividends and capital gains.

- **Sales and use tax**. 5.0 percent. Manufacturers are given an exemption from the state's sales tax.

- **Economic Development Incentive Program**. This program was initiated to stimulate economic development in distressed areas, attract new businesses and encourage existing businesses to expand in Massachusetts. There are 36 designated Economic Target Areas throughout Massachusetts. Certified projects within Economic Opportunity Areas can qualify for additional investment incentives, including a 5 percent state investment tax credit, a 10 percent abandoned building tax deduction, priority for state capital funding and municipal tax benefits that include a special tax assessment and tax increment financing. To be eligible, the company must be an existing Massachusetts business creating permanent jobs or be a business relocating to Massachusetts and creating permanent jobs. To take advantage of the abandoned building tax deduction, the site must be at least 75 percent vacant for at least 24 months.

- **Investment Tax Credit**. Business are eligible for a 5 percent investment tax credit for tangible personal property used in certified projects within an Economic Opportunity Area. A 3 percent investment tax credit is also available to any manufacturer or research and development company located in Massachusetts. The credit applies to buildings, structural components, personal and other property. To be eligible, the investment must be in Massachusetts and must be a depreciable asset. The credit also applies to depreciable lease hold improvements.

- **Research and Development Tax Credit**. Any company investing in research and development is eligible for research and development tax credits. Credits of 10 and 15 percent are permanent with a 15-year or indefinite carry forward provision. The credit applies to the Massachusetts portion of the qualified federal research and development expense, research and development in Massachusetts for multi-state firms and contract expenses for research.

FINANCIAL INCENTIVES:

- **Economic Development Incentive Program**. This initiative is to stimulate economic development in distressed areas, attract new business and encourage existing businesses to expand in Massachusetts. Certified projects within economic opportunity areas can qualify for additional investment incentives, including a 5 percent state investment tax credit, a 10 percent abandoned building tax credit, priority for state capital funding, and municipal tax benefits such as special tax assessments and tax increment financing.

LEGISLATIVE TIMELINE:

1990: Increased taxes by more than 5 percent. Passed an interstate banking bill that gives financial institutions from across the nation the right to buy or operate banks in the state.

1991: Voted to repeal a 5 percent tax on some 600 business services.

1994: Created the Massachusetts Manufacturing Partnership to help state firms gain access to export markets. Extended the 3 percent investment tax credit through the end of 1997.

1995: Changed Massachusetts' capital gains tax, eliminating the tax for assets held for at least six years. Cut the state's bank excise tax from 12.54 percent to 10.5 percent over the next five years.

1996: Passed a new harbor maintenance tax credit that offsets the corporate excise tax against the federal tax imposed. Created the Economic Development Incentive Program to stimulate job creation in blighted areas.

1997: Passed an act deregulating the electric utility industry and enhancing consumer protections therein.

1998: Passed an act to eliminate discrimination against hiring women on state construction projects.

MASSACHUSETTS

- **Predevelopment Assistance Program**. This program provides matching funds for feasibility studies, planning and technical analysis to seed high-impact economic development projects in needy communities. Eligible activities include market and feasibility analysis, environmental testing and analysis, architectural and engineering work, project management, appraisal and other technical services. Funds are awarded annually through an RFP process. Priority is given to projects in communities ranking high under the Massachusetts economic distress index and to projects with the greatest potential economic impact.

- **Mortgage Insurance Program**. This program is designed to help smaller businesses obtain funds to meet growth objectives. Through this program, Massachusetts insures repayment of a portion of a permanent loan for real estate and/or equipment. This insurance can support either conventional loans or industrial development bonds. The program is well suited for financing equipment with low collateral value.

- **Equity Investment Program**. Massachusetts makes both debt and equity investment, usually in the form of a direct purchase of common or preferred stock in combination with a long-term loan. Such investments are generally made as part of a joint venture with conventional private-sector investors. Massachusetts also assists companies in locating compatible private-sector investors for joint ventures.

OTHER INCENTIVES:

- **Corporation for Business, Work and Learning**. The Corporation provides a variety of worker training services including support for defense firms seeking to enter commercial markets and support for firms adding jobs and developing new training methods.

- **Public/Private Partnerships**. The public/private partnerships consist of the following:

    Capital Access Program – The program provides participating banks with a cash collateral guarantee. The program is designed to encourage banks to makes loans to small businesses and is available to Massachusetts companies with annual sales less than $5 million that have borrowing needs to $500,000.
    Massachusetts Capital Resource Company – This private company established in conjunction with the state acts as an economic catalyst by providing capital to businesses throughout the commonwealth.
    Massachusetts Business Development Corporation – This private corporation under state charter provides loans to firms unable to obtain full financing from conventional lenders.

- **Massachusetts Office of Trade (MassTrade)**. This office works to attract foreign investment into Massachusetts by promoting the advantages of locating in Massachusetts. The agency also works to assist companies to develop and expand their presence in international markets. They also offer Export Finance Guarantee Fund through MassDevelopment.

- **Day Care Facilities**. Tax-Exempt Bonds provide low cost financing for nonprofit organizations and long-term care facilities.

Contact:

Brenda A. Doherty
Manager, Marketing & Communications
Massachusetts Office of Business Development
10 Park Plaza, Suite 3750
Boston, MA 02116
(617) 973-8600

TAX INCENTIVES:

- **Corporate income tax.** None.

- **Personal income tax.** 4.4 percent.

- **Sales and use tax.** 6 percent state sales tax; no local sales taxes.

- **Recent Tax Reforms.** Twenty-four tax cuts in the last seven years have put $11 billion back into the pockets of the state's businesses and families. The following are a few examples of the Single Business Tax (SBT) cuts:

  – A 1995 reform instituted a dramatic reduction in the tax base used in levying the SBT. Compensation addbacks (specifically, unemployment insurance, workers' compensation insurance and FICA) were removed from the tax base, thus significantly reducing the SBT (estimated tax reduction: $536.7 million).

  – In 1992, the number of businesses required to file the SBT was reduced when the gross receipts filing threshold was increased to $100,000 from $40,000. The threshold was expanded again in 1994 to $250,000 (estimated tax reduction: $248.9 million).

  – In 1994, the SBT rate was reduced to 2.3 percent from 2.35 percent (estimated tax reduction: $256.1 million).

  – Eligible small businesses may pay an alternative profits tax instead of the SBT. In 1992, the alternative profits tax was reduced to 3.0 percent from 4.0 percent. The alternative profits tax was lowered again in 1995 to 2.0 percent (estimated tax reduction: $127.3 million).

  – Tax reforms have twice re-weighted the SBT's apportionment formula and restructured the application of the capital acquisition deduction (CAD). The most recent reforms were effective in 1999 (estimated tax savings: $246.7 million).

  – A relatively new program, the Michigan Economic Growth Authority (MEGA) program allows SBT and/or personal income tax credits for large-scale economic development projects (estimated tax savings: $11.9 million).

- **Michigan Renaissance Zone Program.** Michigan's Tax-Free Renaissance Zones are regions of the state designated as virtually tax-free for any business or resident presently in or moving to a zone. The zones are designed to provide selected communities with the most powerful market-based incentive – no taxes – to spur new jobs and investment. Each Renaissance Zone can be comprised of up to six smaller zones (sub zones) which are located throughout the community to give businesses more options on where to locate. A business would pay unemployment insurance, social security taxes, workers' compensation, and sewer and water fees which are either federal taxes or fees for service. Businesses would also pay property taxes which result from local bonded indebtedness or special assessments so as not to jeopardize the community's current bonds. Businesses

LEGISLATIVE TIMELINE:

1992: Passed a bill that makes more small businesses eligible for credits under the state's Single Business Tax.

1993: Established the Michigan Jobs Commission to promote a healthy business climate and increase the competitiveness of Michigan businesses.

1994: Lowered property taxes by an average of 30 percent and capped business property taxes for school purposes at 24 percent. Increased the sales tax to 6 percent from 4 percent.

1995: Created the Michigan Economic Growth Authority (MEGA) to award a Single Business Tax Credit to eligible companies.

1996: Approved establishing as many as nine tax-free "Renaissance Zones," the first such initiative in the nation. The Michigan Jobs Commission released a report outlining plans for the establishment of a private venture capital fund to accelerate the development of high technology in the state.

1998: Allowed 85 communities in the state to exempt the personal property of certain businesses.

would also pay Michigan's six percent sales tax. Michigan does not allow local sales taxes.

- **Michigan Economic Growth Authority (MEGA).** The objective of MEGA is to promote high quality economic growth and job creation in Michigan that would not occur without this program. Businesses engaged in manufacturing, research and development, wholesale and trade or office operations are eligible. Retail facilities are not eligible. Businesses must be financially sound with economically sound proposed plans. A business may receive Single Business Tax (SBT) credits for the incremental SBT liability attributable to an expansion/new location project and/or tax credits for the amount of personal income tax attributable to new jobs being created at the project site. Each credit may be awarded for up to 20 years and for up to 100 percent of the amount attributable to the project.

- **Brownfield Redevelopment Program.** "Brownfields" are "abandoned, idled, or underutilized industrial or commercial properties where redevelopment is complicated by real or perceived environmental contamination." Recently enacted legislative reforms and financial incentives have created new opportunities for brownfields. The benefits of brownfield redevelopment include job creation, restoration of tax base, reuse of existing infrastructure, slowing of urban sprawl and preservation of green space. The Michigan Single Business Tax Act has been amended to extend a tax credit for non-liable owners and operators of contaminated facilities who conduct redevelopment activities on their property. The credit is equal to 10 percent of the cost of eligible investment paid or accrued, up to a maximum cumulative credit of one million dollars.

FINANCIAL INCENTIVES:

- **Business and Industrial Development Corporations.** Business and Industrial Development Corporations (BIDCOs) are private financial institutions designed to fill the moderate risk/moderate return gap between the banks and venture capitalists. BIDCOs have substantial flexibility in the types of financing tools that can be used, i.e., subordinate loans with equity features, royalty financing for product development, equity investments and guaranteed loans under the Small Business Administration (SBA) program. There are ten BIDCOs in Michigan.

- **Capital Access Program.** Participating banks throughout Michigan offer the Capital Access Program directly to companies that need credit enhancement. Similar to a loan loss reserve fund, the bank, company and the Michigan Economic Development Corporation place a small percentage of the loan into a reserve that makes it possible for the company to receive fixed asset and working capital financing.

- **Employee-Owned Corporations.** This loan program can assist in the formation of employee-owned corporations. Loans can be used for fixed assets and working capital. Maximum loan amount is $200,000.

- **Industrial Development Revenue Bonds (IDRB).** Industrial Development Revenue Bonds can be used as a financing vehicle for manufacturers, solid waste/cogeneration companies and certain private nonprofit corporations. All issuers can provide up to $10 million on manufacturing projects. Tax-exempt IDRB financing makes the cost of borrowing approximately 75 to 85 percent of prime rate for eligible capital expenditures because the interest paid to the bond buyer is exempt from federal taxes (and state taxes in certain cases).

- **Loan Guarantees.** The Michigan Economic Development Corporation works with the Small Business Administration (SBA) and Rural Development Agency on particular projects that require loan guarantees from one of these federal agencies to secure private financing on eligible projects.

- **SBA 504 Program.** For qualified small businesses, the SBA 504 Program can provide subordinated, fixed asset financing at long-term Treasury bond rates. Maximum loans are limited to $750,000 or 40 percent of project financing requirements (whichever is less).

- **Taxable Revenue Bonds.** Taxable Revenue Bonds also can be issued by the MSF or local economic development corporation. These bonds are tax-exempt at the state and local level if purchased by Michigan taxpayers. These bonds can provide companies with potentially longer term financing (perhaps 10 to 20 years) and are often at a fixed rate and lower cost than conventional financing. Taxable Revenue Bonds are not restricted by the Internal Revenue Service and can be used to finance projects of more than $10 million. Also, these bonds can be used as working capital and to finance commercial, pollution control, agriculture and recreational projects.

SUCCESSFUL INCENTIVES:

- **Customized Business Incentives.** The MEGA program and the Renaissance Zone program mentioned earlier are customized incentive programs and have been especially successful.

Contact:

John Czurnecki
201 N. Washington Square
Lansing, MI 48913
(517) 373-9148

TAX INCENTIVES:

- **Corporate income tax.** 9.8 percent, plus a 5.8 percent tax on any Alternative Minimum Taxable Income over the base tax.

- **Personal income tax.** 6. 0 to 8.5 percent.

- **Sales and use tax.** General statewide sales tax is 6.5 percent. Special tooling, capital equipment for manufacturers, and input used during the manufacturing process and in the production of certain services are exempt.

- **Enterprise Zone Program.** The Enterprise Zone Program provides tax credits to qualifying businesses which create investment, development, or create or retain jobs in the Enterprise Zone cities. Tax credits are allocated by the state to Enterprise Zone cities. Businesses apply for tax credits through the city Enterprise Zone coordinator. The type of tax credits include: property tax credits, debt financing credit on new construction, sales tax credit on construction equipment and materials, and new or existing employee credits. Any business is eligible except the following: a recreation or entertainment facility, one owned by a fraternal or veteran's organization, one owned by a public utility or a financial institution.

FINANCIAL INCENTIVES:

- **Minnesota Investment Fund.** The purpose of this fund is to create and retain the highest quality jobs possible on a statewide basis with focus on industrial, manufacturing and technology related industries; to increase the local and state tax base and improve the economic vitality for all Minnesota citizens. Grants are awarded to local units of government which provide loans to assist expanding businesses. Eligible projects include: loans for land, buildings, equipment and training. Funds may also be used for infrastructure improvements necessary to support businesses located or intending to locate in Minnesota. The maximum available is $500,000 and only one grant per state fiscal year can be awarded to a government unit. The terms on real estate are a maximum of 20 years and on machinery and equipment a maximum of 10 years.

- **Microenterprise Assistance Grants.** This program's purpose is to assist Minnesota's small entrepreneurs with the successful startup or expansion of their businesses and to support job creation in the state. Startup entrepreneurs and expanding businesses receive technical assistance and, in some cases, financial support through selected nonprofit business development organizations. Eligible applicants include businesses which employ less than five people and are being considered for a loan ranging from $1,000 to $25,000. Any type business is eligible to receive assistance, especially nontraditional entrepreneurs such as women, members of minorities, low-income individuals or persons currently on or recently removed from welfare assistance who are seeking work. The assistance should nurture the owner in order to improve the prospects of the business's

LEGISLATIVE TIMELINE:

1991: Created Advantage Minnesota, a nonprofit public corporation designed to market the economic potential of the state. Amended existing corporate takeover statutes, broadening the protections for state corporations.

1992: Repealed a sales tax on used business equipment. Extended the corporate liability protections enjoyed by "C" and "S" corporations to small partnerships.

1994: Eliminated the sales tax on special tooling equipment and enacted a gradual reduction in the sales tax on replacement equipment to 2 percent from 6 percent by 1999. Reduced property taxes on business incubators.

1995: Enacted a measure to phase in a tax cut on replacement equipment from the 6.5 percent to 2 percent by July 1, 1998.

1996: Created the Minnesota Investment Fund to support business start-ups, expansion or retentions and encourage new jobs. Passed legislation that permits property tax abatements if a plant is located in a county adjacent to another county with property tax rates that are 45 percent lower.

1997: Appropriated more than $135 million for economic and community development purposes.

1998: Appropriated over $1.5 million for economic development projects.

longevity. Businesses are eligible for up to $4,000 of technical assistance through this program. Participating organizations are reimbursed by DTED for up to half of this amount for approved expenses they incur on behalf of the grant recipient. The participating organization provides the other matching amount.

- **Small Business Development Loan Program.** The Minnesota Agricultural and Economic Development Board(MAEDB) makes small business loans through the issuance of industrial development bonds backed by a state-funded reserve of 25 percent in order to create jobs and business expansion. Eligible applicants include manufacturing and industrial businesses located or intending to locate in Minnesota, as defined by Small Business Administration size and eligibility standards; generally, those with 500 employees or fewer. Eligible projects include: acquisition of land, building, machinery and equipment; building construction and renovations; and development costs such as engineering, legal and financial fees. Working capital and refinancing are not eligible. The maximum amount available is $6 million with a minimum of $500,000.

- **Tourism Loan Program.** The purpose of this program is to provide low-interest financing to existing tourism-related business providing overnight lodging. Additionally, the program assists with the development of business plans. Businesses with feasible business plans qualify to receive financing for up to half of all eligible costs. Direct loans, or participation loans in cooperation with financial institutions, can be made for up to 50 percent of total project cost. Eligible applicants include: corporations; sole proprietorships or partnerships or partnerships engaged in an existing tourism-related business providing overnight lodging, including resorts, bed and breakfast inns, cabins or cottages, hotels, ski lodges and ski resorts, campgrounds and recreational vehicle trailer parks.

- **Capital Access Program.** This program is used to encourage loans from private lending institutions to businesses, particularly small-and medium sized-businesses, to foster economic development. When loans are enrolled in the program by participating lending institutions, the lender obtains additional financial protection through a special fund created by the lender, borrower and the state. The lender and borrower contribute between 3 percent and 7 percent of the loan to the fund. The amount of funds contributed by the borrower/lender must be equal; however, the funds contributed by the bank may be recovered from the borrower as additional fees or through interest rates.

- **Rural Challenge Grant Program.** The purpose of the Rural Challenge Grant Program is to provide job opportunities for low-income individuals, encourage private investment and promote economic development in rural areas of the state. The Business and Community Development Division has a partnership with six regional organizations to provide low-interest loans to new or expanding businesses in rural Minnesota. Eligible applicants include businesses located, or intending to locate, in rural Minnesota (where "rural" is defined as the 80 counties of Minnesota outside the Twin Cities metropolitan area). The maximum amount available is $100,000. Most loans will be smaller due to the high demand for funds compared with the funds available. Retail loans may be made to a maximum of $20,000. Each dollar of Challenge Grant funds must be matched by at least one dollar of non-public funds, usually owners' equity and/or private financing.

OTHER INCENTIVES:

- **Minnesota Trade Office for Minnesota Exporters.** The Minnesota Trade Office (MTO) promotes international trade and investment activities that have the most positive effect on the state's economy. Resources are focused on developing trade with Canada, the European Union and most Asian countries, as well as targeting Minnesota's leading industries for export promotion. The MTO has strategies and programs in place for developing export opportunities in the emerging markets of China, India, Central and Eastern Europe, South Africa and Latin America. The MTO offers the following programs: export education and training; export counseling and assistance; an international information network that includes a dozen international contacts; export finance; and an international library that includes a variety of resources to assist in exporting.

- **Minnesota Job Skills Program.** This program acts as a catalyst between business and education in developing cooperative training projects that provide training for new jobs or retrain existing employees. Grants are awarded to educational institutions with businesses as partners. Eligible applicants include public and/or private educational institutions within the state. Preference will be given to nonprofit institutions which serve economically disadvantaged people, minorities or those who are victims of economic dislocation, and to businesses located in rural areas. The maximum amount awarded for partnership funds per grant is $400,000.

Contact:

Robert W. Isaacson
Director, Office of Analysis & Evaluation
500 Metro Square, 121 7th Place East
Saint Paul, MN 55101-2146
(800)657-3858
(651)297-3615

MISSISSIPPI

TAX INCENTIVES:

- **Corporate income tax.** 3.0 to 5.0 percent.

- **Personal income tax.** 3.0 to 5.0 percent.

- **Sales and use tax.** Sales and use taxes are applied to all businesses having legal existence within the state. Sales taxes vary, based upon the types of transactions.

- **Job Tax Credit.** Provides a five-year year tax credit to the company's state income tax bill for each new job created by a new or expanding business, effective for years two through six after the creation of the job. The credit amount depends on the development status of the county in which the business is located and is as follows: (1) $2,000 per new job for less developed counties, (2) $1,000 per new job for moderately developed counties, and (3) $500 per new job for developed counties. In less developed counties, businesses must create at least 10 new jobs to be eligible for the credit; in moderately developed counties, 15 new jobs; and in developed counties, 20 new jobs.

- **Research and Development Jobs Tax Credit.** Provides an additional five-year tax credit of $500 per year for each net new research and development job created by new or expanding businesses, effective for years two through six after the creation of the job. There is no minimum number of research and development jobs required to be eligible for this credit. To qualify for this credit, a business must first meet Mississippi State Tax Commission regulations defining the eligible research and development jobs.

- **Headquarters Jobs Tax Credit.** Provides an additional five-year tax credit of $500 per year for each net new job created by the transfer of a national or regional headquarters to Mississippi, provided that at least 35 full-time jobs are created. The credit is effective for years two through six after the creation of the job.

- **Child Care Tax Credit.** Provides a tax credit to new or existing businesses that provide or contract for child care for employees during the employees' work hours. The credit is equal to 25 percent of qualified expenses for child care. The child care facility must have an average daily enrollment of at least six children who are 12 years of age or less for the business to qualify for this credit.

- **Basic Skills Training Tax Credit.** Provides a tax credit to new or existing businesses that pay for certain basic skills training or retraining for their employees. The credit is equal to 25 percent of qualified training expenses. Training programs must be certified by the state Department of Education to qualify for this credit.

- **Rural Economic Development Credits.** Through certain types of bond financing agreements, a company's state income tax liability may be reduced by an amount equal to its annual bond debt service payments.

LEGISLATIVE TIMELINE:

1990: Established a minority loan program. Authorized an initial five-year property tax exemption and job tax credits for air transportation and maintenance facilities and large hotels and movie studios.

1991: Increased funding for the Major Economic Impact Authority, which is dedicated to the impact area surrounding the National Aeronautics and Space Administration's rocket facility to be constructed in north-east Mississippi

1992: Created the Rural Economic Development Assistance Program which provides state income tax credits for new and existing companies creating jobs in rural areas. Appropriated an additional $2 million for industrial training.

1993: Created the Rural Economic Development Assistance Program which provides state income tax credits for new and existing companies creating jobs in rural areas. Appropriated an additional $2 million for industrial training.

1994: Eliminated the capital gains tax and authorized a tax credit for companies using Mississippi ports. Extended the bonding authority of Mississippi's $75 million low-interest infrastructure loan program.

1995: Approved a Marketing Match Grants program to assist communities in their marketing efforts to win new businesses and industry. Approved property tax exemptions and jobs and basic skills tax credits for telecommunications companies. Appropriated additional funding for the Institute for Technology Development.

1996: Passed a measure that increases the bonding authority of the Mississippi Business Investment Act to small communities and provides a credit against state income taxes in the amount of debt service paid by certain companies.

1997: Increased bonding by $110 million for Mississippi Major Economic Impact Act purposes. Authorizes an additional $20 million in bonds for economic development projects under the Economic Development Act.

1998: Passed the Small Enterprise Development Finance Act that allows the bonding authority to have a total of $140 million outstanding at any time. Increased bond money for the Mississippi Business Investment Act to a maximum of $254.8 million.

- **Mississippi State Port Income Tax Credit.** Provides an income tax credit to taxpayers who utilize the port facilities at state, county and municipal ports in Mississippi. The taxpayer receives a credit in an amount equal to certain charges paid by the taxpayer on export cargo.

FINANCIAL INCENTIVES:

- **Small Enterprise Development Program.** The issuance of state general obligation bonds provides funds allowing manufacturing and processing companies to finance fixed assets, including land, buildings, new machinery and new equipment at below market interest rates for terms of up to 15 years. Although a company may qualify for more than one loan under this program, the aggregate amount loaned to any company cannot exceed $2 million. Interest rates on these loans are equal to the net interest rate on the bonds issued by the state plus a service fee. A project must create a minimum of 10 jobs, and loans cannot exceed 90 percent of the market value of the financed assets. A letter of credit from an approved financial institution guaranteeing the loan must be obtained.

- **Loan Guarantee Program.** This program provides guarantees to lenders on loans made to small businesses. Loan proceeds may be used for all project costs including fixed assets, working capital, start-up costs, rental payments, interest expense during construction and professional fees. The maximum guarantee is 75 percent of the total loan or $375,000, whichever is less. The maximum term is 20 years with the interest rate established by the lender. The borrower must have equity in the business and pay a guarantee fee of 2 percent of the guaranteed portion of the loan. Loans cannot exceed 90 percent of the fair market value of the collateral.

- **Minority Business Enterprise Loan Program.** This program provides funds for minority economic development by directly financing up to one-third or $250,000, whichever is less, of eligible project costs of a new or expanding business at below market interest rates. Collateral is typically subordinated to the financial institution participating in the project. Ownership must be at least 60 percent minority.

- **Agribusiness Enterprise Loan Program.** This program provides interest-free loans to agribusiness concerns. The maximum loan is 20 percent of the eligible project costs or $200,000, whichever is less. Proceeds may not be used to purchase land. All loans must be guaranteed by either the Farm Service Agency, the Small Business Administration or a direct lender.

- **Mississippi Business Investment Act.** Through the issuance of general obligation bonds, low interest loans are provided to counties or municipalities to finance improvements that complement investments made by private companies and may include the acquisition, expansion or improvement of land, buildings and infrastructure. Requires a $3 private investment for every $1 in state assistance and minimum of one job created for every $15,000 in assistance.

- **Capital Improvements Program.** This program provides low-interest loans to counties and municipalities for the purpose of making infrastructure or capital improvements to attract local industry.

- **Mississippi Major Impact Authority.** This program allows the state, through the issuance of general obligation bonds, to assist local communities in financing a variety of improvements inherent in large capital projects. Eligibility is based upon a private company or the U.S. government making an initial investment in the community of at least $300 million.

- **Economic Development Highway Program.** Assists political subdivisions with the construction or improvement of highway projects that encourage high economic benefit projects to locate in a specific area. A high economic benefit project is any new private investment of $50 million or more by a company in land, buildings or depreciable fixed assets, or an investment of at least $20 million by a company that has statewide capital investments of at least $1 billion.

- **Mississippi Access Road Program.** This program assists local entities in the construction of highway links to connect new and existing industrial sites to adequate road facilities.

- **Mississippi Airport Revitalization Revolving Loan Program.** Funds from the issuance of state bonds provide loans to airport authorities for the construction and/or improvements of airport facilities that will be used in the promotion of Latin American trade markets. Airport loan funds may be used for 100 percent project financing. The maximum loan amount for any one project is $500,000, with a maximum term of 10 years and an interest rate of 4 percent.

- **Mississippi Port Revitalization Revolving Loan Program.** This program provides loans to state, county or municipal port authorities for the improvement of port facilities. Funding for loans is derived from the issuance of state bonds. Port loan funds may be used for 100 percent project financing. The maximum loan amount for any one project is $500,000, with a maximum term of 10 years and an interest rate of 4 percent.

- **Energy Investment Program.** This program offers low interest loans to companies making energy saving capital improvements or designing and developing energy conserving processes. The maximum loan is $200,000.

OTHER INCENTIVES:

- **The Mississippi Department of Economic and Community Development (MDECD) International Development Division.** This division of the MDECD targets industries and countries. Recruitment missions were completed last year to Europe, Asia and Canada. MDECD maintains foreign offices in Chile, Singapore and Germany for recruitment and trade purposes. The staff provides technical assistance, consultation and referrals to Mississippi exporters. In addition, exporters are represented at a number of foreign catalog and trade fairs.

- **Public/Private Partnerships.** The MDECD and local economic development organizations partner frequently on business recruitment and expansion projects. The public/private partnership also includes: individual businesses participating in foreign investment and trade missions, business leaders serving on Workforce Development Councils (created under the Workforce and Education Act of 1994) to help direct worker training efforts, MDECD and universities are partnering with companies in the MS Space Commerce Initiative to build a remote sensing based industry sector in the state, and state agencies and universities partnering with private sector controlled nonprofit technology development corporations.

Contact:

William T. Barry
Director, Financial Resources Division
Mississippi Department of Economic and Community
   Development
P.O. Box 849
Jackson, MS 39205
(601) 359-3552
(601) 359-3619

MISSOURI

LEGISLATIVE TIMELINE:

1990: Amended state enterprise zone legislation to authorize the formation of five new zones, upping the total to 38.

1991: Provided for the designation of 50 enterprise zones.

1992: Created the Small Business Development Centers Program, providing managerial and technical assistance to small businesses. Created tax credits for qualified investments in Missouri small businesses.

1993: Enacted the Omnibus Economic Development Act, an initiative that extends tax incentives to existing businesses and establishes six regional economic development offices. Raised the corporate income tax rate to 6.25 percent from 5 percent.

1994: Authorized the Missouri Tech. Corp. to make direct seed or venture capital investments in Missouri businesses. Passed the Missouri Capital Access Program Act intended to encourage banks to make risky business loans.

1995: Allowed enterprise zones to request a seven-year extension beyond the 15-year limit. Approved a measure that authorized the Missouri Technology Corp. to contract with state Centers for Advanced Technology and Innovation.

1996: Passed business inducements for a Harley-Davidson plant, and created a statewide program to help industry finance new construction and jobs. Enacted BUILD (Business Use Incentives for Large-scale Development).

1997: Expands the duties of the Agriculture and Small Business Development Authority to provide assistance to businesses involved in processing, manufacturing and exporting Missouri's agricultural products by granting partial loan guarantees.

1998: Authorized tax credits and other incentives for economic development.

1999: Made changes to various economic development programs including tax credit programs and enterprise zones.

TAX INCENTIVES:

• **Corporate income tax.** 6.25 percent.

• **Personal income tax.** 1.5 to 6.0 percent.

• **Sales and use tax.** 4.225 percent

• **New or Expanded Business Facility Credit.** Manufacturers, wholesale distributors, office tenants, truck, barge or rail line operators, interchange telecommunications company facilities, or mining, warehouses, or research/development operators, agricultural farm implement dealers, poultry producers, insurance carriers or recyclers may be eligible to claim this credit if they establish a new facility or expand an existing facility and create new jobs and new investment.

• **Missouri Low Income Housing Credit.** Owners of or investors in rental property, approved for a federal low income housing credit, may be eligible for the Missouri low income housing credit in an amount up to 100 percent of the project's federal tax credit. A statement authorized and issued by the commission certifying that a given project qualifies for the Missouri low income housing credit must accompany your tax return.

• **Enterprise Zone Credit.** You may be eligible for this credit if you established a new facility or expanded an existing facility in an enterprise zone and created new jobs and new investment.

• **Small Business Investment Credit.** If you have made a monetary contribution to an approved small business in Missouri, you may be entitled to this credit.

• **Processed Wood Energy Credit.** Companies producing processed wood energy products from Missouri timber waste are eligible for an energy tax credit. The credit may be claimed for a period of five years and is to be a credit against tax otherwise due. This credit is for producing an end product, not for the building of wood.

• **Wine and Grape Production Tax Credit Program.** Beginning January 1, 1999, a grape grower or wine producer shall be allowed a 25 percent state income tax credit on the amount of the purchase price of all new equipment and materials used directly in the growing of grapes or the production of wine in the state.

FINANCIAL INCENTIVES:

• **Missouri FIRST Linked Deposit For Small Businesses.** The State Treasurer has reserved a portion of available linked deposit funds for small businesses. State funds are deposited with participating lending institutions at up to 3 percent below the one-year Treasury Bill rate, with the lender passing on this interest savings to the small business borrower. A company must have less than 25 employees, be headquartered in Missouri and be operating for profit. Small Business MISSOURI FIRST Linked Deposit loans are available for working capital. The maximum loan amount is $100,000.

• **Market Development Loans for Recovered Materials.** The Environmental Improvement and Energy Resources Authority funds activities that promote the development of markets for recovered materials. Loans of up to $75,000 are available to companies for equipment used in the production or manufacture of products made from recovered materials. After three years, if all contract obligations are met, the loan is forgiven and repayment is not required.

• **Financial Aid for Beginning Farmers.** Beginning farmers can receive federally tax-exempt loans from commercial lenders at rates 20 to 30 percent below conventional rates through this program. A qualified borrower can borrow up to $250,000 to buy agricultural land, farm buildings, farm equipment and breeding livestock in Missouri. The borrower must be a Missouri resident, at least 18 years old and whose chief occupation must be farming or ranching after the loan is closed. The borrower's net worth must not exceed $200,000, and he or she must have adequate working capital and experience in the type of farming operation for which the loan is sought. A beginning farmer is one who has not previously owned more than 30 percent of the medium-sized farm in their county.

OTHER INCENTIVES:

• **Missouri's Export Finance Program.** Missouri companies that need financial assistance exporting to foreign markets can use programs of the Export and Import Bank of the United States (Ex-Im Bank) and the Small Business Administration (SBA) through a joint project that provides local access for Missouri businesses. There are primarily two programs available, Working Capital Loan Guarantees and Export Credit Insurance. These programs are designed to help small and medium-sized businesses that have exporting potential but need funds or risk insurance to produce and market goods or services for export.

The state of Missouri also offers assistance in obtaining export credit insurance through the Ex-Im Bank of the US to take the risk out of selling to customers overseas. The Missouri program, which insures both commercial and political risks, guarantees an exporter that once his goods are shipped he will be paid.

Contact:

Stacy Meyer
Department of Economic Development
301 W. High St.
P.O. Box 1157
Jefferson City, MO 65102
(573) 751-394

MONTANA

1991: Passed the Microbusiness Development Act, which provides loans for businesses having less than 10 employees and less than $500,000 in annual gross revenues. Passed a measure allowing the Science & Technology Alliance to fund up to $2.5 million in venture capital projects. Passed a bill allowing a 50 percent tax break to go to businesses that earn at least 50 percent of their income from out of state, rather than requiring a manufacturing base for the tax break.

1995: Cut the business equipment tax to 6 percent from 9 percent.

1996: Passed a new law that provides infrastructure loans to new companies that will employ at least 50 workers. Authorized cities, towns and counties to levy a local property tax to fund economic development activities. Reduced the tax on business equipment.

1997: Passed an Act that allows the Dept. of Commerce to establish a foreign capital depository to attract legally derived foreign capital for investment, revenue enhancement and other economic development purposes.

1999: Reduced the current minimum loan limit for the Montana Board of Investment Infrastructure Loans from $500,000 to $250,000 and the job creation threshold from 50 jobs to 15 new jobs.

TAX INCENTIVES:

• **Corporate income tax.** 6.75 percent.

• **Personal income tax.** 2.0 to 11 percent

• **Sales and use tax.** None.

• **New or Expanding Industry Wage Credit.** A new or expanding manufacturing corporation may receive a corporation license tax credit of 1 percent of wages paid to new employees for the first 3 years of operation or expansion.

• **Recycling Tax Credit and Deduction.** Taxpayers are allowed a credit on the investment of depreciable property used to collect or process reclaimable material or to manufacture a product from reclaimed material. The credit is equal to 25 percent on the first $250,000 invested; 15 percent on the next $250,000; and 5 percent on the next $500,000. An additional deduction allowed equal to 10 percent of the expenditures for the purchase of recycled material otherwise deductible as a business-rated expense. The credit and the deduction may be applied either to individual income or corporation license tax.

• **Research and Development Firms Exemption.** A research and development firm organized to engage in business in Montana for the first time, is exempt from corporation license taxation for the first 5 years of taxable activity in the state.

• **Small Business Investment Company Tax Exemption.** Capital gains and dividend income received from a small business investment company is exempt from individual and corporation income taxation.

• **Water's Edge Unitary Combination Option.** For corporation license tax purposes, a corporation subject to apportionment may choose between worldwide combined reporting and the water's edge combination method of reporting. The net income of corporations making a water's edge election is taxed at 7 percent. For all other corporations the license tax rate is 6.75 percent.

• **Wind Farms Tax Credit.** A 35 percent credit is available for investing in wind powered electrical generating equipment when that investment exceeds $5,000. The credit is in lieu of exempt property tax status for a portion of the appraised value of electrical generating equipment. It also excludes the taxpayer from qualification for other major state and local tax incentives. The credit can be claimed for individual income or corporation license tax purposes.

• **Business Incubators Exemption.** If approved by the local governing body, a business incubator owned and operated by a local economic development organization is eligible for an exemption from property taxes.

- **Canola Seed Oil Processing Machinery and Equipment Reduced Rate.** Machinery and equipment used in a canola seed oil processing facility with a minimum of 15 full-time employees and located in the state after July 25, 1989, is taxed at the classification rate of 4 percent. Normally, personal property is classified at 6 percent.

- **New Industry Reduced Rate.** New industrial property, including real and personal property, is eligible for a reduced taxable valuation rate of 3 percent for the first three years of operations. Normally real property is taxed at 3.794 percent and personal property is taxed at 6 percent.

- **Research and Development Firms, Pollution Control Equipment, Gasohol Producing Property and Electrolytic Reduction Equipment Reduced Rate.** This property is taxed at the lowest classification rate of 3 percent.

- **Coal Production Incentives.** Persons producing less than 50,000 tons of coal in a year are exempt from severance tax. Persons producing in excess of 50,000 tons per year are exempt from severance tax on the first 20,000 tons produced. A person is not liable for any severance tax upon the first 2,000,000 tons of coal produced as feed stock for an approved coal enhancement facility. This exemption terminates on December 31, 2005. One-half of the contract sales price of coal sold by a coal producer who extracts less than 50,000 tons of coal in a calendar year is exempt from taxation.

- **Oil and Gas Production Incentives.** Incremental production from secondary and tertiary recovery projects and recompleted horizontal wells are taxed at reduced rates. These reduced rates apply when the average price for crude oil is less than $30 per barrel.

FINANCIAL INCENTIVES:

- **Job Investment Loan Program.** Eligible businesses are any that create or retain jobs in Montana. The total funding limit is $500,000 and must be used for working capital, equipment and fixed assets. The company must receive prior private financial institution approval in order to be considered for the Job Investment Loan.

- **Micro-Business Finance.** This program is for businesses with 10 or fewer employees and gross revenues of less than $500,000 per year. These small or start-up businesses will receive business training and technical support through a local development organization, fixed-rate financing and effluent mitigation credit enhancements. The total funding limit is $35,000 and the use of the proceeds must be for working capital, equipment and fixed assets. The credit criteria is based on a business plan noting repayment ability, a credit report and management quality.

- **The Montana Board of Investments (BOI) Loan Participation Program.** Any for-profit and nonprofit Montana businesses are eligible for a maximum of $16 million for any one project (80 percent BOI, 20 percent from private

lender). The funds must be used for working capital, equipment and real property.

- **Montana Science and Technology Alliance.** Medium to rapid-growth, for-profit businesses that have the potential to provide a substantial return to investors are eligible for a maximum of $700,000 in funding. The loan must be for working capital, equipment, and product and market development.

- **Montana Growth Through Agriculture.** The maximum loan is $50,000 for any one round of financing, and a total of $150,000 to any one firm. The borrower may be an individual, corporation or local government and projects must embody innovative agricultural products or processes.

- **Small Business Administration.** Must be a small business by Federal SBA standards and the loan must be used for working capital, equipment and real property. The loan can be either a $700,000 guarantee limit or, for businesses that create or retain jobs, the loan can be up to 40 percent of the project, with a limit of $750,000 (up to $1 million for special public goals).

- **Rural Development by the Rural Business Cooperative Service (RBS).** A rural-area business that creates employment with a preference to areas with less than 25,000 people. Eligible borrowers include any legal entity, including individuals, public and private organizations and federally recognized Indian tribal groups. The loan limit is $10 million and must be used for working capital, equipment and real property.

OTHER INCENTIVES:

- **Export Assistance Programs.** Montana offers technical assistance for new to export or new to market businesses and has Pacific Rim trade offices.

- **Aerospace Incentive.** Montana offers a tax exemption for aerospace business equipment on the Venture Star reusable launch vehicle spaceport.

- **Day Care Incentive.** A 20 percent tax credit for dependent care assistance offered by businesses in Montana.

- **Public/Private Partnership.** The State Commerce Department Regional Development officers assist clients with finding private capital.

Contact:

Jerry L. Tavegia
Business Location Officer
Montana Department of Commerce
1424 Ninth Avenue
Helena, MT 59620
(406) 444-4378

NEBRASKA

LEGISLATIVE TIMELINE:

1990: Passed the Small Business Incubator Act, allowing local governments, educational institutions and other organizations to designate vacant space in public buildings as incubator space for new business development.

1991: Passed the Local Option Municipal Economic Development Act, allowing the use of municipal general tax revenues for local economic development activity.

1992: Approved a measure to facilitate enactment of the Local Option Municipal Economic Development Act.

1993: Enacted enterprise zone legislation and legislation allowing limited liability companies.

1994: Increased state general funds dedicated to finance new employee training. Created a State Unemployment Insurance Trust Fund, interest from which will be used for training and retraining workers and upgrading skills.

1995: Approved the Quality Jobs Act, authorizing a wage benefit credit to new employees of approved companies in Nebraska. Gave all Nebraska electronic utilities the ability to negotiate lower rates for large business customers. Passed the Nebraska Redevelopment Act, authorizing tax-increment financing for large new projects.

1996: Amended the Quality Jobs Act, giving companies the option of taking a wage benefit credit that can be applied against state income tax liability.

1998: Amended the Quality Jobs Act allowing a company 6 years instead of 4 to meet the requirements of the levels of employment or investment.

1999: Amended the Employment Expansion and Investment Incentive Act in order to redefine the terms of the original act.

TAX INCENTIVES:

- **Corporate income tax.** 5.58 to 7.81 percent.

- **Personal income tax.** 2.51 to 6.68 percent.

- **Sales and use tax.** The tax rate is 5 percent of the gross receipts from sales of tangible personal property and certain taxable services. Additional local option taxes of 0.5, 1.0 or 1.5 percent may be approved by local voters.

- **Employment and Investment Growth Tax Incentives.** Businesses, such as manufacturers, processors, research and development facilities, insurance and financial companies, telecommunications companies and administrative headquarters facilities of such firms are eligible for tax incentives by meeting minimum thresholds for employment and investment. Three levels of incentives are available to qualifying businesses:

  1. A business investing at least $3 million in qualified property and creating at least 330 new or additional jobs is entitled to: (1) a refund of all sales and use taxes paid for all purchases of depreciable property, including building materials used in connection with a qualified project; (2) a 5 percent tax credit on the compensation paid to the company's new or additional employees each year for seven years; and (3) a 10 percent tax credit of the investment made in qualified depreciable property (new and relocated to the state) related to a qualified project over the seven-year entitlement period.

  2. A business investing at least $10 million in qualified property and hiring at least 100 new employees shall, in addition to all the incentives specified above, be entitled to : (1) a personal property tax exemption for a 15-year period for mainframe computers and peripheral equipment used with a qualified project; (2) a personal property tax exemption for a 15-year period for turbine-powered aircraft used with a qualified project; and (3) a personal property tax exemption for a 15-year period for business equipment utilized in a business that manufactures or process agricultural products.

  3. A business investing at least $20 million in qualified property but not reaching the above employment thresholds shall be entitled to a refund of all sales and use taxes paid for all purchases of depreciable property used with a qualified project.

  Credits may be used to reduce Nebraska corporate income tax liability or to obtain a refund of sales and use taxes paid on purchases for use at a project. Qualifying businesses are eligible for credits for a seven-year period and accumulated credits may be used during a 15-year period. If required levels of investment and employment are not met within or maintained for seven years, all or part of the incentives shall be disallowed or recaptured.

- **Employment Expansion and Investment Tax Incentives.** Businesses that increase investment by at least $75,000 and increase net employment by an average of two full-time positions during a taxable year are eligible for a credit of $1,500 per each new employee and $1,000 for each $75,000 of new investment. Accumulated credits can be used to reduce corporate income tax liability by up to 50 percent in any one year. Unused credits can be carried over for five immediately succeeding taxable years. The credits also can be applied toward a refund of sales and use taxes paid on purchases used on a project. Businesses utilizing Employment and Investment Growth tax credits are not eligible for Employment Expansion and Investment tax credits.

• **Enterprise Zone Act (EZA).** The EZA provides tax credits for qualifying businesses that increase investment by at least $75,000 and increase net employment by an average of full-time positions during a taxable year. Credits may be used to reduce a portion of the taxpayer's income tax liability or to obtain a refund of sales- and use-taxes paid. Initial expansion must occur in one taxable year, but additional credits may be obtained for increasing employment by two or more full-time employees during the next five years. Credits not used in the first year may be carried over and used against liabilities incurred in the next five taxable years. Failure to maintain required levels of investment and employment for at least two years after creation of the credits will result in the recapture of allowed benefits and loss of carry-overs.

• **Quality Jobs Act.** This act authorizes a wage benefit credit to new employees of approved companies that add at least 500 new jobs and $50 million in new investment or 250 new jobs and $100 million in new investment in Nebraska. The wage and benefit credit is equal to the new employee's actual Nebraska income tax withholding, up to a total of 5 percent of wages for 10 years. The wage credit is paid to the employee to be applied toward company training programs, employee benefit programs, educational institution training programs or company workplace safety programs.

FINANCIAL INCENTIVES:

• **Nebraska Investment Finance Authority.** The Nebraska Investment Finance Authority (NIFA) is an independent, nonprofit, quasi-state agency that provides lower-cost financing for manufacturing facilities, certain farm property, health care and residential development. Project funds are obtained by issuing notes and bonds. The company seeking financing is responsible for finding a purchaser for the bonds. The notes and bonds are only limited obligations of NIFA, payable solely from specific assets of the related borrowing. The interest NIFA pays on its obligations are exempt from federal income taxation, so purchasers of NIFA notes and bonds are willing to accept lower interest rates. Programs and services available to business in Nebraska include:

(1) Industrial Development Revenue Bonds – source of low interest financing.
(2) Nebraska Investment Finance Authority(NIFA) – issues tax exempt bonds to provide low interest financing.

(3) Nebraska Development Finance Service (NDFS) – provides assistance in assembling financing.
(4) Nebraska Energy Office – provides low interest loans for energy efficiency improvements.
(5) Community Improvement Financing — a source of funding public improvements.

OTHER INCENTIVES:

• **Foreign Trade and Investment.** The Department of Economic Development has an office of International Trade and Investment to assist companies that operate in an international market.

• **Ethanol Tax Incentive.** Nebraska stimulates ethanol manufacturing using grains grown in the state through a 20-cent per gallon production tax credit.

• **Regulatory Relief Program.** Nebraska has regulatory relief programs especially for dealing with federal and state environmental regulations, a mandate initiative, and an ombudsman in the Nebraska Department of Environmental Quality provide assistance.

• **Public/Private Partnership.** The Nebraska Investment Finance Authority (NIFA) provides low interest financing for eligible industrial projects. NIFA was created by state law, and its Board of Directors is chaired by the Director of the Department of Economic Development, The Department of Economic Development also uses Nebraska's Community Development Block Grant (CDBG) funds to provide loan guarantees for bank financing of projects it favors.

SUCCESSFUL INCENTIVES:

• **Customized Business Incentives.** Though in existence for more than 5 years, the production tax credit encouraging the manufacture of ethanol from Nebraska grains is a good example of an incentive that influenced the growth of an industry. Ethanol is used in the creation of gasohol, a motor fuel composed of 90 percent gasoline and 10 percent alcohol (ethanol).

Contact:

Tom Doering
Director, Division of Research
Nebraska Department of Economic Development
P.O. Box 94666
Lincoln, NE 68509-4666
(402) 471-3784

NEVADA

LEGISLATIVE TIMELINE:

1991: Imposed a new tax on all state businesses, based on each firm's total number of employees. New or expanding businesses that meet certain job creation and capital investment criteria may apply for an exemption to the tax.

1993: Exempted recycling companies that make a capital investment of at least $15 million from 75 percent of personal property taxes.

1995: Approved a new sales and use tax abatement on manufacturing equipment and machinery. Appropriated $200,000 to fund start-up costs of the Nevada Development Capital Corporation, a quasi-governmental corporation charged with working with private investors and lenders to offer capital for small businesses.

1997: Passed a bill to encourage certain types of industry to locate or expand their businesses within the state with certain abatements, exemptions and deferrals of taxes.

1999: Passed a measure to allow the Director of Nevada's Department of Business and Industry to finance the acquisition, refurbishing, replacement and installation of equipment for a project.

TAX INCENTIVES:

- **Corporate income tax.** None.

- **Personal income tax.** None.

- **Sales and use tax.** 6.5 to 7 percent depending on county; no sales tax on food items for home use, medicine or services; sales and use tax deferral and abatement available.

- **Sales and Use Tax Abatement.** An abatement of sales and use tax on eligible machinery and equipment may be given to businesses with operations consistent consistent with Nevada's state plan for economic diversification and development. Qualifying criteria for certification by the Commission on Economic Development include commitment to doing business in Nevada, minimum job creation, employee health plans and wage requirements.

- **Sales Tax Deferral.** The state of Nevada offers a sales and use tax deferment program to qualified industries that purchase specific types of capital equipment in excess of $100,000. Taxes can be deferred interest-free over a five-year period.

- **Sales Tax Exemptions.** Certain aircraft engaged in air transportation are exempted from taxes imposed on gross receipts from the sale of aircraft and major components of aircraft.

- **Business Tax Abatement.** Partial exemptions from business tax may be obtained by new and expanding businesses that meet the overall objectives of the state plan Focus 2000. There are a number of statutory requirements which must be met to qualify, including a minimum number of jobs created, a minimum capital investment, and wage and fringe benefit requirements.

- **Industrial Insurance.** In determining and fixing premium rates, the Nevada State Industrial Insurance System (SIIS) will take into account an employer's previous experience in the state from which the employer relocates. The company must have three years experience with an industrial insurance provider in the state(s) from which the employer relocates.

- **Personal Property Tax Abatement.** An abatement of personal property may be given to businesses with operations consistent with Nevada's state plan for economic diversification and development. Qualifying criteria for certification by the Commission on Economic Development include a commitment to doing business in Nevada, minimum job creation, employee health plan, minimum capital investment and wage requirements.

- **Property Tax Abatement.** Qualified recycling businesses which engage in the primary trade of preparing, fabricating, manufacturing or otherwise processing raw materials or an intermediate product through a process in which at least 50 percent of the material or product is recycled on site may be certified for a 75 percent personal property tax abatement. Personal property is exempt from taxation for up to ten consecutive years to the extent that the property is used as a facility for the production of electrical energy from recycled material. A real property exemption also applies for up to 20 consecutive years for property used for the same purpose.

• **Property Tax Exemptions.** The following are exempt from property tax:

    1. All personal property stored, assembled or processed for interstate transit.

    2. All raw materials and supplies utilized in the manufacturing process.

    3. Inventories held for sale within Nevada.

    4. All real and personal property which qualifies and is used for the purpose of air and/or water pollution control.

FINANCIAL INCENTIVES:

• **Industrial Development Bonds.** Nevada is authorized to use tax-exempt IDB's to provide low-interest financing of new construction, improvements, rehabilitation or redevelopment of qualified projects, which include manufacturing facilities and certain other projects organized under Section 501 of the Internal Revenue Service.

OTHER INCENTIVES:

• **Nevada International Division.** The International Division provides technical assistance to foreign investors and also works with a variety of businesses and associations developing export markets and assisting them in the process.

• **Job Training.** Nevada offers a customized job training program to qualified businesses that meet established criteria. This program may be used prior to a plant opening and up to 90 days following.

Contact:

Tim Rubald
Director of Research
Nevada Commission on Economic Development
108 East Proctor
Carson City, NV 89701
(775) 687-4325

NEW HAMPSHIRE

LEGISLATIVE TIMELINE:

1991: Added incentives to the business profits tax that include tax credits for job creation and capital investment for expanding firms. Another incentive benefits multi-state firms that locate operations and employees in the state.

1992: Passed a measure that restructured the Business Finance Authority to better serve small- and medium-sized businesses. Passed a bill that made several changes in the Pease Development Authority to facilitate infrastructure development.

1993: Eliminated loopholes allowing professionals to escape business profits taxes. Passed legislation that provides privately owned companies with subsidized training through state technical colleges and institutes.

1994: Passed a law that provides companies with grant-funded marketing assistance and short-term educational and informational services through the University of New Hampshire's corporate income taxes to 7 percent from 7.5 percent.

1995: Restored the business profits tax credit for job creation.

1996: Approved deregulation of the state's electric utility industry, allowing customers to choose an electricity supplier.

1997: Established a Northern New England Interstate Commission on Economic Development which shall not become effective until Maine, New Hampshire and Vermont have adopted it.

1999: Established a division of travel and tourism development within the department of resources and economic development.

TAX INCENTIVES:

- **Corporate income tax.** 8.0 percent.

- **Personal income tax.** 5.0 percent on interest and dividend income only.

- **Sales and use tax.** None.

- **Tax Credits.** A direct dollar-for-dollar credit is offered against any business profits tax liability, for business enterprise tax paid.

- **Capital Investment Tax Credit.** Equal to 10 percent of qualified manufacturing capital expenditures made or incurred during the taxable period, up to a ceiling of 5 percent of the Business Profits Tax Liability.

FINANCIAL INCENTIVES:

- **Capital Access Program.** The Capital Access Program provides incentives to bankers to make loans of $500,000 or less to small businesses that are considered moderate to high risks.

- **Guarantee Asset Program.** The Guarantee Asset Program provides financial institutions with loan guarantees for business that have more than conventional risk.

- **Working Capital Asset Guarantee Program.** The Working Capital Asset Guarantee Program guarantees loans from financial institutions for up to $7 million in working capital to businesses that have more than conventional risk.

- **Aid to Local Development Organizations.** This program helps local development organizations create and maintain employment opportunities by purchasing loans to replenish funds and/or provide additional resources for financing, developing and expanding business opportunities.

- **Export Working Capital Program.** This program helps small New Hampshire businesses that export to obtain export-related working capital loans.

OTHER INCENTIVES:

- **Job Training.** New Hampshire offers subsidized training to privately owned companies through state technical colleges and institutes.

Contact:

Margaret M. Joyce
Programs Information Officer
New Hampshire Division of Economic Development
172 Pembroke Rd.
P.O. Box 1856
Concord, NH 03302-1856
(603) 271-2341

TAX INCENTIVES:

- **Corporate income tax.** 9.0 percent. There is also a net worth tax at rates ranging from 0.2 to 2 mills. The minimum tax is $200. Corporations not subject to the franchise tax are subject to a 7.25 percent income tax. Banks other than savings institutions are subject to the franchise tax. S-Corporation are subject to an entity level tax of 1.13 percent.

- **Personal income tax.** 1.4 to 6.37 percent.

- **Sales and use tax.** 6.0 percent.

- **Business Employment Program.** Annual incentive grants for up to 10 years may be approved for 10 percent to 80 percent of the total amount of state income taxes withheld by a business for new employees hired during the year. The State Treasurer must certify that the amount of withholdings received from the business equals at least the grant amount before any grant monies are disbursed. Qualifying businesses must maintain a project in New Jersey for at least 1.5 times the number of years of the grant. Businesses that will create at least 25 jobs in an Urban Aid community or a minimum of 75 jobs in a non-urban area, are economically viable, and demonstrate that the incentive grant is a material factor in their decision to locate or expand in New Jersey are eligible for this program. Point of final purchase retail facilities are not eligible.

- **Property Tax Abatements and Exemptions.** New Jersey law authorizes municipalities, under the State Constitution, to provide property tax abatements for commercial and industrial properties in areas in need of redevelopment.

- **Urban Enterprise Zone.** In promoting growth and development within the state's economically distressed areas, New Jersey has created 27 Urban Enterprise Zones (UEZ's). Companies that locate within one of the designated zones and create jobs are eligible for a number of benefits and zone incentives that include:
  1. A one-time corporation tax credit of $1,500 for full-time hiring of residents of a city where a zone is located who have been unemployed or dependent upon public assistance for at least 90 days, or
  2. A one-time corporation tax credit of $500 for hiring certain full-time employees who are residents of any UEZ municipality.
  3. Subsidized unemployment insurance costs for certain new employees.
  4. Sales tax exemptions for materials and for tangible personal property.

- **Foreign Trade Zones.** New Jersey has four strategically located Foreign Trade Zones: Port Newark/Elizabeth in Essex County, Mount Olive in Morris County, Port Salem in Salem County, and Mercer County Airport in Mercer County. Within these zones, which are outside U.S. Customs territory, businesses may manufacture, assemble, package, process, and exhibit merchandise with substantial duty and cash flow savings. No duty

LEGISLATIVE TIMELINE:

1990: Increased the sales tax and personal income tax.

1992: Approved a measure to issue $200 million in bonds for the Economic Recovery Fund, which includes a statewide lending pool for small- and medium-sized businesses, an export-import fund, money for economic development infrastructure and funds to renovate schools.

1993: Passed a 2 percent tax credit for manufacturing equipment investments. Repealed the Business Personal Property Tax. Enacted a 10 percent research and development tax credit and set aside tax credits for facility investments that create jobs.

1994: Reduced the corporate tax rate and income tax. Added 10 new zones to the Urban Enterprise Zone Program.

1995: Reduced the personal income tax by 15 percent.

1996: Created the Business Employment Incentive Program. Created the Business Relocation Assistance Grant Program. Passed a measure giving new or expanding companies a rebate of up to 80 percent of their employee payroll taxes. Reduced taxes on small businesses.

1997: Provided $789 million in financing to more than 300 businesses and not-for-profit organizations.

1998: Passed an $18.1 billion state budget that included the formation of the Economic Growth Commission designed to help companies respond to the demands of competition in the global marketplace.

must be paid until the goods are moved in the distribution system for sale in the U.S. If re-exported, no duty will be assessed on the merchandise.

- **Recognition of Subchapter "S" Status for Corporations.** New Jersey "S" corporations are provided a reduced corporation tax rate. The law defines the amount of minimum tax imposed on domestic and foreign corporations, determination of new income and the legal requirements to become an "S" corporation.

- **New Jersey Limited Liability Company Act.** Effective January 26, 1994, a domestic or foreign LLC is taxed in accordance with the corresponding federal classification and provides for LLC's to follow federal treatment of certain taxpayers.

- **New Jobs Investment Tax Credit.** Companies that make certain investments in new or expanded business facilities that are directly related to the creation of new jobs may be eligible for credits against their New Jersey Corporation Business Tax Liability. Other significant job tax credits are available for firms expanding, retaining or relocating new jobs in New Jersey.

- **Manufacturing Equipment and Employment Investment Tax Credit.** Certain investments made by companies for manufacturing equipment with a recovery life of four years or more are eligible for a credit against the New Jersey Corporation Business Tax Liability.

- **Research and Development Tax Credit for Corporation Business Tax.** Businesses may be eligible for a credit against New Jersey's Corporation Business Tax liability for certain increased research expenditures in the state. The base period amounts and qualified expenditures are determined by the guidelines for the federal research credit.

FINANCIAL INCENTIVES:

- **The New Jersey Economic Development Authority (EDA).** The EDA is a statewide financing agency that sponsors several loan and loan guarantee programs to encourage businesses to locate, expand and remain in New Jersey. The Authority evaluates each financing request on whether it meets its public polity criteria of stimulating jobs and other economic growth and whether the potential borrower has the ability to repay the loan and provide collateral to secure the loan. The Authority is not a substitute for bank financing but works in partnership with banks to close financing gaps and supplement/complement bank lending activities.

- **Statewide Loan Pool for Business.** Through an arrangement between EDA and New Jersey banks, loans from $50,000 up to $1 million for fixed assets and up to

$500,000 for working capital are available. The total financing for a combination of fixed assets and working capital is $1 million. The EDA provides up to 25 percent of the financing subordinate to 75 percent bank participation. EDA may guarantee up to 25 percent of the bank portion. Loans above $1 million up to $3 million are available and can include both fixed assets and working capital as long as the latter does not exceed $500,000. EDA will provide up to $250,000 of the loan and also may guarantee up to 30 percent of the bank portion.

- **Loan Guarantees.** Guarantees of conventional loans of up to $1 million for working capital and guarantees of conventional loans or bond issues for fixed assets of up to $1.5 million are available. Guarantees can be arranged for a maximum of 10 years although the loan may be for a longer term. Generally, guarantees are limited to 30 percent - 50 percent of the loan amount but cannot exceed the dollar limitations above. Creditworthy business that need additional security to obtain financing are eligible. Preference is given to businesses that are either job intensive, will create or maintain tax tables, are located in an economically distressed area, or represent an important economic sector of the state and will contribute to New Jersey's growth and diversity.

- **Direct Loans.** Loans are made for up to $500,000 for fixed assets and up to $250,000 for working capital for up to 10 years. Businesses that are unable to get sufficient bank credit on their own through the Statewide Loan Pool or with an EDA guarantee are eligible. Preference is given to job-intensive enterprises located in economically targeted areas or representing a targeted business sector.

- **New Jersey Seed Capital Program.** Loans are made from $25,000 to $200,000 at a market rate of interest and can be used for working capital and fixed assets. Funding may be secured as a single loan or may be offered in tiered increments based on specific goals set and met by borrowers. Loans will be available to qualified applicants for up to 5 years. Various repayment terms will be utilized including royalties and warrants. Technology businesses that have risked their own capital to develop new technologies and need additional funds to bring their products to market are eligible for this program.

- **New Jersey Technology Funding Program.** EDA participates with commercial banks to make term loans from $100,000 to $3 million. EDA direct participation may be up to $250,000 for working capital and up to $500,000 for fixed assets. Eligible companies are second stage technology enterprises that meet the majority of the following characteristics: received venture capital, other investor financing and/or is raising funds through an IPO or private placement; received or is close to obtaining regulatory approval, if applicable; has licensing arrangements with or is selling to established companies; has historical financial statements showing limited cash flow/profitability; has reasonable forecasts of profits/cash flow; has a detailed business plan.

- **Technology Business Tax Certificate Transfer Program.** This program allows new or expanding technology and biotechnology businesses to "sell" their Unused Net Operating Loss (NOL) Carryover and Unused Research and Development Tax Credits to corporate taxpayers in the state for at least 75 percent of the value of the benefits.

- **Fund for Community Economic Development.** Loans and loan guarantees are made to urban-based community organizations that in turn make loans to micro-enterprises and small businesses which may not qualify for traditional bank financing. Affordable capital is provided to fill financing gaps in the development of community facilities and other real estate based economic development projects. Funds are available to local groups to finance feasibility studies and other pre-development costs to determine if a real estate project is viable.

- **Business Employment Incentive Program.** Annual incentive grants for up to 10 years may be approved for 10 percent to 80 percent of the total amount of state income taxes withheld by a business for new employees hired during the year. Qualifying businesses must maintain a project in New Jersey for at least 1.5 times the number of years of the grant. Businesses that will create at least 25 jobs in an Urban Aid community or a minimum of 75 jobs in a non-urban area, are economically viable, and demonstrate that the incentive grant is a factor in their decision to locate or expand in New Jersey will be eligible for this program.

- **Workforce Training Grants.** New Jersey, through its nationally recognized Workforce Development Partnership, offers customized skills training, education and support services to workers and employers. The program is a coordinated effort by New Jersey's 19 community colleges, state government and the private sector that helps business maximize their potential through access to affordable training services in numerous critical areas. Under this program, matching grant dollars can be awarded to employers for classroom based and on-the-job training. Grant allocation can be applied to the direct cost of training (training vendor fees, training supplies, etc.) as well as the partial reimbursement of wages of workers in the training.

OTHER INCENTIVES:

- **Foreign Investment.** The EDA's programs are available to foreign firms seeking to locate or expand operations in New Jersey.

- **Export Assistance.** Under an arrangement between EDA

and New Jersey banks, up to a $1 million one-year revolving line of credit will be provided to finance confirmed foreign orders. Funds can be drawn to buy raw materials, pay production costs and ship product. The borrowing is repaid when the account receivable is collected. Generally, the borrower must have an irrevocable letter of credit from the purchaser or insurance acceptable to the EDA to collateralize borrowings under the line of credit. The bank will provide 75 percent of the funds at its normal lending rate and EDA will provide the remaining 25 percent at its lending rate.

- **Bright Beginnings Child Care Facilities Loan Fund.** The Loan Fund program is designed to support the creation, expansion and establishment of child care facilities in New Jersey through debt financing and technical assistance. Any for-profit or not-for-profit Licensed Child Care Center, Registered Family Day Care Providers or Prospective Child Care Center Operator in New Jersey can apply for a loan.

- **Regulatory Relief Program.** The Office of the Business Advocate and Business Information is charged with assisting businesses that are having difficulty navigating state regulations.

- **Public/Private Partnerships.** The Statewide Loan Pool for Business targets businesses that create or maintain jobs; are located in a financially targeted municipality; or represent a targeted industry such as manufacturing, industry, agriculture or one of the other sectors targeted for assistance by the EDA. Through an arrangement between EDA and New Jersey banks, loans from $50,000 up to $1 million for fixed assets and up to $500,000 for working capital are available.

SUCCESSFUL INCENTIVES:

- **Employment and Technology Incentives.** The Business Employment Incentive Program has been highly effective in creating jobs. The Technology Center of New Jersey offers affordable state-of-the-art facilities to high technology/emerging technology companies.

Contact:

Lisa Kruse
Vice President, Marketing & Communications
NJ Commerce Commission
20 West State St.
P.O. Box 820
Trenton, NJ 08625
(609) 984-6677

NEW MEXICO

LEGISLATIVE TIMELINE:

1990: Increased funding for the state's industrial training program and passed legislation that enables service-oriented businesses to utilize this program. Enacted a sales tax exemption for companies that invest $50 million or more.

1991: Amended the Investment Tax Credit Program, eliminating the maximum credit limits established under the previous law. Passed the Border Development Act, which created port facilities and increased economic development along the state's border with Mexico.

1992: Provided tax breaks for movie makers, the Air Force and telecommunication companies.

1993: Approved a 6-cent hike in gasoline taxes and a 2-cent increase on the diesel fuel tax.

1994: Cut income taxes by $35 million.

1995: Repealed the 6-cent gasoline tax.

1996: The state planned to spend $1.4 billion on highway projects during the next five years.

1997: Amended Development Training by moving the industrial development training program to the Economic Development Department from the State Department of Education.

1998: Made Industrial Development Training Appropriation of $6,070,000.

1999: Made Industrial Development Training Appropriation of $6,160,000. Reduced Oil and Gas Severance Tax Rate and an exemption for the first two years of oil and gas production.

TAX INCENTIVES:

- **Corporate income tax.** 4.8 to 7.6 percent.

- **Personal income tax.** 1.8 to 8.2 percent; sliding scale rate of imposition dependent on Federal Net Taxable Income.

- **Sales and use tax.** 5.0 percent and local option imposition.

- **Rural Job Tax Credit.** Under this program, an employer located in a rural area of New Mexico may apply for a tax credit for each qualifying job the employer creates in the period beginning July 1, 2000 and ending June 30, 2005. The maximum tax credit amount is equal to: 1) 25 percent of the first $16,000 in wages paid for the qualifying job if the job is performed or based at a certain area of Tier Two rural New Mexico; and 2) 12.5 percent of the first $16,000 in wages paid if the qualifying job is performed or based in a different area of Tier One rural New Mexico. A qualifying job is one that qualifies under the state Industrial Development Training Program. A qualifying employer is one that qualifies under the state Industrial Development Training Program. To receive a rural job tax credit, the employer must apply to the New Mexico Taxation and Revenue Department.

- **Investment Credit.** New Mexico offers manufacturers a credit of 5 percent of the equipment and machinery used specifically for manufacturing. If new equipment, the 5 percent is applied against the purchase price. If the equipment is owned by the company and being moved from another location to New Mexico, the book value of the equipment is used to determine the value of the credit. The credit may be used against other gross receipts, compensating or withholding taxes due in the state. If the full amount of the credit cannot be used in the first year, the credit carries over. Qualification requirements of new, full-time jobs are as follows: (1) for an investment up to $2 million, one full-time job must be created per $250,000 of investment; (2) from $2 million to $30 million, one full-time position for every $500,000 of investment; (3) more than $30 million, one full-time job for every $1 million in investment.

- **Corporate Child Care Tax Credit.** A credit against corporate income tax is allowed for certain child care services provided or paid for by a corporation for employees' children for 30 percent of eligible costs, up to $30,000. Unused credit amounts may be carried over for three years.

- **Cultural Property Preservation Tax Credit.** A credit against personal or corporate income tax of 50 percent of costs, up to $25,000 per project, for the restoration or preservation of property listed on the New Mexico register of cultural properties.

- **Enterprise Zones.** The Enterprise Zone was enacted to stimulate the creation of new jobs and revitalize economically distressed areas. It authorizes local governments (municipality, county, Indian nation, tribe or pueblo), based on public input, to designate as an Enterprise Zone an area within its jurisdiction not exceeding 25 percent of its land area or encompassing more than 25 percent of its population. An Enterprise Zone Plan must be developed. The Enterprise Zone Plan is the road map which the local government uses to revitalize an area and create jobs. Technical assistance is available through workshops and one-on-one meetings in order to assist local governments in coordinating their targeted development efforts.

- **Investment in Participation Interests in New Mexico Real Property-Related Business Loans.** Severance Tax Permanent Fund investment in participations of up to 80 percent in a loan by a financial institution to a start-up or expanding business. Eligible uses of funds include the purchase of land and attached buildings, and refinancing existing debt if the loan is for expansion purposes. Loan amounts may range from $500,000 to $2 million. Loan maturities are not less than five years or more than 15 years.

FINANCIAL INCENTIVES:

- **North Central New Mexico Economic Development Revolving Loan Fund.** The Revolving loan fund assists small businesses located within targeted counties. The intent of the program is to create and/or save jobs. Loans of $10,000-$100,000 are provided for fixed asset and working capital purposes. Eligible counties are Colfax, McKinley, Mora, Rio Arriba, San Miguel and Taos.

- **Community Development Revolving Loan Fund.** Loans are provided to local governments to encourage economic development activities within a community. Eligible activities include infrastructure improvements; acquisition of land, building, machinery and equipment; and construction of facilities. The maximum loan is $250,000 with no minimum. The interest rate is fixed at one half the Treasury bond equivalent rate and the maximum term is 10 years. The business must locate on publicly-owned property and the local government must be the applicant.

- **Industrial Revenue Bonds.** Local governments may authorize industrial revenue bonds to enable a business to access property tax and compensating tax abatements. A lease agreement enables the business to take normal depreciation and a deduction of interest on the bonds. A purchaser of the bonds must be identified by the business, and the industrial revenue bond inducement and property tax abatement is negotiated with the local government.

- **Rural Development Business and Industry Loan Program.** Guarantee of loans made by financial institutions to start-up and expanding businesses in rural areas. Eligible uses of funds include real estate, fixed assets, working capital and pollution control. Guarantees range from 70 percent to 90 percent for loans up to $10 million.

- **Small Business Administration 504 Program.** The SBA 504 loan program provides long-term (up to 20 years), low down payment (10 percent), fixed rate loans for land, buildings and equipment. This program is most appropriate for existing and expanding businesses. It has been used in New Mexico in conjunction with industrial revenue bonds.

- **Small Business Administration 7(a) Program.** The SBA 7(a) loan guarantee program provides guarantees on loans made by lenders. The program provides a maximum 80 percent guarantee on fixed or variable rate loans for land, buildings, equipment and working capital. This program is available to start-up, existing and expanding business.

- **New Mexico Community Development Loan Fund (NMCDLF).** NMCDLF is a nonprofit organization whose primary purpose is to provide capital to support the creation and preservation of jobs, affordable housing and the provision of human services. Financial assistance is provided in the form of small loans up to $200,000 for up to ten years at an interest rate of approximately 10 percent. The applicant must first attempt to obtain bank financing.

- **Women's Economic Self-Sufficiency Team (WESST Corp).** WESST Corp is a nonprofit organization whose purpose is to assist small business owners with technical and financial assistance. Technical assistance is provided through individual consultations and small group workshops. Financial assistance is provided in the form of small loans up to $5,000 for up to three years at an interest rate of approximately 12 percent.

OTHER INCENTIVES:

- **Special-Interest Exemptions.** New Mexico Statute includes several "special-interest" exemptions and deductions from the Gross Receipts and Compensating Tax Act to provide tax relief for certain activities:
  1. Exemptions - Insurance companies and Railroad equipment and aircraft.
  2. Deductions - Railway roadbed materials, sale of aerospace services to certain organizations, spaceport operation, launching and recovery of space launch vehicles, payload services, intrastate transportation, services in interstate commerce, internet services, hosting World Wide Web sites, hospitals and sales to qualified film production companies.

- **Child Care Credits.** A taxpayer that pays for child care services in New Mexico for dependent children of an employee of the taxpayer may claim a 30 percent credit of the total expenses of such services against corporate income tax. The credit may not exceed $30,000 in any taxable year.

• **Public/Private Partnerships.** New Mexico Venture Capital Fund Investment is a severence tax permanent fund investment of $500,000 to $3 million in New Mexico venture capital funds. The fund must have an office located in New Mexico and must have at least two general partners who have worked together previously.

SUCCESSFUL INCENTIVES:

• **Industrial Revenue Bonds.** Will accord a business or company an exemption from property taxation for up to 30 years. Will also allow a business or company an exemption from gross receipts and compensating tax on the purchase or importation of land, building(s), equipment, furniture and fixtures for their facility.

• **The Investment Credit Act.** Will allow for a gross receipts and compensating tax deduction on the purchase or importation of equipment used specifically for manufacturing.

• **The Industrial Development Training Program.** New Mexico will reimburse a company to train its employees. Reimbursement ratio for rural areas is 75 percent (urban 50 percent) of wage and training expenses for up to 1,040 hours. Qualified employees must have been residents of New Mexico for one year prior to training. Employees must be guaranteed full-time employment at the commencement of training.

Contact:

Galen Garcia
Economic Development Division
Recruitment Team
New Mexico Economic Development Dept.
P.O. Box 20003
Santa Fe, NM 87504-5003
(505) 827-0300

NEW YORK

TAX INCENTIVES:

- **Corporate income tax.** 9.0 percent. Or 1.78 mills(0.1 percent for banks) per dollar of capital (up to $350,000), or 5 percent of the minimum taxable income, or a minimum of $1,500 to $325 depending on payroll size; if any of these is greater than the tax computed on net income. An additional tax of 0.9 mills per dollar of subsidiary capital is imposed on corporations.

- **Personal income tax.** 4.0 to 7.125 percent.

- **Sales and use tax.** New York's sales/use tax rate is 4 percent. Most counties impose a local sales/use tax at rates ranging from 1 to 4.25 percent, which is combined with the state rate. Exemptions available.

- **New Capital Investment Tax Credits.** A credit against the corporation franchise tax on business corporations is available at 5 percent of new capital invested in buildings and/or depreciable tangible personal property used primarily in the production of goods by manufacturing, processing, assembling and certain other types of activities. The credit drops to 4 percent for investments by corporations in excess of $350 million or for investment made by personal income taxpayers. The credit first applies to the tax payable for the year the investment is made. A new business may elect to receive as a refund any unused part of the tax credit earned. All businesses may carry forward any unused portions of the credit for up to 15 years.

Securities Industry ITC – Effective for property placed in service after October 1, 1998, but before October 1, 2003, the investment tax credit (ITC) (and economic development zone ITC) is extended to tangible personal property principally used in the ordinary course of business:
1. As a broker or dealer in connection with the purchase or sale (which shall include but not be limited to the issuance, entering into, assumption, offset, assignment, termination or transfer) of stocks, bonds or other securities, or of commodities (as defined in the Internal Revenue Code);
2. Of providing investment advisory services for a regulated investment company (as defined in the IRC), or lending, loan arrangement or loan origination services to customers in connection with the purchase or sale of securities; or
3. As an exchange registered as a national securities exchange (within the meaning of the Securities Exchange Act of 1934) or a board of trade (as defined in the NYS Not-for-Profit Corporation Law).

- **Research and Development Credit.** A credit against the corporate franchise/income tax is available at 9 percent of the cost or other basis for the federal income tax purpose of qualified research and development tangible property acquired, constructed or reconstructed after June 20, 1982. The research and development credit under the personal income tax is 7 percent. In order for property to qualify it must be used for research and developmental purposes in the experimental or laboratory sense, be lo-

LEGISLATIVE TIMELINE:

1990: Approved a bill to assist businesses in exporting.

1992: Executive order issued to ease regulatory pressures on business development and investment.

1993: Created a linked-deposits loan program and expanded the existing economic development zones program. Passed legislation to assist exporting.

1994: Created a tax credit for wages paid to new employees in qualified economic development zones. Increased funding for worker-skills training and initiated managed care for certain workers' compensation cases.

1995: Enacted a reduction in the personal income tax that was phased in over three years. Cut various business taxes, including the petroleum business tax on aviation fuels.

1996: Created the Jobs Now program to attract new businesses that create at least 300 jobs. Created the Empire State Development Fund to provide business loans and grants.

1999: Passed an act that provides tax incentives in New York City for the creation of private sector jobs.

cated in New York State, have a useful life of four or more years, be depreciable pursuant to Section 167 of the IRS code and be acquired by purchase as defined by Section 179(d) of the Internal Revenue Code.

• **Pollution Control Credit.** Expenditures for the construction or improvement of industrial waste/or air pollution facilities are eligible for the investment tax credit in the year the expenditures are made or incurred, provided the facilities are certified as being in compliance with applicable New York State laws, codes and regulations.

•**Emerging Industries Jobs Act.** Two new credits for emerging technology companies, effective January 1, 1999:

1. Qualified Emerging Technology Employment Credit – A credit of $1,000 per new full-time employee (employees in excess of 100 percent of base year employment level), available for one three-year period (the year the credit is first claimed and in each of the next two years provided minimum employment levels are maintained.

2. Qualified Emerging Technology Company Capital Tax Credit – A taxpayer is allowed a credit equal to a percentage of each qualified investment in a qualified emerging technology company and certified by the Commissioner of Taxation and Finance as follows: 10 percent of qualified investments, provided the taxpayer certifies that the qualified investment will not be sold, transferred, traded or disposed of during the four years following the year in which the credit is first claimed; or 20 percent of qualified investments, provided the taxpayer certifies that the qualified investment will not be sold, transferred, traded or disposed of during the nine years following the year in which the credit is first claimed.

• **Credit for Hiring Persons With Disabilities.** A credit is available for employers who employ individuals with disabilities. The credit equals 35 percent of the first $6,000 of first year wages paid to the disabled employee (maximum of $2,100 per employee). However, if the first year wages qualify for the federal work opportunity tax credit, the New York credit will apply to second year wages. To be eligible for the credit, an employee must work for the employer on a full time basis for at least 180 days or 400 hours, and must be certified as disabled by the State Education Department or, in the case of a visual handicap, by the New York State Commission for the Blind and Visually Handicapped. In cooperation with these agencies, the New York State Department of Labor currently administers the certification program.

• **Alternative Fuels Vehicle Credit.** A credit is allowed for electric vehicles; clean fuel vehicles using natural gas, methanol and other alternative fuels; and clean fuel re-

fueling facility property. The tax credits equal: 50 percent of the incremental cost of new electric vehicles registered in New York (capped at $5,000 per vehicle); 60 percent of the cost of new clean-fuel components for alternative fuel vehicles registered in New York (capped at $5,000 per vehicle with a gross vehicle weight rating of 14,000 pounds or less, and $10,000 for those over 14,000 pounds); and 50 percent of the cost of new clean-fuel refueling property used in a trade or business.

• **Statewide Property Tax Exemptions.** Pollution-control facilities are exempt from local real property taxes and ad valorem levies (upon application by taxpayer to local taxing authorities) to the extent of any increase in value resulting from the construction or reconstruction of such facilities to comply with New York State environmental conservation and/or health laws, codes and regulations.

• **Real Property Tax Exemptions Outside of New York City.** Commercial and industrial facilities, constructed or reconstructed outside of New York City at a cost of more than $10,000, may be eligible for a partial exemption from the real property tax levied by counties, cities, towns, villages and/or school districts. The maximum exemption amounts to 50 percent of any increase in value in the first year following completion, and declines by five percent in each of the succeeding nine years. Local taxing jurisdictions have a number of options in implementing this program.

• **Economic Development Zone (EDZ) Investment Tax Credit.** A credit against the corporation franchise tax or personal income tax is available for new capital invested in buildings and/or depreciable tangible personal property used primarily in production by manufacturing, processing, assembling, pollution-control and certain other activities in a designated Economic Development Zone. The credit under the corporation franchise tax is 10 percent of the cost or other basis of eligibility property employed in such zone, and under the personal income tax, 8 percent of such cost. The eligibility requirements are the same as those for the regular investment tax credit.

• **EDZ Employment Incentive Credit.** An additional credit, at 30 percent of the Zone Investment Tax Credit, is deductible from the tax payable in each of the three years next succeeding the firm's eligible investment if the firm maintains an average employment in the Zone of 101 percent of the average number of employees employed by the taxpayer in the Zone in the year immediately preceding the year of the eligible investment in the Zone. A corporate taxpayer not subject to the tax and not having a taxable year immediately preceding the year the investment is made may use the year of the eligible investment as the base for calculating the employment incentive credit.

• **EDZ Wage Tax Credit.** A credit against the corporation franchise tax, personal income tax, insurance tax or bank tax is available to eligible firms who create full-time jobs in Economic Development Zones. The credit for "targeted" employees is $1,500 for the first year and for each of the four succeeding taxable years. A "Targeted" employee is one receiving Zone wages who is eligible for targeted jobs tax credit, eligible under the job training partnership act (JTPA), a recipient of public assistance, or a person whose personal income or family's income is below Federal government poverty guidelines and whose rate of pay exceeds 135 percent of the State minimum wage. The wage credit in any year cannot exceed 50 percent of the tax otherwise due, without regard to other available tax credits, but unused zone wage New Businesses may get a refund of 50 percent of the unused credit.

- **EDZ Capital Credit.** A credit is allowed against the corporation franchise tax or the personal income tax for up to 25 percent of any of the following investments or contributions: Investments in or contributions to EDZ capital corporations; Qualifying investments in certified Zone businesses that employ no more than 250 persons within New York State (not counting general executive officers), investments made by or on behalf of a partner proprietor or stockholder in the business are not eligible for the credit; Cash contributions to community development projects in an EDZ. Credits received by a taxpayer may not exceed $300,000 in aggregate or $100,000 in each of the above categories.

- **EDZ Sales/Use Tax Credit.** Purchases of building materials that will become an integral part of non-retail commercial or industrial real property located in an economic development zone are exempt from the State sales/use tax and may also be exempt from the local sales/use tax if a local law authorizes such an exemption.

- **EDZ Real Property Tax Credit.** Under Section 485-e of the Real Property Tax Law, businesses or homeowners constructing, reconstructing or improving real property located within an economic development zone may be eligible for a partial exemption from real property taxes for up to ten years. The exemption begins at a total exemption of the improvement to real property for up to seven years and is reduced by 25 percent per year over the next three years (a 10 year average exemption of 85 percent).

This exemption is a local option, and is available from each local taxing jurisdiction in the zone. This credit cannot be combined with real property tax exemption available under Section 485-b of the Real Property Tax Law.

FINANCIAL INCENTIVES:

- **The Empire State Development (ESD) Financial Assistance.** The financial assistance can be provided for: acquisition of land and buildings or machinery and equipment, construction or renovation of buildings to house business operations, including leasehold improvements, construction or improvement of the infrastructure required for the location or expansion, working capital, training, expanding export opportunities, and productivity enhancement assistance. The assistance to implement any of these activities may be made available through: Direct loans and/or grants to business for a portion of the cost of the above-noted project to be implemented, interest rate subsidies to reduce the cost of borrowing from private- or public-sector financial institutions, in the form of a grant or linked deposit with the lending institution, loans and grant for working capital assistance in specialized situations, and infrastructure assistance in the form of a loan and grant combination for a portion of the cost of the infrastructure project to be implemented. ESD can assist the following types of business: Manufacturing, services, warehouse and distribution, research and development, tourism destination, minority- and women-owned business.

OTHER INCENTIVES:

- **Foreign Investment.** Foreign companies can leverage expertise at ESD to locate investment opportunities within New York State in manufacturing, distribution, services, headquarters or sales operations, joint ventures and strategic alliances. ESD can identify potential sites and buildings and facilitate introductions to local government officials and private business people to aid transactions.

- **Export Assistance.** ESD provides assistance to New York business that are committed to growth through export sales and the development of international markets. Our services include training in developing export skills; consultations with specialists on exporting products or services; and providing assistance in identifying a foreign sales agent or distributor with whom a company may negotiate an agreement. Matching grants are available for individual businesses and business or industry groups for assistance in creating export market development plans. ESD also leads targeted trade missions and participates in selected trade shows. The ESD network of 10 regional and 11 foreign offices directly assists New York State business to succeed in global markets.

- **Regulatory Relief Program.** Governor Pataki established *Governor's Office of Regulatory Reform* (GORR) in 1995 and provided it with the authority to oversee the exercise of regulatory power — a first in the history of New York State. The top priority of GORR is to help grow private-sector jobs in New York State by making regulations more sensible and by making the permitting process more efficient. New York has adopted an aggressive regulatory reform program designed to accelerate all aspects of the permitting process (environmental permit assistance included), to eliminate duplicative requirements, and eliminate the duplication of effort for business wishing to locate anywhere in the state.

PUBLIC/PRIVATE PARTNERSHIP:

- **Project Long Island.** This program began last year by the Long Island Authority to identify and strengthen the high technology manufacturing industries already on Long Island that have the best chance of rapid growth and rapid job creation during the next five years. The industries are biotechnology/bioengineering, emerging electronics, graphic communications, medical imaging and health information systems, and computer software. The LIA forecasts that, with the cooperation of Long Island's business, civic, academic and governmental communities, about 28,000 new high-paying, high-quality jobs can be directly created in these industries. Project Long Island's action agendas include some initiatives that affect all of the identified industries, some that are specific to each industry and many that overlap areas. A comprehensive Long Island report on the process to determine the industries, the Working Group process, the action items and implementation timetable will be available in the fall. The Project Long Island action agendas do not request a single dollar of appropriated state or local government funds.

- **New York-Interamerican Commerce for Consulting Engineers (NYICCE).** This is a trade development initiative including partnerships between ESD, the American Consulting Engineers and its New York member organization, the Consulting Engineers Council of New York State, Inc., the New York Association of Consulting Engineers, Inc., The U.S. Department of Commerce and the Pan-American Federation of Consulting Engineers. The three-year initiative is designed to build business relationships between consulting engineering firms in New York and Latin America to increase exports of their services. The program was selected to the 1999 William T. Hackett Award for excellence in Economic Development by the National Association of State Development Agencies.

- **NYSERNet.** This program advances network technologies and applications that enable collaboration and promote technology transfer for research and education, and expand these to government, industry, and the broader community. In the mid-1980's, NYSERNet was formed as a not-for-profit corporation to serve the remote networking needs of several organizations.

- **New York State's Energy Research and Development Authority (NYSERDA).** NYSERDA provides grants to New York State firms seeking to develop or commercialize innovative products or processes that will lead to improvements in energy or waste minimization.

- **Emerging Industry of NYS.** This six member association (New York Biotechnology Association, New York New Media Association, Photonics Development Corporation, Environmental Business Association of New York State, New York Software Industry Association, Aerospace Diversification and Defense Conversion Association) represents the dynamic high technology sectors of New York State's economy. Each is partially funded by ESD and involved in a number of initiatives to facilitate the job growth and economic prosperity of their constituents.

SUCCESSFUL INCENTIVES:

- **American International Insurance Company.** A member company of American International Group, Inc. (AIG), one of the world's leading insurance/financial services companies, will locate a new call center in Vestal, Broome County, investing $7.5 million and creating 500 new jobs. In consideration for its commitment to invest and create jobs in New York State, ESD has provided an incentive offer including a capital grant of $1.325 million and a training grant of $500,000. In addition, AIG was offered a legislative grant for $200,000, local real estate abatements and discounted electricity rate.

- **Gap Inc.** Gap Inc. is planning to establish a major distribution facility in Dutchess County creating more than 1,000 new jobs over the next five years. The company intends to invest up to $150 million in Fishkill over the next several years to create a major regional distribution center for its Old Navy division. If fully developed according to plan, the company will construct a three phase, 2.3 million square foot campus-like complex on 200 acres in Merrit Park in Fishkill. In consideration of the company's commitment to invest in New York, Gap Inc. will be eligible to apply to Empire State Development for a $1.5 million capital grant, a $500,000 training grant, and a $250,000 grant, and Transportation will provide up to $1 million from the Industrial Access Program to fund road improvements at the site.

Contact:

Anthony M. Quenelle
Director of Industry Development
Strategic Business Division
Empire State Development
30 South Pearl Street
Albany, NY 12245
(800) STATE-NY

NORTH CAROLINA

LEGISLATIVE TIMELINE:

1990: Expanded the Business incubator program to allow communities of all sizes to participate. Provided funding for an Industrial Building Renovation Fund, designed to create jobs in 50 of North Carolina's 100 counties.

1991: Expanded the number of counties eligible for the Jobs Tax Credit Program from 25 to 33. Increased the state sales and use tax from 3 percent to 4 percent.

1992: Expanded the definition of distressed areas, increasing the availability of incentives. Increased the corporate income tax to 7.75 percent and enacted an additional personal income tax bracket of 7.75 percent.

1993: Extended the Job Creation Tax Credit to 17 more counties, increasing the number of eligible counties to 50. Refined the Qualified Business Tax Credit. Created the Industrial Recruitment Competitive Fund.

1994: Appropriated $7 million to the state's Industrial Recruitment Competitive Fund. Appropriated $1.25 million to expand the state's network of incubator facilities. Appropriated $900,000 to implement a new economic development information system, a strategic planning staff and a video conference center.

1995: Cut individual and corporate income taxes by $380 million.

1996: Passed the William S. Lee Quality Jobs and Expansion Act that provides tax reductions and credits. The law includes a new investment tax credit, an increase in an existing credit for job creation (expanded to include all 100 counties), a worker training tax credit, a research and development tax credit and a business property tax credit.

1999: Amended the William S. Lee Act to extend sunset from 2002 to 2006 and to provide additional tax incentives.

TAX INCENTIVES:

- **Corporate income tax.** 7.25 percent. Financial institutions are also subject to a franchise tax equal to #30 per one million in assets. The rate decreased to 7.0 percent for 1999.

- **Personal income tax.** 6.0 to 7.75 percent.

- **Sales and use tax.** 6 percent (4 percent state and 2 percent county).

- **Investment Tax Credit.** The investment tax credit is equal to 7 percent of the value (above the applicable Economic Tier Threshold) of machinery and equipment placed in service in North Carolina by eligible new or expanding firms. The credit is taken in equal installments over the seven years subsequent to when the machinery and equipment is first placed in service (generally when it is capitalized on the books; this credit applies to both capital purchases and capital leases). The tier of the county in which the firm operates determines the Tier Threshold. If the taxpayer places eligible machinery and equipment into service at one site over the course of a two-year period, the applicable threshold is applied only in the first year of that period. A letter of commitment must be filed prior to the start of the project. For taxpayers with more than one site in a given tier, the threshold applies only once for that tier.

  Large Investment Enhancement – Qualifying taxpayers can take carry forwards over a twenty-year period. A taxpayer is eligible for this enhancement if the taxpayer certifies that it will purchase or lease, and place in service in connection with an eligible business within a two-year period, at least $150 million worth of one of the following: real estate, machinery and equipment or central administrative office property. If the taxpayer fails to make the level of investment certified within the two-year period, the taxpayer forfeits the enhancement.

- **Job Creation Tax Credit.** Firms with at least five full-time employees working 40 or more weeks during the taxable year can take a credit for each new full-time additional job(s) created during that taxable year. Credit is to be taken in equal installments over four years following the year of hire. The tier of the county in which the jobs are created determines the amount of tax credit per job.

- **Research and Development Tax Credit.** The R&D tax credit enables firms that qualify for the federal Research and Experimentation Tax Credit to take a state tax credit equal to 5 percent of the state's apportioned share of the taxpayer's expenditures for R&D. A taxpayer claiming the alternative incremental credit under section 41(c)(4) of the IRS Code is allowed a credit equal to 25 percent of the state's apportioned share.

- **Central Administrative Office Credit.** For purchased property, the credit equals 7 percent of the property cost. For leased property, the credit equals 7 percent of the taxpayer's lease payments over an eight-year period, plus expenditures made by the taxpayer to improve the property if the expenditures are not reimbursed or credited by the lessor. The maximum credit allowed is $500,000. A central administrative office must hire at least 40 full-time administrative positions to fill new positions at the office. These jobs may be created within the taxable year or in the preceding 24 months while using temporary space for administrative functions during completion of the central administrative office property. The credit is taken in equal installments over the 8 years following the taxable year in which the property is used in this manner.

• **Development Zone Enhancements.** Taxpayers located in development zones gain additional tax credit enhancements. The taxpayer must already qualify for credit under Article III A of the act. For purposes of the wage standard test, investment tax credit threshold, and worker training tax credit, the taxpayer is considered to be in Tier One. The taxpayer must only pay wages that are 100 percent of the county level, the threshold for investment is zero, and $1,000 credit may be claimed for each worker trained. There is also an additional $4,000 credit for each job created. For all other purposes and calculations, the taxpayer has the same tier designation as the county in which it is located.

• **Change in Ownership of Business.** The acquisition of a business is considered a new investment with regards to these tax credits if any of the following conditions are met: (1) the new business closed before it was acquired; (2) the business was required to file a notice of plant closing or mass layoff under the federal Worker Adjustment and Retraining Notification Act before it was acquired; or (3) the business was acquired by its employees through an employee stock option transaction or similar mechanism.

• **Industrial Parks Located in Two Counties.** Two-county industrial parks will have the lower tier tax designation of the two counties in which it is located if all of the following conditions are met: (1) the park must be located in two contiguous counties; (2) at least one-third of the park must be located in the county with the lower tier designation; (3) the park is owned by the two counties or by a joint agency of the two counties; and (4) the county with the lower tier designation contributed at least one-half of the cost of developing the park.

• **Business Property Tax Credit.** This credit is available under Article III B of the act and equals 4.5 percent of tangible personal business property capitalized under the tax code, up to a maximum single-year credit of $4,500. It is taken in five equal installments beginning in the taxable year property is placed in service. Tax credits can be taken against the income or franchise taxes and have a five-year carry forward for each eligible year. A company qualifying as a central administrative office may claim credits against the gross premiums tax. Election is made

when taking the first installment. The total value of credits cannot exceed 50 percent of annual tax liability. (Note: There are no tier thresholds, wage tests, industry classifications or applications for this credit.)

FINANCIAL INCENTIVES:

• **Industrial Revenue Bond Program (IRB).** Revenue Bonds have a variety of names and purposes but essentially are of three basic types. First, these bonds whose proper name is Small Issue Industrial Development Bonds are referred to as Industrial Revenue Bonds (IRBs). The state's principal interest in these bonds is assisting new and expanding industry while seeing that North Carolinians get good jobs at good wages. The regulations governing bond issuance are a combination of federal regulations and North Carolina statutes. The amount each state may issue annually is designated by population. There are three types of bond issuances:
1. Tax Exempt
2. Taxable
3. Pollution Control/Solid Waste Disposal Bond

• **Business Energy Loans.** The Business Energy Improvement program provides loans between $100,000 and $500,000 to industrial and commercial business located in or moving to North Carolina. Loans can be financed for up to seven years at interest rates equal to 50 percent of the average (high and low) T-bill rate for the past year or five percent, whichever is lower. Current rate is around 5 percent, which is the maximum. Funds are provided from a pool of $2.5 million designated for energy-related capital improvement such as cogeneration, energy-saving motors, boiler improvements and low energy use lighting. Loans will be processed first-come-first-served based upon the date of receipt of a letter of credit by a participating bank.

• **Community Development Block Grants (CDBG).** The Community Development Block Grant program has been administered by the State of North Carolina since 1982. The funds may be accessed by a local government applicant (municipal or county, excluding entitlement cities or designated urban counties). Proposed projects will involve a specific business that will create new jobs (or, in some instances, retain existing jobs). Assisted project activities must benefit persons (60 percent or more) who were previously (most recent 12 months) in a low or moderate family income (LMI) status, based on income levels published for the state annually by the US Department of Housing and Urban Development (HUD).

• **Economic Development Category.** This project may involve assistance for public facilities needed to serve target business, or loans to the private business to fund items such as machinery and equipment, property acquisition or construction. Public facility projects may provide grants of up to 75 percent of the proposed facility costs, with a 25 percent cash match to be paid by the local government applicant. (Note: Based on 1996 North Carolina General Statutes, no local match is required for projects to take place in designated Enterprise Tier One areas.)

Loan projects are assisted in conjunction with a participating bank, which will provide 50 percent or more of the funds needed by the project company. Application for economic development assistance may be made by eligible local governments to the North Carolina Department of Commerce's Commerce Finance Center.

- **Industrial Development Fund.** The purpose of the Industrial Development Fund is to provide an incentive for jobs creation in the state's most economically distressed counties (also identified as Tier 1, 2 and 3 areas). Funds for the renovation of manufacturing buildings and the acquisition of infrastructure are made available by the Department of Commerce to eligible counties or their local units of government, which apply for the funds on behalf of their existing or new manufacturing businesses.

- **Special Utility Account Funding.** Within the Industrial Development Fund, a special Utility Account provides grants to assist local units of governments in Tier 1 areas (the state's 10 most economically distressed counties) in creating jobs in manufacturing and processing, warehousing and distribution, and data processing. Utility funds are used only for construction of or improvements to new or existing water, sewer, gas or electrical lines. Funding amounts are not specified per job or per project, and local matching is not required. A pre-application conference is necessary when a utility project is expected to exceed $50,000.

- **Local Assistance with Land, Site Preparation and Shell Buildings.** North Carolina counties and cities are authorized to engage in a number of economic development activities. Counties and cities may acquire and develop land for an industrial park; acquire, assemble, and hold for resale property suitable for industrial or commercial use; and/or acquire or construct shell buildings. Appropriations for these purposes must be approved by the local governing body following a public hearing.

OTHER INCENTIVES:

- **Economic Opportunity Act (EOA).** The Economic Opportunity Act of 1998 is an act that allows certain recycling facilities an investment tax credit, a refundable income tax credit, a sales tax reduction for cranes and materials handling equipment, a sales tax refund for construction materials, a sales tax exemption for electricity, and a property tax exemption for recycling property. This act also allows certain tax exemptions for air couriers as well as expands the industrial development fund and utility account addressed in the William S. Lee Act. The EOA also uses tax credits to enhance the state development zones.

- **Public/Private Partnerships.** These partnerships are a joint public/private economic development initiative comprised of North Carolina counties. The counties of North Carolina have been organized into seven regional partnerships for economic development. North Carolina's regional partnerships enable regions to compete effectively for new investment and to devise effective economic development strategies based on regional opportunities and advantages.

SUCCESSFUL INCENTIVES:

- **Customized Business Incentives.** Federal Express announced in early 1998 that it would locate its new Mid-Atlantic Cargo Hub at Greensboro's Piedmont Triad International Airport in North Carolina, creating 1,500 new jobs and investing more than $300 million in the hub's construction. The tax incentives totaled nearly $133 million over a 20-year period to the company. Wisconsin Tissue announced in January of 1999 that it will build its newest paper recycling and production facility in Halifax County, the third most economically distressed county in North Carolina. Wisconsin Tissue is eligible, according to the Economic Opportunity Act of 1998, for a tax credit equal to 20 percent of the value of the machinery and equipment it places into service during the next two years. The credit is valued at $31 million over the next 25 years. A steel recycling company, the Nucor Corporation, was enticed by an incentive package in 1998 that was worth up to $155.2 million.

Contact:

Todd Tucker
Director of Marketing & Customer Services
N.C. Department of Commerce
301 North Wilmington Street
Post Office Box 29571
Raleigh, NC 27626-0571
(919) 733-4151

NORTH DAKOTA

LEGISLATIVE TIMELINE:

1991: Increased tax exemptions for new and expanding businesses. Under the new legislation, a company may now apply for a five-year income-tax exemption.

1994: Approved additional tax exemptions to help lure a $245 million corn-processing plant to the state.

1995: Approved pioneering tort reform legislation to increase the state's attractiveness to aircraft manufacturers.

1997: Amended seed capital investment tax credit provisions to eliminate the requirement of gross sales receipts of less than $2 million in the most recent year.

1999: Passed a bill that provides for a beginning entrepreneur loan guarantee program. Also amended the Business Corporations Act, the development corporations law, venture capital corporations law, and the nonprofit corporation law.

TAX INCENTIVES:

- **Corporate income tax.** 3.0 to 10.5 percent or 6 percent Alternative Minimum Tax. The bank tax rate includes a 2 percent privilege tax; minimum tax is $50.

- **Personal income tax.** 2.67 to 12.0 percent. Taxpayers have an option of paying 14 percent of the adjusted federal income tax liability, without a deduction of federal taxes. An additional $300 personal exemption is allowed for joint returns or unmarried heads of households.

- **Sales and use tax.** 5 percent.

- **Exemption for Manufacturing Equipment.** Machinery or equipment that a new or expanding plant uses primarily for manufacturing or agricultural processing is exempt from sales and use taxes. Also exempt is machinery and equipment that a new or expanding plant uses solely for recycling. The expansion must increase production volume, employment or the types of products that can be manufactured or processed. To qualify for the exemption at the time of the purchase, the manufacturer must receive prior approval from the State Tax Commissioner. If prior approval is not obtained, the manufacturer must pay the tax and apply to the State Tax Commissioner for a refund. The exemption is not available to contractors, but manufacturers may apply for a refund of the appropriate portion of the tax actually paid by contractors on eligible machinery and equipment.

- **Exemption for Agricultural Processing Plant Construction Materials.** Construction materials used to construct an agricultural processing facility are exempt from sales and use taxes. The processor must apply to the State Tax Commissioner for a refund of the tax paid by a contractor.

- **Income Tax Exemption.** A new or expansion project in a primary sector business or tourism qualifies for an income tax exemption for up to five years. Primary sector business means an enterprise which creates wealth by using knowledge or labor to add value to a product, process or service. The exemption is limited to income earned from the qualifying project. The project operator is required to file a state income tax return even though an exemption is granted. A project is not eligible for an exemption if the project received a tax exemption under tax increment financing; or there is a recorded lien for delinquent property, income, sales or use taxes against the project operator or principal officers; or the exemption fosters unfair competition or endangers existing business.

- **Wage and Salary Credit.** Any corporation, doing business in North Dakota for the first time, may take an income tax credit equal to 1 percent of all wages and salaries paid the first three years of operation and 1/2 percent of wages and salaries paid in the fourth and fifth years. A corporation qualifies for the credit if the corporation did not receive a new business income tax exemption; and the corporation did not result from a reorganization or acquisition of an existing North Dakota business; and the corporation is engaged in assembling, fabricating, manufacturing, mixing or processing of an agricultural, mineral or manufactured product.

- **Seed Capital Investment Credit.** An individual, estate or trust is allowed an income tax credit for investing in a business certified by the Department of

Economic Development and Finance. The credit is 30 percent of the investment (of at least $5,000 but no more than $50,000). The credit is limited to gross receipts from out of state sales; not more than 50 percent of the credit is allowed in the year of investment; and not more than 5 percent of tax liability may be offset by the credit. Any unused credit may be carried forward up to 15 years. An individual, estate or trust may take the credit only on the long form method of filing.

• **Nonprofit Development Corporation Investment Credit.** An income tax credit is granted to an individual, estate, trust or corporation for buying membership in, paying dues to, or making a contribution to a certified nonprofit development corporation. The credit is equal to 25 percent of the qualifying payments or $2,000, whichever is less. The unused credit may be carried forward seven years. An individual, estate or trust may claim the credit only on the long form method of filing.

• **Credit for Investment in a North Dakota Venture Capital Corporation.** An income tax credit is granted to an individual, estate, trust or corporation for investing in a qualified North Dakota venture capital corporation. The credit is equal to the lesser of 25 percent of the amount invested or $250,000. The unused credit may be carried forward seven years. An individual, estate or trust may claim the credit only on the long form method of filing.

• **Credit for Investment in a Small Business Investment Company.** An income tax credit is allowed to an individual, estate, trust, corporation, financial institution or insurance company for investing in the North Dakota Small Business Investment Company. The credit is equal to 25 percent of the amount invested (50 percent in the case of a financial institution or insurance company). The unused credit may be carried forward seven years. An individual, estate or trust may claim the credit only on the long form method of filing.

FINANCIAL INCENTIVES:

• **Small Business Loan Program.** The Small Business Loan Program is designed to assist new and existing businesses in securing competitive financing on reasonable terms and conditions. This program allows the Bank of North Dakota (BND) to participate in a total loan financing of up to $250,000. BND's share of this loan may not exceed the lesser of $187,500 or 75 percent. The actual amount of BND's participation will depend upon the legal lending limit of the lead lender and the quality of the loan.

• **Business Development Loan Programs.** The Business Development Loan Program is designed to assist new and existing businesses in obtaining loans that would have a higher degree of risk than would normally be acceptable to a lending institution. The total outstanding amount under this program by BND may not exceed $25 million.

• **Match Program.** The MATCH program is designed to encourage and attract financially strong companies to

North Dakota. The program is targeted to manufacturing, processing and value-added industries. Through this program, BND will participate in loans to financially strong companies and provide interest rates at some of the lowest in the nation. The primary candidates for this program are businesses that create new wealth for the state and provide new jobs outside of the retail sector.

• **STEP (Start-up Entrepreneurial Program).** The STEP Program assists entrepreneurs involved in non-farming business activity. This program is designed to work in conjunction with other estate and federal small business loan programs. Borrowers for these programs include all small business activities including home-based businesses, retail, services and manufacturing.

• **Oil and Gas Development Loans.** The Oil and Gas Development Loan Program is designed to assist North Dakota developers in increasing oil and gas production in existing wells. This program provides for BND to participate in loans for oil and gas rework, recompletion and enhanced recovery operations, and for the purchase of producing oil and gas wells.

• **Bank Stock Loan Program.** BND Stock Loan Program assists in the acquisition or refinancing of bank stock loans by individuals and bank holding companies residing in North Dakota. This is a direct loan with BND. Loans may be made to individuals or bank holding companies.

• **Bank Participation Program.** BND's participation loan program is founded on the principle that all loans should serve the legitimate credit needs of the state and be made on a sound and collectible basis. The total loans and extensions outstanding at any one time to a single borrower may not exceed 10 percent of BND's total capital. All loans are reviewed in accordance with BND's lending policies and sound banking practices including, but not limited to, the intended purpose of the loan, the ability to repay, the business and its management and the feasibility of the project.

OTHER INCENTIVES:

• **The Job Training Partnership Act (JTPA).** The JTPA provides eligible individuals with an opportunity to get trained or retrained so they may gain the skills necessary to obtain employment.

Contact:

Cindy Finneman
North Dakota Department of Economic Development
   & Finance
1833 E. Bismark Expressway
Bismark, ND 58504-6708
(701) 328-5300

OHIO

1990: Passed a measure to provide 3 percent loans to fund fixed assets of businesses locating or expanding in economically distressed areas of the state. Provided statutory authority for the state's counties to open county economic development offices.

1991: Broadened the state sales and use tax to include security firms, nursery firms and companies that sell services using 900 telephone numbers.

1993: Passed the Ohio Jobs Bill to encourage the creation of high-quality jobs by providing tax credit, encouraging research and development and promoting export industries. Passed a franchise tax credit to benefit corporations and individuals who increase Ohio exports, state payroll or capital expenditures.

1994: Passed a bill to provide a nonrefundable corporate franchise or state income tax credit for a company purchasing new manufacturing machinery or equipment for use in an Ohio production facility. Passed a law that eliminates the distinction between private and public warehouses in Ohio. Broadened sales tax exemptions for equipment used primarily in storing, transporting, mailing or handling inventory in a warehouse or similar facility.

1995: Expanded a 1994 law to create a nonrefundable 7.5 percent corporate franchise or state income tax credit for manufacturing machinery and equipment.

1996: Created the Rural Industrial Park Loan Program to promote economic development in rural areas. Authorized credits against corporate franchise and state income taxes for companies completing a voluntary environmental cleanup of a contaminated site.

1999: Passed an act that allows municipal corporations, counties, townships, the state, and certain persons and private entities to enter into cooperative economic development agreements.

TAX INCENTIVES:

- **Corporate income tax.** 5.1 to 8.9 percent or 5.8 mills time the value of the taxpayer's is used and outstanding share of stock; minimum tax is $50.

- **Personal income tax.** 0.731 to 7.201 percent.

- **Sales and use tax.** 5 percent on retail sales and rental of tangible personal property, on repair or installation of such property, and on sale of selected services; counties and transit authorities can impose sales and use taxes of up to 1.5 percent.

- **Ohio Job Creation Tax Credit.** The business must agree to create 25 new full-time jobs within three years of operation and maintain operations at the project site for twice the term of the credit. A business can receive a refundable tax credit against its Ohio corporate franchise/income tax based on the state income tax withheld on new full-time employees.

- **Ohio Manufacturing Machinery and Equipment Investment Tax Credit.** This program encourages expansion of existing operations and supports additional investment in the state. The credit is based on the amount of the investment in excess of the company's base three-year annual average. Equipment must be new to Ohio or be a retooling of current manufacturing machinery or equipment.

- **Ohio Enterprise Zone Program.** This includes local and state tax incentives for businesses that expand or locate in Ohio. In municipalities, there is up to a 75 percent exemption of the value of real property improvements and/or new tangible personal property for up to 10 years. In unincorporated areas, incentives can be up to a 60 percent exemption of the value of new real and/or personal property for up to 10 years.

- **Community Reinvestment Areas (CRAs).** This program offers up to a 100 percent exemption of the value of real property improvement for up to 15 years. Property owner must undertake new real property investment. The term of the exemption is established by the local legislative authority, but cannot exceed 15 years on new construction or 12 years on major renovation projects.

- **Tax Increment Financing.** This program permits service payments in lieu of real property taxes to be used to finance public infrastructure improvements directly supporting an improvement project declared to have a "public purpose." Up to 75 percent of the value of real property taxes can be exempted for up to 10 years. The rate and term can be extended up to 100 percent for up to 30 years with school board approval.

- **Research and Development Sales Tax Exemption.** A sales tax exemption for machinery and equipment used in research and development. The exemption applies only to equipment, and the equipment must be used in qualified research and development activities.

• **Brownfield Site Clean-Up Tax Credit.** The credit will be 10 percent of the eligible remediation costs up to $500,000. In designated Priority Investment Areas, the credit is extended to 15 percent of the eligible remediation costs up to $750,000.

FINANCIAL INCENTIVES:

• **166 Direct Loan Program.** Eligible businesses are those which undertake an ongoing manufacturing concern. The maximum loan amount is $1 million and the minimum is $350,000 where a private lender is required and the term of the loan can be up to 15 years for real estate and 10 years for machinery and equipment.

• **166 Regional Loan Program.** The project must be an acquisition of land and building, new construction, renovation of existing building, or acquisition of new and/or used machinery and equipment. The maximum amount is $350,000 or 30-40 percent of eligible costs and the term can be up to 10 years on machinery and equipment and 15 years on real estate.

• **Ohio Enterprise Bond Fund.** The enterprise must be manufacturing or industrial and commercial and the project must be acquisition of land and building, new construction, renovation of existing building, or acquisition of machinery and equipment. The maximum amount is $10 million and the minimum is $1 million.

• **Port Authority Bond Reserve Fund.** The purpose of the Port Authority Bond Reserve Fund Program is to provide direct financial assistance to eligible port authorities for economic development activities. The funds shall be used to supplement local matching funds in establishing a bond reserve fund for economic development activities.

• **SBA 504 Loan Program.** Must be a small business as defined by SBA and the enterprise must be manufacturing, commercial or retail. The maximum is $1 million and the minimum is $50,000 and the term can be up to 10 years for machinery and equipment and 20 years for real estate.

• **Pioneer Rural Loan Program.** Eligible projects include acquisition of land and building, new construction, renovation of existing building, and acquisition of new or used machinery or equipment in labor surplus counties, distressed counties and situational distressed counties.

• **Buckeye Fund Loan Program.** The Buckeye Fund blends the 166 Direct Loan with the Ohio Enterprise Bond Fund. The maximum amount of the Direct Loan portion of the financing is $1 million. The Enterprise Bond Funds maximum is $10 million.

• **Rural Industrial Park Loan Program.** Nonprofit organizations which promote economic development in rural areas and improve the economic welfare of Ohioans are eligible. Eligible applicants include the following: port authorities, community improvement corporations, community-based organizations that provide social services and have experience in economic development, and other nonprofit economic development entities.

• **Pollution Prevention Loan Program.** Eligible projects are those that acquire or renovate machinery or equipment for pollution prevention. The maximum is $350,000 and the minimum is $25,000 and the term is up to 7 years.

• **Scrap Tire Loan and Grant Program.** Eligible projects are those that focus on the recycling of scrap tires. The maximum is $250,000 and the minimum is $50,000 and the term may be up to 10 years on machinery and equipment and 15 years on real estate.

• **Business Development (412) Account.** Grant dollars are available to induce companies to move forward with a project in Ohio. Eligible uses of the 412 funds are on- or off-site infrastructure improvements, including water and sewer improvements, road improvements and rail work.

OTHER INCENTIVES:

• **Export Tax Credit.** The credit is based on the average increase in export sales during the two years prior to the year in which the credit is claimed. Export sales are defined as those sales that qualify for special Foreign Sales Corporation (FSC) federal tax treatment.

• **Public/Private Partnerships.** The Ohio Economic Development Council works with Development on marketing efforts outside the state's borders.

SUCCESSFUL INCENTIVES:

• **Manufacturing Tax Credit Program.** Statewide, between the start of the program on July 1, 1995 and March 15, 1999, manufacturers qualified for about $469 million in tax credits. The manufacturing companies' total capital spending was about $7.4 billion over seven years.

Contact:

Steve Kelley
Senior Economist
Ohio Department of Development
77 S. High Street
Columbus, OH 43215
(614) 466-2116

OKLAHOMA

LEGISLATIVE TIMELINE:

1990: Simplified and consolidated enterprise zone designation criteria, provided additional flexibility in venture capital investment and enhanced confidentiality of business information received by government agencies. Approved increases in the state's sales, corporate and personal income taxes.

1991: Passed a 20 percent tax credit for investments in qualified venture capital companies.

1992: Approved a sales tax exemption for certain telecommunications services operating in the state and extended a similar exemption for distribution facilities. Also approved a sales tax exemption and refund for information companies buying computers and related high-tech equipment.

1993: Approved the Quality Jobs Program.

1994: Modified the enterprise zone law to allow any city or town within a county already designated as an enterprise zone to also be designated as an enterprise zone. Provided that funds invested in a qualified venture capital company to finance a new business at a former military installation would be eligible for an income tax credit equal to 35 percent of the amount invested.

1995: Expanded financial incentives available under the Quality Jobs Program. The eligibility threshold was reduced to $1.5 million of new payroll for food processing and research and development companies. Benefits for defense contractors also were expanded.

1996: Authorized new tax incentives to increase the manufacture and export of value-added agricultural products in Oklahoma.

1999: Passed a corporate income tax credit for investment made in a new or expanding facility.

TAX INCENTIVES:

• **Corporate income tax.** 6 percent.

• **Personal income tax.** 0.5 to 10 percent.

• **Sales and use tax.** 4.25 percent.

• **Ad Valorem Tax Exemption.** New and expanding qualifying manufacturers, research and development companies, certain computer services and data processing companies with significant out-of-state sales, aircraft repair and aircraft manufacturing may be eligible for ad valorem exemptions for up to five years.

• **Sales Tax Exemptions.** This is a sales tax exemption for manufacturers that have a manufacturer's exemption permit and a sales tax permit from the Oklahoma Tax Commission.

• **Computer Services and Data Processing.** Oklahoma recognizes the importance of certain service companies by increasing favorable tax treatment for companies engaged in computer services or data processing activities by offering exemptions from sales tax on certain items such as machinery and equipment.

• **Aircraft Maintenance Facilities.** Oklahoma has several special benefits for sales to aircraft maintenance facilities owned by an air common carrier that employ at least 2,000 workers. The primary sales tax exemption is on aircraft and aircraft parts.

• **The Investment/New Jobs Income Tax Credit.** Manufacturers who hold a manufacturer's exemptions permit may choose this income tax credit based on either an investment in depreciable property or on the addition of full-time-equivalent employees engaged in manufacturing, processing or aircraft maintenance. Such a choice prohibits a manufacturer from participating in the Quality Jobs Program.

• **Technology Transfer Income Tax Exemption.** The taxable income of any corporation is decreased for transfers of technology to qualified small business located in Oklahoma. Such transferor corporation shall be allowed an exemption from taxable income of the amount of royalty payment received as a result of such transfer, provided the exempted amount shall not exceed 10 percent of the amount of gross proceeds received by such corporation as a result of the technology transfer.

• **New Products Development Income Tax Exemption.** Royalties earned by an inventor on products developed and manufactured in Oklahoma are exempt from state income tax for seven years when registered with the Oklahoma Center for the Advancement of Science and Technology.

• **Agricultural Commodity Processing Facility.** Owners of agricultural commodity processing facilities which include buildings, fixtures and improvements used to process or package agricultural commodities as long as more than mere storage, cleaning or transporting takes place in the facility, may exclude a portion from Oklahoma taxable income based on investment.

- **Small Business Capital Formation Tax Credit.** The act authorizes an income tax credit of 20 percent of equity or near-equity investment for investors in qualified businesses either through a qualified small business capital company or, in Oklahoma small business ventures, by an angel investor in conjunction with investment by a qualified small business capital company. The credit may be taken annually up to ten years.

- **Recycling, Reuse and Source Reduction Incentive Act.** Manufacturing and service industries may receive an income tax credit of up to 20 percent of investment cost for equipment and installation of processes used to recycle, reuse or reduce the source of hazardous waste. Credits are limited to $50,000.

- **Income Tax Exemption for Interest Paid on Bonds Issued by or on Behalf of Public Agencies.** Beginning in 1999, interest payments received as a result of bonds issued by 501 (C) (3) corporations on behalf of towns, cities or counties for housing purposes in Oklahoma are not subject to Oklahoma income tax if such payments are exempt from federal income tax.

- **Tax Incentives on Former Indian Reservation Lands.** Business locating in these areas benefit by accelerated depreciation of investment or by employment tax credits when employing tribal members or their spouses. The taxpayer must be in an active trade or business.

- **The Welfare-to-Work Tax Credit.** The Welfare-to-Work Tax Credit is available to employers who hire individuals certified as Long-Term Assistance Recipients. The hires must work at least 400 hours or 180 days.

- **Enterprise Zones.** Enterprise Zones can be designated in either disadvantaged counties, cities or portions of cities. These zones provide extra incentives for business. Double the Investment/New Jobs Tax Credit is allowed and low interest loans may be made available through enterprise district loan funds.

FINANCIAL INCENTIVES:

- **Quality Jobs Program.** This program provides quarterly cash payments to a qualifying company of a percentage, not to exceed 5 percent, of new taxable payroll. A fully executed contract must be in place before any new direct jobs salaries are included in the new taxable payroll.

- **Oklahoma Finance Authorities (OFA).** The OFA provides permanent financing for real estate and equipment. OFA have both tax-exempt and taxable financing available for most types of industries, including manufacturing, agricultural processing, and certain mining or recreational/tourism facilities.

- **Small Business Linked Deposit.** The Small Business Linked Deposit Program provides below-market interest rates for qualified small businesses and certified industrial parks through local financing sources.

- **Oklahoma Capital Investment Board.** Through its venture capital program the Oklahoma Capital Investment Board facilitates investment in venture capital companies that focus on investing in quality Oklahoma companies.

- **Capital Access Program.** The Oklahoma Capital Investment Board manages this easy-to-use economic service that encourages additional business lending activity.

OTHER INCENTIVES:

- **Foreign Investment.** The Oklahoma Department of Commerce (ODC) has recruiters who focus on reverse investment as well as foreign trade offices that work in this area.

- **Export Assistance.** The DOC works with Oklahoma firms by identifying financing options for exports. Assistance is available through a relationship with the Export-Import Bank of the United States to facilitate export financing with working capital guarantees, credit insurance and foreign buyer financing.

SUCCESSFUL INCENTIVES:

- **The Quality Jobs Program.** This program provides a cash rebate to qualifying basic (exporting) firms of up to 5 percent of new payroll for up to ten years. Through the first five plus years of the program, around 190 firms have committed to adding 80,000 new jobs. More than 35,000 new basic jobs are actually on the ground and $1.7 billion in qualifying payroll has been added. The program is simple, easy to monitor, and its payments require performance.

Contact:

Dan Gorin
Research Director/Chief Economist
Oklahoma Department of Commerce
P.O. Box 26980
Oklahoma City, OK 73126-0980
(405) 815-5178

OREGON

LEGISLATIVE TIMELINE:

1991: Strengthened a number of business financing programs and added a new entrepreneurial development loan for start-up businesses. The new program provides loans of up to $15,000 at commercial rates to new businesses.

1993: Enhanced the existing enterprise zone program, extending its benefits to seven additional nonurban areas, and gave the director of the state's economic development department authority to designate new zones. Instituted a new Strategic Investment Program to facilitate financing of certain key industry plants costing more than $100 million. Other programs provide easier financing for smaller firms and an extension service for industrial modernization.

1995: Enacted a $266 million income tax cut. Extended several key business tax credits, including the pollution control facility tax credit, the reclaimed plastic tax credit, the business energy tax credit and the research and development tax credit. Created a new Rural Investment Fund that gives rural areas greater access to economic development financing to address the unique needs of smaller communities. Passed legislation encouraging the reuse of industrial sites where the removal of hazardous substances has been completed. Established a new International Trade Advisory Committee within the Department of Economic Development.

1997: House Bill 2143 provides added property tax abatement and corporate income tax exemptions for companies locating in enterprise zones with chronic high unemployment.

1998: OEDC modified the Oregon Economic Development Department's mission statement to state "Assist Oregon business and governments to create economic opportunities and build quality communities throughout Oregon." The new focus will enable the department to be more flexible and responsive to the needs of Oregon communities and business. It will focus department efforts on solving problems rather than just running programs.

1999: House Bill 2804 creates the Oregon Internet Commission to examine policies concerning Internet commerce.

TAX INCENTIVES:

- **Corporate income tax.** 6.6 percent.

- **Personal income tax.** 5.0 to 9.0 percent.

- **Sales and use tax.** None.

- **Enterprise Zone Program.** The Oregon Enterprise Zone Program was created in 1985 by the Oregon Legislature as a business incentive to create new jobs by encouraging business investment in economically lagging areas of the state. If a facility is located in an enterprise zone, new construction and most of the equipment installed in the plant would receive a 100 percent property tax abatement for a minimum of three years. Manufacturing and distribution are eligible activities.

- **Strategic Investment Program.** The Strategic Investment Program exempts a major portion of large capital investments (over $100 million) from property taxes with local approval. To offset the fiscal impacts to the community where the project locates, the manufacturer pays a community service fee equal to 25 percent of the abated taxes, up to a maximum of $2 million annually.

- **Construction In Progress Exemption.** Under provisions of Oregon law, new commercial facilities will be exempt from property taxes while they are under construction and not in use on January 1 of the taxing year. This construction exemption may be valid for two years with manufacturing projects. The exemption also applies to any machinery or equipment located in the unoccupied facility on January 1. The exemption does not apply to the land. Depending on the construction status and occupancy of the project on January 1, substantial tax savings can be realized by a company during the construction period.

- **Pollution Control Tax Credits.** Oregon provides corporate tax credits to companies that utilize pollution control technologies or facilities that meet or exceed Environmental Protection Agency, Oregon Department of Environmental Quality or regional air authority requirements. The maximum credit is 50 percent of the certified cost of the qualifying investment in the pollution control facility and equipment. The annual credit is determined by the useful life for up to ten years. No limit is placed on the amount of the investment.

- **Business Energy Tax Credit (BETC).** The BETC is an Oregon excise tax credit program equal to 35 percent of the eligible project costs. Eligible project costs are costs for equipment that is at least 10 percent more efficient than currently required by the Oregon Uniform Building Code. Other eligible costs include company van pool vehicles and telecommuting equipment. The Department of Energy has engineering staff available to provide technical assistance and a utility provider can assist with the application.

- **Reclaimed Plastics Product Tax Credit.** The reclaimed plastics product tax credit provides a credit of 50 percent of the certified cost of equipment used to recycle plastic. This credit is applied against state corporate income tax. The Department of Environmental Quality has staff available to provide technical assistance.

- **Research Tax Credit.** The research tax credit applies to qualified research expenditures during the tax year. The credit is equal to 5 percent of the increase in qualified research expenditures over a base amount for the taxable year. Alternatively, the credit is five percent of the increased qualified research expenditures that exceed 10 percent of Oregon sales for the year.

FINANCIAL INCENTIVES:

- **Industrial Development Revenue Bond Program.** The Oregon Economic Development Commission issues Industrial Development Revenue Bonds for manufacturing and processing facilities in Oregon. Only manufacturing projects, exempt facilities (such as docks or solid waste facilities), and bonds for nonprofit organizations are federally tax exempt. A major goal of the program is the creation of employment through the formation and movement of capital to value-added manufacturing.

- **Oregon Business Development Fund (OBDF).** The OBDF is a revolving loan fund administered by the Oregon Economic Development Department. Manufacturing, processing and regionally significant tourism projects are eligible. The fund provides long-term, fixed-rate financing for land, buildings, equipment, machinery and permanent working capital. Loans will be made only where the creation of new jobs or retention of existing jobs can be demonstrated. The program places particular emphasis on rural and distressed areas, and on businesses with fewer than 50 employees.

- **Capital Access Program.** The Capital Access Program is designed to increase the availability of loans from banks to small businesses in Oregon. The program provides a form of loan portfolio insurance so lenders may make business loans that carry higher than conventional risks, but that are within the soundness and safety requirements of federal and state banking regulations.

- **Oregon Credit Enhancement Fund.** The Credit Enhancement Fund provides guarantees to increase capital availability to small business firms in Oregon, thereby assisting them in creating jobs. The fund, administered by the Oregon Economic Development Department, guarantees bank loans, primarily for working capital. Banks originate and service the loans. The Oregon Economic Development Department reviews and approves the loan guarantees.

OTHER INCENTIVES:

- **Dependent Care Tax Credits.** Oregon provides corporate tax credits for dependent care assistance, dependent care facilities, and the costs of dependent care information and referral services for employees. Maximum credits are $2500 per employee for direct assistance, 50 percent of cost or $100,000 for facilities, and 50 percent of cost for information and referral services. The employer must maintain cost details for audit verification.

Contact:

Ted Werth
Industry Development Coordinator
Oregon Economic Development Department
775 Summer St., NE
Salem, OR 97310
(503) 986-0156

PENNSYLVANIA

LEGISLATIVE TIMELINE:

1990: Passed a strong corporate anti-takeover-bill.

1991: Passed legislation authorizing millions of dollars in low-interest loans as an incentive to encourage the relocation of new companies to the state.

1992: Increased corporate net income tax to 12.25% from 8.5%. The Industrial Development Authority increased the amount of low-interest money available to businesses that create high-quality jobs to $20,000 per job.

1993: Created a private/public economic development partnership, passed an export assistance program and instituted a minority venture capital fund.

1994: Enacted a bill that gradually reduces the state's corporate income tax to 9.99% from 12.25%. Cut business taxes by a total of $111 million.

1995: Cut business taxes by $283 million. Transferred the Customized Job Training Program to the Commerce Department and boosted funding for the program to $9 million.

1996: Created the $25 million Opportunity Grant Program. Doubled funding for customized job training. Boosted funding for international trade by $1.6 million. Appropriated $1 million to develop a business resource center.

1997: Amended Job Enhance Act by establishing the Export Financing Loan Fund and the Family Savings account program to provide financial assistance to small businesses.

1998: Created "Keystone Opportunity Zones" that provide tax exemptions, tax deductions, tax abatements, and tax credits.

1999: Amended Tax Reform Code. Providing for a tax credit for coal waste removal and for ultra-clean fuels; reducing the capital stock and franchise tax; and, eliminating utilities gross receipts tax on natural gas.

TAX INCENTIVES:

- **Corporate income tax.** 9.99 percent.

- **Personal income tax.** 2.8 percent.

- **Sales and use tax.** Sales and use tax is imposed at a rate of 6 percent on retail sales, consumption, rental, or use of tangible personal property (within Pennsylvania) and a limited number of business services relating to such property and on the charge for a limited number of business services. Exemptions available.

- **Employment Incentive Payment Credit.** These credits are extended to employers who hire eligible public assistance clients under an Employment Incentive Program. The maximum amount of credit the first year is $1,800, the second year it is $1,200, and the third year it is $600. An additional credit of $600 in the first year of employment, $500 in the second year, and $400 in the third year are available per new employee for providing child care. The amount of credits may not exceed 90 percent of the tax liability for the employer.

- **Enterprise Zone Credit.** These credits are available to businesses making investments in the rehabilitation, expansion, or improvement of buildings or land in enterprise zones. Businesses that are interested must submit a plan that describes their activities and the benefits that will result, a budget itemizing costs, and make a commitment to avoid dislocation of current residents. Tax credits are awarded in the amount of 20 percent of the total funds invested by the firm, up to a maximum of $250,000 per firm.

- **Homeowner Mortgage Credit.** These credits are available to businesses that make contributions to the Pennsylvania Mortgage Assistance Fund. The credit is available for up to 70 percent of the contribution to the fund. Any unused credit may be carried forward to the next calendar year.

- **Job Creation Tax Credit.** These credits are used to promote and secure job creation and economic development in Pennsylvania. A business must agree to create at least 25 new full-time jobs or to increase its number of employees by at least 20 percent within 3 years of the start day (the first day of the business quarter in which the business is approved for the credit). To be counted, the new employee must earn 150 percent of the federal minimum wage, excluding benefits. A business can earn a maximum of $1,000 for each new employee. The business must be able to demonstrate its ability to create jobs, its financial stability and project viability.

- **Neighborhood Assistance Tax Credit.** These credits are available to businesses which contribute money or other resources to nonprofit corporations which provide education, job training, crime prevention, community services, and physical improvement projects in impoverished neighborhoods. The credits are also available to private companies which provide the services. Up to 50 percent of the contribution by the firm or 20 percent of qualified investments by a private company can be used as a credit. It is limited for any one business at $250,000 a year.

- **Research and Development Tax Credit.** The credits are provided to qualified companies to offset the cost of additional research and development. The total credits are capped at $15 million per year. Firms can receive up to 10 percent of the amount spent on research and development. There is $3 million set aside for small businesses (book value assets of $5 million or less) that if unused will carry over to the larger companies in that fiscal year. The credit can be used to offset up to 50 percent of each of the companies' tax liabilities with a 15 year forward provision.

- **Waste Tire Tax Credit.** These 10 percent tax credits are available to a business which reduces, reuses or recycles waste tires. Certification must be obtained from the Dept. of Revenue to receive the credit. To qualify for the credit a business must demonstrate that at least 25 percent of the waste tires were processed from a priority tire site. The credit is capped at $2 million each year.

- **Keystone Opportunity Zone.** This program provides tax relief to economically distressed urban and rural communities in an attempt to revive these areas. Economic activity in a defined geographic area of deteriorated property designated by the Department of Community and Economic Development to be a keystone opportunity zone is exempt from all local and certain state taxes for a maximum of twelve years beginning January 1, 1999. In addition to benefiting from a limited sales and use tax exemption, zone residents and qualified businesses are exempt from the corporation and personal income taxes. The tax expenditure is the value of all state taxes waived within the zone.

FINANCIAL INCENTIVES:

- **Industrial Sites Reuse Program.** Also known as the Brownfields Program, this program provides grant and low interest loan financing to companies, public and private nonprofit economic development entities to perform environmental site assessment and remediation work at former industrial sites. No financing is available to companies or others who caused the environmental contamination on the property. Funds may be used to finance up to 75 percent of the costs of environmental assessment or remediation. Recipients of funds under this program may receive special consideration under other financing programs.

- **Job Creation Tax Credits.** Provides a $1,000 tax credit to approved businesses that agree to create new jobs in the Commonwealth within 3 years. A business must agree to create at least 25 jobs or jobs equaling at least 20 percent

of the existing work force. 25 percent of the tax credits allocated each year must go to businesses with less than 26 employees. The tax credits may not be utilized by a business until the jobs are actually created.

- **Pennsylvania Industrial Development Authority.** Offers loans to businesses for land and building acquisition, building construction and renovation, industrial park development, and multi-tenant spec building construction, acquisition and renovation. Job creation loans are for manufacturing, industrial research and development, agricultural processors, or firms establishing a national or regional headquarters. Job retention loans are for manufacturing firms that meet certain quality standards and wage thresholds in that county. Loans up to $1 million (within Enterprise Zone $1.5 million); may be for no more than 30 to 40 percent of total eligible project costs depending upon firm size and area unemployment rate.

- **Small Business First.** Provides low interest loan financing to small businesses (generally 100 employees or less) for land and building acquisition and construction, machinery and equipment, and working capital. The program provides financing for businesses that need to come into compliance with environmental regulations or that are involved in municipal commercial recycling, and companies impacted by the reduction in defense-related activities, and companies involved in export-related services. The program also provides financing for businesses that operate a hotel, motel, or lodging facility and restaurant or food service operation. Funding is up to $200,000 or 50 percent of the total eligible project costs, whichever is less.

- **Machinery and Equipment Loan Fund (MELF).** A loan fund for machinery and equipment acquisition and upgrading and related engineering and installation costs, for manufacturing and industrial businesses. Loans can be up to $500,000 or 50 percent of the total eligible project costs, whichever is less.

- **Pennsylvania Minority Business Development Authority (PMBDA).** A loan program for minority-owned businesses for land and building acquisition; building, construction and renovation; machinery and equipment acquisition and installation, and working capital. Loans can be up to $500,000 ($750,000 within an Enterprise Zone) or 75 percent of total eligible project costs, whichever is less.

- **Pennsylvania Economic Development Financing Authority (PEDFA), Tax-Exempt Bond Program.** This program is targeted to manufacturing, nonprofit, energy, solid waste disposal, and transportation facilities. Uses of funds are for land and building acquisition, building renovation and new construction, machinery and equipment acquisition and installation, designated infrastructure and tax exempt bond refunding. Loans are no less than $400,000 and no more that $10 million.

- **PEDFA, Taxable Bond Program.** This bond program is for all types of business needing access to low-cost capital. Funds are used for land and building acquisition, building renovation and new construction, machinery and equipment acquisition and installation, designated infrastructure, refinancing and working capital. Loans are no less than $400,000; and fund up to 100 percent of the total project costs.

- **Pennsylvania Capital Access Program (CAP).** This is a loan guarantee program administered in conjunction with participating Commonwealth banks. Targeted to all businesses with capital needs; loan guarantee use is for land and buildings, equipment and working capital. There is no minimum; the maximum is up to $500,000.

OTHER INCENTIVES:

- **Export 2000.** Export 2000 is a three-year Statewide Outcome-Based Strategy consisting of four programs and two initiatives:

    Programs – Pennsylvania 100, Market Access Grant (Regional), Trade Finance, and PA SourceNet.
    Initiatives – PA Goes to Market, and Bring the World to PA.

    The Small Business First Program maintains the Export Financing Program, which provides working capital term loans and accounts receivable financing to small to medium sized companies that export goods and services. Maximum loan amount is $350,000 at market interest rates.

- **Ben Franklin Partnership Program - Challenge Grant Program.** A grant program to assist technology, research and development and start-up companies. The Ben Franklin Program assists companies, primarily small and medium sized companies, to do applied research and development projects, and to develop and introduce new products and processes. The Ben Franklin Technology Centers also support services at small business incubators and other innovative special initiatives designed to promote the development and introduction of new technologies.

- **Day Care Program.** The 1998-99 budget provided funds in order to authorize grants to assist small companies to collaboratively plan and develop child care options for their employees.

- **Public/Private Partnership.** Team Pennsylvania, headquartered in Harrisburg just minutes from the State Capital's Complex, is a dynamic public-private partnership that brings together Pennsylvania's businesses, its government and community and economic development leaders. Guided by a board of directors chaired by Governor Ridge, Team Pennsylvania builds a vision for the future in the Commonwealth by providing the resources businesses need to launch or expand business success in the Commonwealth.

SUCCESSFUL INCENTIVES:

- **The Opportunity Grant Program (OGP) and The Job Creation Tax Credit Program.** Created as part of the Job Enhancement Act of 1996, the programs are part of the Governor's initiative to give Pennsylvania economic development professionals and businesses state of the art tools to create and retain jobs in the Commonwealth.

Contact:

Francis Dougherty
Director, External Affairs
Pennsylvania Dept. of Community and Economic Development
433 Forum Building
Harrisburg, PA 17120
(717) 787-3003

TAX INCENTIVES:

• **Corporate income tax.** 9.0 percent.

• **Personal income tax.** 26 percent of federal income tax liability.

• **Sales and use tax.** 7.0 percent. The following are exempt from the state sales and use tax: manufacturers' production machinery and equipment, including replacement parts; goods consumed in the manufacturing process; professional services, such as those provided by physicians, attorneys, accountants, engineers and others, including any tangible personal property that may be sold at retail by such professionals; occupational services; interstate commerce sales; sales or transfers of intangible personal property, such as stocks, bonds, accounts receivable, money or insurance policies; sales of air and water pollution control equipment; sales of precious metal bullion; and sales of scientific equipment, computers, software and related items to a qualifying firm to be used predominantly by that firm for research and development purposes.

• **Investment Tax Credit.** To stimulate investment in machinery, equipment and information technology, Rhode Island offers the highest investment tax credit in America. Manufacturers and traded service firms paying above average wages or investing significantly in worker training are able to take a 10 percent credit on purchased or leased equipment. To qualify, the firm must be either a manufacturer or a traded service firm and meet one of the four "High Performance" tests.

• **Research and Development Expense Credit.** A 22.5 percent tax credit is allowed for increases in qualified research expenses - the highest rate in America. If the increase above base period expenditures exceeds $111,111, the credit equals 16.9 percent of the excess. The credit is available to corporations, sole proprietors or passed through from partnerships, joint ventures or subchapter S corporations.

* **Research and Development Property Credit.** A taxpayer is allowed 10 percent tax credit for expenditures paid or incurred during the taxable year for the construction, reconstruction, erection or acquisition of any property which is used or to be used for the purpose of research and development in the experimental or laboratory sense. The property must be depreciable and have a useful life of 3 years or more.

* **Job Development and Training.** The Rhode Island Job Training Tax Credit allows companies to take a tax credit up to $5,000 per employee over any three-year period against their state business tax. The tax credit is equal to 50 percent of approved worker training expenses up to $5,000 per individual employee over any three-year period. Up to $1,000 of the $5,000 may be for employee wages.

• **Corporate Income Tax Rate Reduction.** The Rhode Island Jobs Development Act grants incremental income tax reductions to companies that

LEGISLATIVE TIMELINE:

1990: Enacted a bill designed to protect Rhode Island companies against takeover attempts by out-of-state firms.

1991: Enacted a major enterprise-zone bill that sets up a series of investment tax credits for businesses establishing operations in designated zones.

1992: Cut the state economic development budget by 15 percent. Imposed an 11 percent business corporation income tax on firms whose fiscal years end before 1997.

1993: Reduced corporate income taxes to 9 percent. Doubled the investment tax credit to 4 percent. Created the Office of Defense Economic Adjustment to help Rhode Island companies make the transition to a post-defense-dependent economy.

1995: Passed the Bank Modernization Act, which gives banks a dollar-for-dollar credit against the state tax they pay on funds held on deposit for customers. Passed the Passive Investment Act, which allows all income derived from assets managed on behalf of clients and passed through to clients to be exempt from the state corporate income tax.

1996: Provided a permanent reduction in the corporate tax rate for companies creating jobs. Broadened the applicability of the sales and use tax exemption for equipment, machinery and related items used in manufacturing and research and development. Authorized a tax credit for worker training and retraining.

1997: Raised the R&D credit to 22.5 percent. Established an Investment Tax Credit where manufacturers investing in worker training will be able to take a 10 percent credit on all purchased or leased equipment. Appropriated $2.7 million for the Slater Innovation Partnership (for cellular medicine).

1998: Enacted a wholesale and retail inventory tax phase out on wholesale and retail inventories over a ten-year period for every municipality. The Jobs Development Act was extended to allow corporate income tax rate reductions for jobs created before July 2001.

1999: Insurance companies were allowed an Investment Tax Credit to be applied against Gross Premium Tax.

create new employment in Rhode Island between January 1, 1995 and July 1, 2001. The new jobs reduce a company's corporate income tax rate (currently 9 percent) by a quarter percentage point (0.25) for each 50 new jobs created during a three-year period.

- **Enterprise Zones Tax Incentives.** A business which has been certified by the Enterprise Zone Council is allowed a credit against chapters 44-11, 44-14, 44-17 and 44-30; Rhode Island General Laws. The credit is 50 percent of the Rhode Island salaries and wages paid only to those newly hired enterprise job workers comprising the employees included in the "5 percent growth test" used for certification by the council.

- **Small Business Incentives.** Deductions, modifications, capital gain exclusions and wage credits are permitted only to business entities or venture capital partnerships certified by the Rhode Island Economic Development Corporation. The certification number must be shown on all incentive claims.

FINANCIAL INCENTIVES:

- **Industrial Revenue Bonds.** Industrial Revenue Bonds may be used to finance qualified commercial and industrial projects. The bonds offer a competitive interest rate and state sales tax rebate on building materials that may be significant for projects involving new construction. Financing is available through the Rhode Island Industrial Facilities Corporation and covers the entire project cost. The project and the credit of the user provide the security for the bonds which may be issued on the financial strength of the user when the user is appropriately rated.

- **Tax-Exempt "Small Issue" Bonds.** Under the small-issue bonds provisions of the Omnibus Budget Reconciliation Act of 1993, interest on certain bonds with face amounts of less than $10 million is excluded from income if at least 95 percent of the bonds' proceeds are used to finance manufacturing facilities. Industrial Revenue Bonds are tax-exempt obligations of the issuer, the interest on which is exempt from federal and state income tax. The interest rate on such obligations is normally below that available for conventional mortgages.

- **Bond and Mortgage Insurance Program.** The program reduces the capital necessary for new manufacturing facilities, renovation of manufacturing facilities, the purchase of new machinery and equipment in financing projects up to $5 million.

- **The Small Business Loan Fund.** The SBLF provides eligible Small Business Fixed Asset Loans from $25,000 to a maximum of $250,000 and Working Capital Loans to a maximum of $30,000.

OTHER INCENTIVES:

- **International Trade Data Network.** Multi-media search and retrieval databases that provide timely, detailed information relating to trade opportunities and market intelligence worldwide. Distributed on CD-ROM through a network of businesses, state and federal agencies, libraries, colleges and universities, associations and other providers.

- **State Managed Trade Missions.** Successful trade missions, such as the recent mission to Singapore, provide a company with the political inroads and the financial clout of top government officials and other industry leaders. These joint public-private efforts have consistently led to real economic benefits for the participating companies and the state.

- **Ocean Technology Companies.** The Ocean Technology Center is a research center located at the University of Rhode Island supporting the advancement of ocean technology in Rhode Island. Federal and State support for the Center allows it to provide grants, loans, and other assistance to the marine technology business community.

- **Biotechnology**. The Rhode Island Center for Cellular Medicine (RICCM) was created in 1996 to address the needs of the Rhode Island biotech industry. The focus of the RICCM is on job creation and economic development, helping to take great ideas from the lab to the marketplace. The Center focuses on the development of companies working in the areas of cellular medicine and tissue engineering, and restricts its sphere of operation to collaboration with companies located in or interested in locating to Rhode Island.

- **Child and Adult Day Care Tax Credit.** A taxpayer who purchases or provides for adult or child day care services for adult family members or dependent children of the taxpayer's employees or to employees of its commercial tenants in Rhode Island is allowed a tax credit in the amount of 30 percent of the total amount expanded during the taxable year for services purchased and 30 percent of the total amount expended during the taxable year for the establishment and/or operation of a day care facility by the taxpayer alone or in conjunction with others.

Contact:

Beth Ashman Collins
Policy & Research Manager
Rhode Island Economic Development Corporation
1 West Exchange St.
Providence, RI 02903
(401) 222-2601

TAX INCENTIVES:

• **Corporate income tax.** 5.0 percent.

• **Personal income tax.** 2.5 to 7.0 percent.

• **Sales and use tax.** 5 percent. A local option sales tax of 1 percent applies in nearly half of the state's 46 counties.

• **Income Tax Moratorium.** Companies creating net new jobs in certain counties may benefit from a 10 year corporate income tax moratorium. In order to qualify, at least 90 percent of the company's total investment must be in a county where the unemployment rate is twice the state average. The length of the moratorium depends on the number of net new jobs created. For companies creating at least 100 net new jobs in one taxable year the moratorium will last ten years while companies creating at least 200 net new jobs will be eligible for a 15 year moratorium.

• **Job Tax Credits.** Corporate income tax credits are available to manufacturing, distribution, corporate office, and qualified service facilities creating 10 or more new jobs. The value of the credits ranges from $1,500 per new job created for five years to $4,500 per new job created for five years depending on the development status of the county in which the facility is located. These credits may be used to offset 50 percent of the company's state corporate income tax liability and, if unused, may be carried forward for 15 years from the year earned.

• **Corporate Headquarters Credit.** The State of South Carolina provides a corporate income tax credit to companies establishing a headquarters facility in the state. To qualify as a corporate headquarters the facility must be:

1. The location where corporate staff members or employees are domiciled and where the majority of the company's financial, legal, personnel, planning and/or other staff functions are handled on a regional or national basis; and
2. The sole such corporate headquarters within the region or nation. (Regional is defined as geographical area comprised of either five states [including South Carolina]; or two or more states [including South Carolina] if the corporation's entire range of business operations is performed in fewer than five states.)

The credit only applies to facilities, or the portion of facilities, established for the direct use of the headquarters staff. To qualify for this credit, the company must create a minimum of 40 new full-time jobs which are engaged in corporate headquarters or R&D activities and at least 20 of the 40 must be classified as staff employees. Facilities qualifying as a corporate or regional headquarters operation will receive a credit to the corporate income tax or corporate license fee for 20 percent of costs incurred in the design, preparation, and development of either establishing or expanding a corporate headquarters and direct construction or direct lease costs

LEGISLATIVE TIMELINE:

1991: Eliminated the sunset provision on property tax moratoriums; removed the sales-tax cap for research and development facilities; and extended the jobs tax credit to tourism facilities and agricultural, aquaculture and mariculture developments. Also re-authorized the South Carolina Coordinating Council for Economic Development until 1997.

1992: Amended the Corporate Headquarters Tax Credit Act to include research and development jobs in the total number required to meet the criteria to qualify for corporate income tax or license fee credits. The South Carolina Coordinating Council for Economic Development received increased funding for road construction and economic development.

1994: Reduced to 40 the number of jobs necessary for a corporate headquarters to qualify for credit against the state corporate income tax; passed legislation that allows part-time jobs to count towards job totals for qualification for property tax abatement; expanded the number of counties offering the maximum job tax credit; and made it easier for companies to qualify for the fee-in-lieu-of-property-tax option by reducing the minimum investment.

1995: Created a new enterprise zone program. Passed a law that provides a tax cut for employers hiring former welfare recipients.

1996: Approved the Rural Development Act under which the entire state is designated an enterprise zone. Job tax credits were increased for almost every county and increased significantly for the poorest counties.

1998: Amended Enterprise Zone Act to allow a moratorium on corporate income taxes for qualifying businesses that invest in a county which the average unemployment rate during the past two years is at least twice the state average, but not less than 10 percent.

during the first five years of operations. Unused portions of this credit may be carried forward for 10 taxable years. Note that this credit is not limited to 50 percent of a firm's tax liability.

- **Economic Impact Zone Investment Tax Credit.** In order to help offset the impact of federal downsizing in the state, legislation was passed to spur economic growth in 26 of the state's 46 counties surrounding the Charleston Naval Base, Myrtle Beach Air Force Base and the Savannah River Site. This legislation allows manufacturers locating in "Economic Impact Zones" a one-time credit against the company's corporate income tax of up to 5 percent of the company's investment in new production equipment. The actual value of the credit depends on the applicable recovery period for property under the Internal Revenue Code.

FINANCIAL INCENTIVES:

- **Job Development Credit.** Approved qualifying industries may retain up to 5 percent of new employees' gross hourly wages for a period of up to 15 years. The monies may be used to offset eligible capital expenditures associated with the project. The actual percentage the company may keep depends on both the compensation level of the individual employee and the development status of the county.

- **Infrastructure Assistance.** Each year the South Carolina Legislature sets monies aside to finance infrastructure improvements needed by economic development projects across the state. These funds, used primarily for offsite road improvements, are administered by the South Carolina Coordinating Council for Economic Development.

- **Working Training.** South Carolina, through its highly regarded network of technical colleges, will recruit, screen, test and train workers needed to fill new manufacturing jobs. This training is done in concert with the company's human resources department and is designed specifically to meet the needs of the company.

- **Financing Assistance.** The South Carolina Department of Commerce has staff on hand to help industries arrange financing.

OTHER INCENTIVES:

- **Child Care Credit.** South Carolina offers business a credit to state corporate income tax for child care expenses. Companies may claim corporate income tax credits for capital costs and operating costs associated with establishing and operating a child care program.

- **Regulatory Relief Programs.** South Carolina's Department of Health of Environmental Control (DHEC) works

hand in hand with businesses seeking air and water permits to make it as painless as possible.

Contact:

Daniel Young
Assistant Director of Research & Presentations Systems
South Carolina Department of Commerce
P.O. Box 927
Columbia, SC 29202
(803) 737-0448

TAX INCENTIVES:

• **Corporate income tax.** None.

• **Personal income tax.** None.

• **Sales and use tax.** 4.0 percent.

• **Sales Tax & Contractors' Excise Tax.** South Dakota offers tax refunds (sales and contractors' excise taxes) for new and expanded value-added agriculture processing facilities. To be eligible for the refund, the total cost of a project must be a minimum of $4.5 million. The refund is one hundred percent and refund permits in South Dakota are valid for 36 months.

• **Property Tax Abatements.** South Dakota counties and municipalities may forgive from 0 percent to 100 percent of the property taxes on a new structure or an addition to an existing one. The abatement may be available on industrial, commercial and non-residential agricultural structures valued at $30,000 or more.

FINANCIAL INCENTIVES:

• **Revolving Economic Development and Initiative (REDI) Fund.** The main objective of the REDI Fund is to create "primary jobs" in South Dakota. Primary jobs are defined as "jobs that provide goods and services which shall be primarily exported from the state, gain market shares from imports to the state or meet an unmet need in the area resulting in the creation of new wealth in South Dakota. Primary jobs are derived from businesses that bring new income into an area, have a stimulative effect on other businesses or assist a community in diversification and stabilization of its economy."

• **Economic Development Finance Authority.** The Economic Development Finance Authority allows enterprises to pool tax-exempt or taxable development bonds for the purpose of constructing any site, structure, facility, service or utility for the storage, distribution or manufacturing of industrial or agricultural or nonagricultural products or the purchase of machinery and equipment used in an industrial process. Generally, the Authority will not consider loan requests for enterprises for amounts less than $300,000 and will not pool projects unless the pool volume is $1 million or more.

• **SBA 504 Loan Program.** The SBA 504 Loan Program offers subordinated, fixed rate financing to healthy and expanding small businesses. Long-term, fixed rate financing (10-20 years) and reasonable rates (near long-term U.S. Treasury bond rates), make the 504 Program an attractive and effective economic development financing tool. The 504 Program is available for fixed asset purchases only: land, building and equipment with a useful life of 10 years or more. No working capital, inventory, venture capital or

LEGISLATIVE TIMELINE:

1990: Approved an anti-takeover law intended to protect South Dakota jobs and investments by establishing a process that must be followed in takeover bids for publicly traded corporations.

1992: Enacted a venture capital bill to provide seed money for new businesses.

1994: Extended the sales and use tax and contractors' excise tax refund or credit to all large facilities and lowered the threshold for eligibility. Lawmakers also created a $2 million loan program for small businesses.

1995: Authorized the formation of limited liability partnerships.

1996: Passed a tax incentive that exempts the international sale of agriculture and industrial equipment from the gross receipts tax.

1997: Clarified the definition of real property for the purposes of property taxes. Machinery and equipment were defined as personal property and therefore exempt from property taxes. Revised the sales and use tax and contractors' excise tax refund to new agriculture facilities worth $4.5 million plus.

1998: Authorized the formation of limited liability companies. Reduced residential property taxes by five percent for a total reduction of 25 percent in the last three years.

refinancing are eligible. The net worth of an eligible business may not exceed $6 million.

- **Micro-Loan Program.** This program was established to help small businesses grow and help rural communities remain viable. Its biggest advantages are that it is the first Governor's Office of Economic Development (GOED) financing program that offers businesses access to working capital and it is subordinated debt. By working with the GOED and local bankers, small businesses will be able to secure a loan that can be used for working capital, equipment, real estate or other fixed asset project costs. The maximum loan amount is $20,000, with the minimum amount set at $1,000.

- **Workforce Development Program.** The South Dakota Workforce Development Program is an opportunity to extend training and educational resources so that South Dakota employers will be provided with a well-trained and skilled workforce. Training is provided in conjunction with an educational institution approved by the Workforce Development Coordinator. Technical instructors, curriculum materials, instructional materials and equipment are available through the coordinating educational institution to help deliver quality programs.

OTHER INCENTIVES:

- **The South Dakota International Business Institute (SDIBI).** Developed as a cooperative effort between the state of South Dakota and Northern State University, the SDIBI supports the Governor's Office of Economic Development (GOED) in facilitating and enhancing international trade. International trade creates jobs which corresponds with GOED's mission of creating quality job opportunities for South Dakotans.

South Dakota exporters now have better access to trade finance assistance through SDIBI and the Export-Import Bank of the United States (Ex-Im Bank). Trade finance assistance includes, but is not limited to, working capital guarantee, export credit insurance, and direct loans and guarantees.

Contact:

**Ron W. Wheeler
Commissioner
Governor's Office of Economic Development
711 E. Wells Avenue
Pierre, SD 57501-3369
(605) 773-5032**

TENNESSEE

TAX INCENTIVES:

• **Corporate income tax.** 6.0 percent.

• **Personal income tax.** Limited to dividends and interest only.

• **Sales and use tax.** Retail sales taxed at a 6.0 percent rate.

• **Job Tax Credit.** As an incentive to locate and expand business operations in Tennessee, the General Assembly enacted a job tax credit in 1993. The credit amounts to $2,000 for each new full-time job created during a fiscal year and still in existence at the end of the year, $3,000 if the business is located in an economically distressed county as defined by the Department of Economic and Community Development (ECD). To qualify as full-time, a job must be for 12 consecutive months, for at least 37.5 hours per week, and must include certain health care benefits.

To qualify for the program, a business must have created at least 25 net new jobs in the first, threshold year, with the jobs created pursuant to a capital investment after Jan. 1, 1993, that increased the corporation's total capital investment in the state by $500,000. After the first year, additional credits can be taken for each net new job related to the capital investment.

• **Enterprise Zone Contributions.** Corporations are entitled to reimbursements of up to 50 percent of their excise tax payments for net new employment in an enterprise zone ($1,000 per new employee) and for 1.3 percent of the purchase price of industrial machinery for use in such a zone. If the reimbursement on account of industrial machinery exceeds the 50 percent limit, it may be carried forward for two years.

• **Industrial or Farm Machinery.** The state sales tax on industrial and farm machinery - which was formerly 1 percent - has been phased out. Local tax has also been eliminated by the same law as interpreted by a 1985 state Supreme Court decision, prior to which the local rate was 0.33 percent in counties or cities with local option rates of 1 percent or less and 0.5 percent in counties or cities with higher rates.

• **Construction Machinery.** A limited exemption exists for construction machinery that is transferred or leased between a parent company and its wholly-owned subsidiary as long as tax has previously been paid on the machinery. If a parent company buys machinery, pays tax on it, and then leases it to its subsidiary, the event is not taxable. The same applies to transfers or leases from a subsidiary to a parent. The industrial machinery exemption, however, does not apply since construction machinery is not used to make tangible personal property. And contractors whose business is improving real property are not considered manufacturers.

• **Pollution Control.** Pollution control equipment purchased by manufacturers is exempt from sales tax under the industrial machinery rules. But as of 1992 non-manufacturing businesses can obtain a sales tax credit for

LEGISLATIVE TIMELINE:

1991: Approved a tax exemption bill to expand the pollution-control exemptions for the state's sales, franchise and property taxes.

1993: Passed the new Jobs Tax Credit Bill, which provides incentives of up to $3,000 for a variety of companies that create new employment.

1994: Revised the franchise tax credit to expand the types of businesses that qualify, permit the credit to be taken sooner and delete the requirement that 25 new jobs must be added every year that the credit is taken.

1995: Passed a tax exemption for certain finished goods from the franchisee tax minimum measure and apportionment formula.

1996: Passed a new warehouse and distribution facility measure facility measure that places a cap on the inventory tax and authorizes a 1 percent credit on qualified equipment. Created the new Small and Minority-Owned Business Telecommunications Assistance Program that provides loan guarantees to help businesses break into the telecommunications industry.

1999: Created the Tennessee Forest Industries Economic Development and Taxpayer Act which increases state expenditures to produce environmental impact studies.

the amount of sales tax paid on pollution control equipment purchased to comply with government emission control standards.

- **Manufacturers Exemption.** The manufacturer's exemption applies to any materials that become a component part of the finished product; containers, labels, and packaging materials if they are sold with or accompany the item at no additional charge; and any materials coming into direct contact with the manufactured product and consumed in the manufacturing process within 25 days.

- **Headquarters Credit.** A credit exists for all but 0.5 percent of the state sales tax on building materials, machinery and equipment used in a new or expanded corporate headquarters facility that meets certain requirements. It applies only if the facility houses the corporate headquarters and if the new or expanded facility cost at least $50 million, along with other restrictions. It expires Dec. 31, 2002.

FINANCIAL INCENTIVES:

- **Tennessee Industrial Infrastructure Program (TIIP).** Tennessee's ECD allocates funds to assist local governments in providing infrastructure to support new or expanding industries. Eligible activities are water systems, wastewater systems, transportation systems and site improvements. Eligible businesses include manufacturing, businesses in which more than half of their product or service enters into the production of exported products, and other economic activities that have a beneficial impact on the economy of Tennessee.

- **Community Development Block Grants (CDBG).** Small city CDBGs are available in Tennessee for new or expanding industrial manufacturing and distribution companies. Eligible activities are those including infrastructure, buildings, and capital equipment. The maximum amount of the loan or grant for any community/company is $500,000.

- **Appalachian Regional Commission Program (ARC).** All 50 Appalachian counties are eligible. Eligible activities include infrastructure projects (water, wastewater, roads, rail) required to secure the creation, expansion or retention of job opportunities; job training programs; basic skills development in reading, writing, computation and computer literacy; housing projects; and multi-jurisdictional programs in enterprise development assistance demonstration projects. The state's maximum ability to pay is $500,000.

- **Small and/or Minority-Owned Telecommunications Business Assistance Program.** This program encourages the creation and support of small and/or minority-owned telecommunications businesses by issuing loan guarantees to banks for qualified borrowers. Eligible businesses are those with gross receipts of $4 million or less. The maximum loan amount is $400,000.

- **Small Business Energy Loan Program.** The Tennessee Small Business Energy Loan Program is designed to help identify, install and incorporate approved energy efficiency measures in existing Tennessee facilities. The maximum loan is $100,000. Eligible businesses are those with 300 or less employees and less than $3.5 million of annual gross sales or receipts, averaged over the last three years.

OTHER INCENTIVES:

- **Foreign Investment.** Tennessee has three consultants with the Department of Travel in Japan, Europe and Canada, and representatives under contract based in Japan, London and Toronto.

Contact:

Ray Dickerson
Director of Research
TN Department of Economic and Commerce Development
8th Floor Rachel Jackson Bldg
320 6th Avenue N
Nashville, TN 37243
(615) 532-1912

TAX INCENTIVE:

- **Corporate income tax.** None.

- **Personal income tax.** None.

- **Sales and use tax.** 6.25 percent.

- **Enterprise Zone Program.** To offer certain incentives to a business, a city and/or county must establish an enterprise zone. To establish a zone, a city and/or county must nominate a specific geographic area within its jurisdiction to The Texas Department of Economic Development (TDED). The area must meet certain size and distress criteria, reflect the economic objectives of the community, and specify local incentives that may be offered to a business in the zone. Zone designation is effective for a period of seven years.

- **Defense Economic Reinvestment Zone Program.** Communities affected by defense downsizing have an important tool for business recruitment, private investment and job creation through the Defense Economic Readjustment Zones. The program offers financial incentives to businesses that make hiring and location commitments to an affected community. Defense readjustment projects are eligible for a refund of state sales or use taxes paid on machinery and equipment, building materials and labor used for remodeling, rehabilitating, or constructing a structure in the readjustment zone, and electricity and natural gas purchased for use in the readjustment zone.

FINANCIAL INCENTIVES:

- **Texas Capital Fund Infrastructure Development Program.** This program is an economic development tool designed to provide financial resources to non-entitlement communities. Funds from this program can be utilized for public infrastructure needed to assist a business which commits to create and/or retain permanent jobs, primarily for low and moderate income persons. This program encourages new business development and expansions.

- **Texas Capital Fund Main Street Improvements Program.** This program is designed to foster and stimulate the development of small businesses by providing financial assistance to non-entitlement cities (designated by the Texas Historical Commission as Main Street Cities) for public improvements. This program encourages the elimination of slum or blighted areas. The minimum awards are $75,000 and the maximum awards are $150,000.

- **Texas Capital Fund Real Estate Development Program.** This program is designed to provide financial resources to non-entitlement communities. Funds must be used for real estate development to assist a business which commits to create and/or retain permanent jobs, primarily for low and moderate income persons. This program encourages new business devel-

LEGISLATIVE TIMELINE:

1990: Increased the state's sales and use tax from 6 percent to 6.25 percent.

1991: Amended the Rural Economic Development Act to delete the requirement that only industrial and manufacturing enterprises may receive assistance. Any otherwise eligible enterprise also may receive assistance under the law.

1992: Authorized the Texas Economic Development Corporation to issue revenue bonds in an unlimited amount for any eligible project.

1993: Approved the Smart Jobs Fund, which offers matching grants for new job training or on-the-job training.

1994: Phased out the sales and use tax on manufacturing machinery and equipment.

1995: Established a new Telecommunications Infrastructure Fund to provide $150 million annually in grants and loans for projects in distance education, information sharing and telemedicine. Increased tax incentives in enterprise zones.

1999: Passed an act exempting certain purchases of machinery and equipment used for research and development from sales and use taxes.

opment and expansions located in non-entitlement communities. The minimum award is $50,000 and the maximum is $500,000.

- **Texas Leverage Fund (TLF).** TLF is an "economic development bank" offering an added source of financing to communities that have passed the economic development sales tax. The TDED may loan funds directly to a local Industrial Development Corporation (IDC) to finance eligible projects. Loan proceeds must be used to pay eligible "costs" of "projects" as defined by the Development Corporation Act of 1979, as amended. Examples of eligible costs include land, buildings, machinery and equipment for manufacturing and industrial operations.

- **Texas Capital Access Fund.** The Capital Access Fund was established to increase the availability of financing for businesses and nonprofit organizations that face barriers in accessing capital. Through the use of the Capital Access Fund, businesses that might otherwise fall outside the guidelines of conventional lending may still have the opportunity to receive financing. The essential element of the program is a reserve account established at the lending institution to act as a credit enhancement, inducing the financial institution to make a loan. The borrower must be a small business with fewer than 100 employees, a medium business with 100 to 500 employees, a nonprofit organization, domiciled in Texas or have at least 51 percent of its employees located in Texas.

- **State of Texas Linked Deposit Program.** The "Linked Deposit Program" was established to encourage lending to historically underutilized businesses, child care providers, nonprofit corporations, and/or small businesses located in an Enterprise Zone by providing lenders and borrowers a lower cost of capital.

- **State of Texas Industrial Revenue Bond Program.** The State of Texas Industrial Revenue Bond Program is designed to provide tax-exempt financing to finance land and depreciable property for eligible industrial or manufacturing projects.

OTHER INCENTIVES:

- **Export Assistance.** The Texas Office of International Business helps Texas companies expand their businesses worldwide. Through international trade missions, trade shows, seminars and inbound buyer missions, the Office of International Business gives Texas companies the opportunity to promote their products and services to international buyers and partners. The State of Texas office in Mexico City is a valuable resource for facilitating business between Texas and Mexico.

- **Regulatory Relief Programs.** The Texas Natural Resource Conservation Commission (TNRCC) and the Texas Department of Economic Development (TDED) have established a relationship to assist companies that experience delays in the environmental permitting process for projects that could affect job creation or have a high economic impact. Pre-permit meetings are arranged for businesses to meet and discuss their projects in detail with the appropriate TNRCC staff.

- **Public/Private Partnerships.** These partnerships are through the aforementioned Texas Capital Access Fund, Texas Linked Deposit Fund and the Industrial Revenue Bond Program.

- **Smart Jobs Fund Program.** The Smart Jobs Fund Program provides grants to employers to train their employees. The fund is a business incentive program designed to increase the competitiveness of Texas businesses in the global economy. The program is "employer driven," which means the employer determines which employees they will train, what type of training will be performed, and who will administer the training. The legislature appropriated $108 million for the 1998-99 biennium. The maximum grant amount available to a single employer is $1.5 million per state fiscal year.

SUCCESSFUL INCENTIVES:

- **Smart Jobs Fund Program.** In Fiscal Year 1998, the Smart Jobs Fund program awarded a total of 529 grants to 510 employers. The awards totaled $53,385,402. It is projected that this funding will provide training for 42,441 jobs in Texas of which 18,189 represent new jobs.

- **Economic Development Sales Tax.** The sales tax for economic development has been one of the most popular and effective tools used by cities to promote economic development. Since 1989, Texas cities have had the option to impose a local sales and use tax to finance community economic development efforts. Since going into effect in 1989, nearly 400 cities have levied the tax and have cumulatively generated in excess of $200 million annually in additional sales tax revenue that is dedicated to local economic development.

Contact:

Rosemary Lucio Suniga
Senior Information Specialist
Texas Department of Economic Development
P.O. Box 12728 Capitol Station
1700 N. Congress
Austin, TX 78711
(512) 936-0223

TAX INCENTIVES:

- **Corporate income tax.** 5.0 percent.

- **Personal income tax.** Maximum rate of 7.2 percent with a deduction against state taxes for federal income taxes which have been paid.

- **Sales and use tax.** 6.125 percent.

- **Manufacturing Equipment Sales Tax Exemption.** An exemption of sales and use taxes are available for the purchase or lease of new equipment or machinery for manufacturing facilities. The 1995 Utah State Legislature passed new legislation which extends the sales and use tax exemption to manufacturing replacement equipment.

- **Economic Development Area/Tax Increment Financing.** Tax Increment Financing (TIF) is utilized in areas that have been targeted for economic development. Redevelopment areas are determined by local municipalities. Portions of the new property tax generated by new development projects are returned to project developers in the form of infrastructure development, land cost write down or other appropriate means.

- **Enterprise Zones.** The act passed by the Utah State Legislature provides tax credits for manufacturing companies locating in rural areas that qualify for assistance. A $750 tax credit is given for all new jobs created plus a credit of $1,250 for jobs paying at least 125 percent of the average wage for the industry.

FINANCIAL INCENTIVES:

- **Industrial Assistance Fund.** The State of Utah has an Industrial Assistance Fund (IAF) that can be used for relocation costs. This incentive loan can be repaid as Utah jobs created meet the IAF requirements resulting in higher quality jobs, and as Utah purchases merit enough earned credits to convert the loan to a grant.

SUCCESSFUL INCENTIVES:

- **The Industrial Assistance Fund.** The Industrial Assistance Fund has been far more successful than any other incentive.

Contact:

Richard Nelson
Utah Department of Community and Economic Development
324 S. State St., Ste. 500
Salt Lake City, UT 84111
(801) 538-8716

LEGISLATIVE TIMELINE:

1990: Passed a sales tax exemption for pollution-control facilities, aircraft parts and equipment installed in Utah and sales of aircraft manufactured in the state.

1991: Created a $10 million Industrial Assistance Fund to provide companies with loans or other financial assistance to help in the establishment, relocation or development of industry in the state.

1993: Repealed several business exemptions from the state sales tax.

1994: Amended a law to give rural areas broader access to the state's Industrial Assistance Fund.

1995: Broadened the manufacturers sales tax exemption to include the purchase of replacement manufacturing equipment. Businesses hiring disabled individuals now qualify for a state income tax credit.

1996: Cut income taxes by $40 million, with the top rate dropping to 7 percent from 7.2 percent. Expanded the enterprise zone program to include 17 counties and many cities. Created a fund for economic development infrastructure.

1997: Energy Savings Tax Credit Extension; increases the maximum amount allowable as a credit for residential energy systems.

1998: Rural Enterprise Zones now allow Indian Tribes to apply for enterprise zone designation.

1999: Modified the individual income tax and corporate franchise and income tax credits for research activities and research equipment and allowed certain taxpayers to make an irrevocable election to be treated as a start-up company for purposes of calculating the base amount.

VERMONT

1990: Increased the state's personal income tax liability for a two-year period.

1991: Extended the maximum repayment period for state loans made to local community development corporations for the construction of speculative buildings or improvements.

1993: Encouraged worker training and cut some taxes; increased funding for the Job Start Program; created the Financial Access Program to provide loans to new companies; passed a new jobs tax credit for companies that create 15 or more jobs paying at least $20,000; passed the Manufacturer Investment Tax Credit to benefit "C" corporations investing at least $4 million over two years.

1995: Extended a sales tax increase for another year, keeping the rate at 5 percent.

1996: Increased the state's minimum wage to $5.15 per hour. A training wage of $4.75 applies to a new worker's first 90 days of employment.

1999: Passed an act which provides that ski lifts and fixtures and snow-making equipment affixed to the land are exempt from the education property tax, effective March 31, 1999.

TAX INCENTIVES:

- **Corporate income tax.** 7.0 to 9.75 percent.

- **Personal income tax.** 25.0 percent of federal tax liability. If Vermont tax liability for any taxable year exceeds the tax liability determinable under federal tax law in effect on December 31, 1995, the taxpayer will be entitled to a credit of 106 percent of the excess tax.

- **Sales and use tax.** 5.0 percent.

Payroll Tax Credit. A person may receive a credit against income tax liability equal to a percentage of its increased payroll costs, defined as salaries and wages.

1. If reporting less than $10 million in sales in the tax year the credit is claimed, they may receive equal to 10 percent of their increased costs of salaries and wages in the applicable tax year.
2. Sales of $10 million through $12,500,000, a 9 percent credit.
3. Sales of $12.5 million through $15 million, an 8 percent credit.
4. Sales of $15 million through $17.5 million, a 7 percent credit.
5. Sales of $17.5 million through $20 million, a 6 percent credit.
6. Sales over $20 million, a 5 percent credit.

- **Research and Development Tax Credit.** A person may receive a credit against income tax liability in the amount of 10 percent of qualified research and development expenditures. Qualified R&D expenditures shall have the same meaning as qualified research and development expenditures included in the IRS code.

- **Workforce Development Tax Credit.** A person may receive a credit against income tax liability in the amount of 10 percent of his/her qualified training, education and workforce development expenditures. A 20 percent credit may be taken for qualified training, education and workforce development expenditures for the benefit of welfare to work participants. Qualified training, education and workforce development expenditures shall mean:

1. Expenditures eligible for financial assistance under the Vermont Training Program; or
2. Expenditures defined by the United States Code concerning the employee educational assistance initiative; or
3. Expenditures for employer-provided child care and transportation subsidies that allow for training and educational activities of welfare to work participants.

- **Small Business Investment Tax Credit.** A person may receive a credit against income tax liability in the amount equal to five to ten percent of its investments within the state of Vermont in excess of $150,000 in plans, facilities and machinery and equipment.

1. Employing fewer than 150 full-time employees, a 10 percent credit.
2. Employing between 150 and 174 full-time employees, a 9 percent credit.
3. Employing between 175 and 199 full-time employees, an 8 percent credit.
4. Employing between 200 and 224 full-time employees, a 7 percent credit.
5. Employing between 225 and 250 full-time employees, a 6 percent credit.
6. Employing more than 250 full-time employees, a 5 percent credit.

FINANCIAL INCENTIVES:

• **Financial Services Incentives.** The financial services industry in Vermont has been designated as a strategic development priority for the state of Vermont. This sector results in the growth of well-paying jobs, diversification and expansion of the Vermont economy and the development of a business sector that has a low impact on the environment. Vermont has also passed an income tax credit of up to 75 percent for the money management industry. It can be taken every year and is easy to understand and therefore to claim.

OTHER INCENTIVES:

• **Export Tax Credit.** A person who makes sales outside Vermont may take as a credit against his/her income tax liability, the difference between the income tax calculated under the existing state apportionment formula and the proposed formula which double weights the sales factor and disregards "throwback" provisions. This incentive is favorable to exporters, encouraging Vermont businesses that export to declare a greater amount of taxable income in Vermont.

Contact:

Linda Royce
Customer Service Representative
Commerce & Community Development
National Life Building
Montpelier, VT 05620-0501
(802) 828-3080

VIRGINIA

LEGISLATIVE TIMELINE:

1990: Created the Rural Economic Development Planning Grant Fund, which is designed to assist local governments in rural areas in identifying and evaluation public industrial sites; expanded the state's enterprise zone program.

1992: Created the $4.5 million Governor's Economic Development Contingency Fund to attract industrial prospects and secure expansions.

1993: Increased the number of enterprise zones from 19 to 25; approved a manufacturing program to promote the development of the high-tech, renewable energy industry in Virginia.

1995: Passed the Major Business Facility Job Tax Credit and the Clean Fuel Vehicle Job Creation Tax Credit. Doubled the number of state enterprise zones to 50 and added new tax incentives for investments in the zones.

1996: Created the Economic Development Partnership to bring increased involvement in the state's economic development efforts and initiated the Dept. of Business Assistance to function as a liaison between the state and existing Virginia businesses.

1999: Passed an amendment that expanded the research and development investment tax credit.

TAX INCENTIVES:

- **Corporate income tax.** 6.0 percent.

- **Personal income tax.** 2.0 to 5.75 percent.

- **Sales and use tax.** 4.5 percent (state and local combined rate). The following are exempt from the sales and use tax: manufacturers' purchases used directly in production, including machinery, tools, spare parts, industrial fuels and raw materials; items purchased for resale by distributors; certified pollution control equipment and facilities; custom computer software; and items used in research and development.

- **Major Business Facility Job Tax Credit.** Qualifying companies locating or expanding in Virginia receive a $1,000 corporate income tax credit for each new full-time job created over a threshold number of jobs. Unused credits may be carried over 10 years.

- **Recycling Equipment Tax Credit.** An income tax credit is available to manufacturers for the purchase of certified machinery and equipment for processing recyclable materials. The credit is equal to 10 percent of the original total capitalized cost of the equipment. In any taxable year, the credit allowed cannot exceed 40 percent of the company's Virginia income tax liability before the credit. Unused credits may be carried over for 10 years.

- **Clean Fuel Vehicle Job Creation Tax Credit.** Businesses manufacturing or converting vehicles to operate on clean fuel and manufacturers of components for use in clean fuel vehicles are eligible to receive an income tax credit for each new full-time job created over and above the previous year's employment level. The credit is equal to $700 in the year the job is created, and in each of two succeeding years if the job is continued, for a maximum of $2,100 per job. Unused credits may be carried over 5 years.

- **Enterprise Zone Program.** Qualified businesses locating or expanding in an enterprise zone are eligible for the following incentives:

– General Tax Credit. A 10-year general credit against state tax liability (80 percent first year and 60 percent in years two through 10). New businesses must have 25 percent of their full-time employees either meeting low-income standards for the area or living within the zone. Existing businesses must increase full-time employment by at least 10 percent with 25 percent of the 10 percent increase meeting low-income standards for the area. For projects investing at least $15 million and creating 100 full-time jobs, the credit amount is negotiable.

– Real Property Improvements Tax Credit. A credit against state tax equal to 30 percent of qualified zone real property improvements is available for rehabilitation projects investing at least $50,000 or an amount equal to the current assessed value of the real property, whichever is greater. New construction projects must invest at least $250,000. The maximum cumulative credit is $125,000 in any five-year period. The credit is applied first to tax liability; the remaining balance, if any, is then refunded.

– Investment Tax Credit. Large projects that invest at least $100 million and create at least 200 jobs are eligible for a negotiable credit of up to 5 percent of the total investment (real property, machinery and equipment). This credit is in lieu of the refundable real property improvement tax credit, and credits may be carried forward until used fully.

– Job Grants. Businesses creating new, full-time positions are eligible to receive grants of up to $500 per person filling a position and up to $1,000 per zone resident filling a position for three years. Existing businesses can receive grants for new positions that are in excess of 110 percent of base employment. New start-up companies receive grants for all new full-time jobs. The maximum grant to any one firm is $110,000 a year for three consecutive years. Businesses receiving this grant are not eligible to receive the Major Business Facility Job Tax Credit.

• **Property Tax Incentives.** Virginia does not tax property at the state level; real estate and tangible personal property are taxed at the local level. In addition, Virginia differs from most states in that its counties and cities are separate taxing entities. A company pays either county or city taxes, depending on its location. If the company is located within the corporate limits of a town, it pays town taxes as well as county taxes. Virginia localities also do not have separate school district taxes.

FINANCIAL INCENTIVES:

• **Industrial Development Bonds.** Tax-exempt Industrial Development Bonds (IDBs) are issued through local industrial development authorities and the Virginia Small Business Financing Authority. These bonds finance new or expanding manufacturing facilities and exempt projects, such as solid-waste disposal facilities. Through IDBs, creditworthy businesses can finance up to 100 percent of the cost of acquiring, constructing and equipping a facility, including site preparation, at favorable interest rates. IDBs may also be used to allow manufacturers to lease facilities and equipment at tax-exempt rates.

• **Community Development Block Grants.** Community Development Block Grants (CDBGs) are available to eligible cities, counties and towns to support local economic development. Funds may be used for off-site activities such as water- and sewerline extensions or treatment facilities, and road and rail access. Funds may also be used for site preparation and development, land purchase, building construction, or expansion loans for machinery and tools, working capital, refinancing plant purchase, and other

activities supporting economic development. CDBG funds are also available for micro-enterprise development, central business revitalization and, on a limited basis, shell building construction.

• **Governor's Opportunity Fund.** The Governor's Opportunity Fund supports economic development projects that create new jobs and investment in accordance with criteria established by state legislation. Funds can be used for such activities as site acquisition and development; transportation access; training; construction and build-out of publicly owned buildings; or grants and loans to industrial development authorities. Grant requests can be made by localities for a project if all of the following conditions are met:

1. Projects must meet investment and job creation minimums;
2. Matching local financial participation is required on a dollar-for-dollar basis;
3. Grants are made at the discretion of the governor.

• **Virginia Coalfield Economic Development Authority (VCEDA).** The VCEDA works to enhance the economic base of the seven counties and one city of far-southwestern Virginia (Buchanan, Dickerson, Lee, Russel, Scott, Tazewell and Wise counties and the City of Norton). The authority provides low-interest loans and grants to qualified new or expanding industries through its financing program. The loans may be used for real estate purchases, construction or expansion of buildings and the purchase of machinery and equipment.

To be eligible for the VCEDA loans, private businesses must be basic employers who will bring new income to the area. Priority will be given to loans requiring $10,000 or less for each new basic job created, and the average minimum hourly wage should equal or exceed 1.5 times the current federal minimum wage rate at the end of one year of employment. Any project providing at least 25 jobs within 12 months of start-up will be given priority.

• **Virginia Small Business Financing Authority.** The Virginia Small Business Financing Authority, which is housed within the Virginia Department of Business Assistance, offers programs to provide business with access to capital needed for growth and expansion.

• **Virginia Capital.** Virginia Capital is a private venture-capital firm investing in profitable companies with revenues between $5 and $30 million. Virginia Capital provides growth capital to expand existing businesses, acquisition capital to finance management buyouts, and equity capital for leveraged recapitalizations. Typical investments range between $1 million and $5 million per company. Virginia Capital's industry preferences are health-care services, communications products or services, small-market media and publishing. The firm does not generally invest in retail, real estate, financial services or natural-resource-related business; nor does it invest in start-up, early-stage or turnaround situations.

- **Small Business Environmental Compliance Assistance.** The 1997 General Assembly established the Small Business Environmental Compliance Assistance Fund to make loans or guarantee loans to small businesses for the purchase and installation of pollution control and prevention equipment. The equipment must be certified by the Department of Environmental Quality as either:

  1. Air pollution control equipment needed by the business to comply with federal Clean Air Act (42 U.S.C. Section 7401 et seq.).
  2. Pollution control equipment that allows the business to implement voluntary pollution prevention measures.

  This revolving loan program is scheduled to begin in late 1998 and will be available to businesses employing 100 or fewer people and meeting the federal Small Business Act definition of a small business.

- **Export Financing Assistance.** The Financing Authority provides guarantees of up to the lesser of $750,000 or 90 percent of a bank loan for export working capital. It also works in partnership with the Export-Import Bank of the United States (Ex-Im Bank) and the U.S. Small Business Administration (SBA) to provide Virginia exporters with easier access to federal financing programs and export credit insurance. The Financing Authority assists businesses in gaining access to Ex-Im Bank and SBA working-capital loan guarantees by packaging and submitting applications according to federal guidelines. In addition, the Financing Authority administers an Ex-Im Bank Export Credit Insurance Umbrella Policy to assist Virginia exporters in obtaining credit insurance on their foreign receivables.

- **Virginia's Center for Innovative Technology.** The Center for Innovative Technology (CIT) exists to stimulate economic growth within the Commonwealth by serving Virginia's technology businesses. Created by the General Assembly in 1984, CIT increases Virginia's economic competitiveness by providing businesses access to the state's technology resources and assisting in the creation and retention of technology-based jobs and businesses.

- **Regulatory Relief Program.** Virginia has streamlined environmental permitting and local building permitting.

- **Public/Private Partnerships.** The Virginia Economic Development Department is an authority that can partner with the private sector to support economic development.

Contact:

Mark Kilduff
Acting Executive Director
Virginia Economic Development Partnership
901 East Cary Street
Richmond, VA 23206-0798
(804) 371-8100

WASHINGTON

TAX INCENTIVES:

- **Corporate income tax.** None.

- **Personal income tax.** None.

Sales and use tax. 6.5 percent. Washington offers a sales and use tax exemption for manufacturers, processors for hire, and manufacturers who perform research and development. Charges for labor and services for installing the machinery and equipment are also not subject to the sales or use tax. In addition, charges for repair labor and parts (if the parts have a useful life of at least one year), cleaning, altering, or improving the qualified machinery and equipment are exempt from the tax as well.

- **Distressed Area Sales and Use Tax Deferral/Exemption.** Manufacturers, research and development, or computer related businesses (excluding light and power businesses) are able to waive sales and use tax if they locate in a specific geographic area. The tax is waived when the project is certified as operationally complete and all purchases are verified as eligible.

- **Employee Training Business and Occupation Tax Credits.** A B&O tax credit is available to businesses which have received approval for the Distressed Area Sales and Use Tax Deferral/Exemption Program and provide employee job training to their employees at no cost to the employee. The maximum annual credit a business may use is $5,000. The credit is computed by multiplying the approved training cost by 20 percent.

- **Distressed Area Business and Occupation Tax Credit.** A $2,000 or $4,000 (if wages and benefits exceed $40,000) credit against the B&O tax is available for each new employment position created and filled by certain businesses located in eligible areas. Additional requirements include:
    - A business must be a manufacturing, research and development, or computer related service business (excluding light and power businesses).
    - Businesses must create a new work force or expand the existing work force by 15 percent (full-time employment positions) over the preceding year.
    - New full-time employment positions must be maintained for 12 consecutive months by either a new or expanding business.
    - The positions must be new. Positions may not be transferred from an established site in Washington to a new site or other qualified location unless the vacated positions are filled.
    - Individual businesses are limited to a maximum credit of $300,000 over the life of the program.
    - An application must be filed with the Washington State Department of Revenue before filling the new positions.

LEGISLATIVE TIMELINE:

1990: Passed a growth management bill to empower local governments to collect fees for the effects of growth on roads, parks, open space, recreational facilities, schools and fire protection.

1991: Passed the Pacific Northwest Economic Region bill, which addresses regional strategies to boost exports, tourism, environmental industries, value-added forestry products and regional recycling.

1993: Increased the Business and Occupation Tax for services by 6.5 percent.

1994: Approved tax credits to high-tech firms for research and development and deferred sales taxes for those firms' investments in building, machinery and equipment.

1995: Enhanced tax incentives available under the Distressed Areas Program and the High Technology Program.

1996: Extended the existing sales or use tax exemption on manufacturing machinery and equipment to cover items used for research and development of new products.

1999: The department of community, trades and economic development were divided into two separate agencies, the department of community development and the department of trade and economic development.

- **High Technology Sales and Use Tax Deferral/Exemption.** Businesses in the following research and development categories may be eligible for a sales and use tax deferral/exemption if they start new research and development or pilot scale manufacturing operations, or expand or diversify a current operation by expanding, renovating or equipping an existing facility: advanced computing, advanced materials, biotechnology, electronic device technology and environment technology.

- **High Technology Business and Occupation Tax Credit.** An annual credit of up to $2 million is allowed for businesses that perform research and development in specified high technology categories and meet minimum expense requirements. Expenditures on research and development during the year the credit is claimed must exceed .92 percent of the business' taxable amount during that same year. The credit cannot exceed the amount of the business and occupation tax due for that calendar year. The rate for the credit is .515 percent of expenses for nonprofit corporation or association and 2.5 percent of expenses for a profit business. Qualified technology businesses are: advanced computing, advanced materials, biotechnology, electronic device technology and environmental technology. Allowable expenditures include operating expenses, wages and benefits, supplies, and computer expenses directly incurred while conducting the research and development.

FINANCIAL INCENTIVES:

- **Community Economic Revitalization Board.** CERB provides low-cost financing for public facilities improvement that are required for private development. Loans, and occasional grants, are available to cities, counties, ports and special utility districts to offset infrastructure costs and assist in the development and retention of jobs. Eligible projects include access roads, sewer and water extensions as well as other public improvements required to make specific sites attractive for private sector development. Infrastructure funded by CERB must serve basic industries including manufacturing, processing, assembly, production, warehousing and distribution, or external services such as businesses that significantly support the trading of goods and services outside the state's borders. A maximum of $750,000 is available per project under CERB's traditional program, $500,000 for industrial projects under the CERB timber area program, and $250,000 for tourism projects

- **Industrial Revenue Bonds.** The IRB Program permits public corporations to issue federal tax-exempt bonds on behalf of private companies. The key advantage of this type of financing lies in its tax-exempt status. Interest payments to IRB bond buyers are not subject to U.S. income tax. As a result, bond buyers are willing to accept lower rates of interest on these bonds, thus reducing project financing costs for the participating companies. Up to $10 million in bonds may be issued to finance one project. In Washington State, IRBs are issued through special public corporations formed by local units of government and through the Community Economic Revitalization Board at the state level. Small and medium sized issues can be pooled through the state Umbrella Bond Program. At least 73 such corporations currently operate in the state. Projects eligible for financing by bond proceeds are limited to manufacturing or processing firms and include acquisition of land, construction and/or improvement of facilities; new machinery and equipment; architectural designs, engineering work, and feasibility studies; consulting, accounting and legal fees; and financing arrangements and interest accrued during construction.

- **Washington Economic Development Finance Authority.** WEDFA is authorized to issue taxable nonrecourse economic development bonds, a form of conduit financing to tax-exempt industrial revenue bonds, which the state and local public corporations in Washington have been issuing for years. They are a means by which the state, without lending its credit or incurring any financial liability, can assist those companies whose projects do not meet the requirements of the federal tax code for the issuance of tax-exempt IRBs to access the long-term debt market. While there is no set size limit for a WEDFA bond financing, current legislation limits the total par value of WEDFA debt that can be outstanding at any given time to $250 million. Eligible projects include the following activities: manufacturing, processing, research, production, assembly, tooling, warehousing, pollution control, energy generating, conservation, transmission, sports facilities or industrial parks.

- **Washington State Job Skills Program.** The JSP was created in 1983 to bring together employers who have specific training needs with educational institutions that can provide customized employee training. JSP supports up to one-half of the total cost short-term, job-specific training; the participating employers provide a dollar-for-dollar cash or in-kind match. Most business related operations are eligible for JSP training programs. These include private corporations, firms, institutions, business associations, and industry groups concerned with manufacturing, trade, or services. JSP grants can be awarded to support training for prospective employees before a new facility opens or when an existing company expands operations, upgrading for current employees when new vacancies are created for unemployed persons, and retraining employees when necessary to preserve their jobs.

OTHER INCENTIVES:

- **Foreign Investment.** The Trade Division of the Washington State Department of Community, Trade and Economic Development (DCTED) maintains offices in Europe, Japan, Russia, Taiwan, and Shanghai which facilitate trade activities as well as serve as contact points for businesses interested in Washington State. The Business Development Team works with individual business that are interested in learning more about or locating in Washington State to facilitate the site selection process, permitting, accessing business incentives, accessing capital investors, and contacting local Economic Development Councils, port authorities, and utility companies.

- **Export Assistance.** The International Trade Division conducts export assistance programs that serve all areas of the world and every industry. The Japan Program, the China, Hong Kong, and Taiwan Program, the Canada and Latin America program, the European Program, and the Korean program together cover all of the world markets. The Trade Division also has specific programs to target the aerospace, software, light industrial machinery, and value-added wood products and building materials sectors. The Office of the Special Trade Representative advises the governor, coordinates with other agencies, and represents the state in major initiates with foreign trading partners. The Department of Agriculture also operates several export assistance programs for agricultural products, including the Export Readiness Program in which the department provides one-on-one consultation services and problem-solving advice for businesses that would like to expand their export markets.

- **Washington's Child Care Advantages Program.** This program offers the Child Care Facility Fund, which makes loans and grants available for employers that provide or want to provide child care services to benefit their employees. The program also provides information to employers about different ways to assist employees with child care issues besides in-house child care facilities. Working Mother magazine recently rated Washington State one of the top ten states in innovative child care and early childhood health and safety and education programs.

- **Regulatory Relief Programs.** Washington State offers a number of regulatory relief programs for businesses on specific issues. The Department of Ecology offers incentives, for example, for businesses that successfully control emissions. The Department of Labor and Industries offers reductions in industrial insurance rates for businesses that participate in programs such as the Return to Work Program, in which injured employees are returned to work in light-duty jobs for the same employer, or for companies who institute drug testing policies. Businesses should contact the specific agency involved for more information.

- **Public/Private Partnerships.** The state Business Development Team works in partnership with local Economic Development Councils, local and state government agencies, port authorities, and utility companies on business development activities such as arranging site visits by potential business investors, and assisting businesses in accessing local business recruitment incentives.

SUCCESSFUL INCENTIVES:

- **Machinery and Equipment Sales Tax Exemption.** This program has been very successful in the past five years. Prior to the establishment of the exemption, Washington was the only state charging sales tax on the purchase of machinery and equipment for use in manufacturing. In order for Washington to continue to attract new businesses and retain the businesses already located in the state, it became necessary to establish this sales tax exemption. This incentive has been especially successful in the case of Hewlett Packard, one of Washington's largest employers. Hewlett Packard, turns over its entire inventory of equipment every two years. The sales tax exemption has resulted in large savings for the company, and has been instrumental in the company's decision to continue operations in Washington State. The Warehouse Bill, which provided for relief from state and local retail sales and use tax incurred by eligible warehousing firms, and relief from the sales tax and state general fund portion of the motor vehicle excise tax paid on trucks which are directly related to the warehousing operation, has also been particularly successful. Because the state assumes the burden of the local portion of the tax relief, local governments and port authorities have been happy with the results, and the incentive has resulted in the attraction of new warehousing business into the state.

Contact:

Stephen D. Smith, Ph.D.
Economist, WA State Department of Revenue
Room 300 Evergreen Plaza Building, PO Box 47459
Olympia, WA 98504-7459
(360) 586-5661

WEST VIRGINIA

LEGISLATIVE TIMELINE:

1990: Established a customized job-training program. Authorized the creation of High-Tech 2000 research zones and parks in which businesses are eligible for deferral of all state corporate net income tax.

1991: Passed the Governor's Guaranteed Work-force Program, which provides one-stop shopping for all economic development related job-training needs. Approved a tax credit for investments in facilities producing coal-based liquids used in the manufacture of synthetic motor fuel

1992: Created a $10 million Jobs Investment Trust to provide business and college students with an opportunity to develop innovative economic development programs and investment opportunities.

1993: Created the Steel Futures Program to promote the steel industry, established a $15 million revolving loan program for industrial development and instituted an export assistance program.

1994: Created the Office of Business Registration to provide one-stop shopping for new and expanding businesses.

1995: Provided an additional $600,000 for the Governor's Guaranteed Work-force Program.

1996: Reduced the franchise tax to 0.7 percent from 0.75 percent. Increased funding for the Governor's Guaranteed Work-force Program by $630,000.

1999: In order to attract new business and industry to this state, it is necessary to promote adequate higher education, arts, sciences and tourism facilities, including infrastructure

TAX INCENTIVES:

- **Corporate income tax.** 9.0 percent.

- **Personal income tax.** 3.0 to 6.5 percent.

- **Sales and use tax.** 6.0 percent.

- **Business Investment and Jobs Expansion Tax Credit (Super Tax Credit).** The State of West Virginia offers a Super Tax Credit program that provides substantial tax savings for qualified companies that create jobs such as manufacturing, information processing, warehousing, goods distribution and destination-oriented tourism. This program is based upon a formula calculated by using factors of qualified investment and job creation. The amount of qualified investment is based on the useful life and cost of real and personal property.

- **Corporate Headquarters Credit.** Additional credit is available to a company that relocates its corporate headquarters to this state. If at least 15 new jobs are created, the allowable credit is 10 percent of adjusted qualified investment. If the relocation results in 50 or more new jobs, the allowable credit is 50 percent (or such other allowable new jobs percentage) of adjusted qualified investment.

- **Small Business Credit.** Small business also are eligible under the Super Tax Credit program. In order to qualify as a "small" business, a company must have an annual payroll up to $2,081,000 and annual sales not exceeding $6,939,000. Also, the median salary of the company's employees must be at least $15,250 per year. The small business must create at least ten new jobs in order to qualify for this tax credit. If ten new jobs are created, the firm is allowed 30 percent of its qualified investment as credit. For every job created over ten, but not over 50, the company is allowed an additional one-half of 1 percent of its qualified investment as credit. If the firm creates 50 or more jobs, it is then subject to the qualified applied investment percentages of the general Super Tax Credit as outlined in the previous section.

- **West Virginia Capital Company Credit.** Investors in qualified West Virginia capital companies are entitled to a state tax credit equal to 50 percent of their investment. Credits may be claimed against Personal and Corporation Net Income Taxes, Business Franchise Tax, Business and Occupation Tax, Telecommunications Tax and Severance Tax. Capital companies must have a capital base of at least $1 million but not greater than $4 million. The state has authorized a total of $5.5 million in credits to be allocated per fiscal year. Unused credit may be carried forward 15 years.

- **Warehouse "Freeport" Tax Exemption.** The Freeport Tax Exemption Amendment allows goods in transit to an out-of-state destination to be exempt from local ad valorem property tax when "warehoused" in West

Virginia. The exemption is specifically applicable to "property in the form of inventory in the flow of interstate commerce or while in transit is consigned to a warehouse, public or private, within this state for final destination outside this state."

• **Research and Development Project Credits.** West Virginia manufacturers may qualify for the Research and Development Project Credit for research activities conducted within the state. The credit generally equals 10 percent of the qualified investment in depreciable personal property, wages and other expenses incurred for conducting a qualified research or development project. The credit is pro-rated over a ten-year period and may reduce Business Franchise Tax and Corporation Net Income Tax liabilities by up to 50 percent.

• **Industrial Expansion and Revitalization Credit.** Industrial expansion and revitalization investment by manufacturers within the state qualifies for a 10 percent tax credit pro-rated over a period of ten years. The Industrial Expansion and Revitalization Credit generally equals 10 percent of the annual investment by manufacturers in real property and tangible personal property with an economic useful life of at least eight years. Property with an economic useful life of at least four years is one-third qualified and property with an economic useful life of at least six years, but less than eight years, is two-thirds qualified.

• **Consumer-Ready Wood Products Manufacturing Credit.** Wood product manufacturers who establish a new consumer-ready wood product line within the state may claim a $250 credit for each new job created at the qualified facility between July 1997 and June 2002. The credit may offset Business Franchise Tax and Corporation Net Income Tax or Personal Income Tax liabilities.

• **The "Five-for-Ten" Program.** This program provides a tax incentive to businesses that make qualified capital improvements of at least $50 million to an existing base of $100 million or more. It assesses the net capital addition at a salvage value of 5 percent for the first ten years. Capital additions may include all forms of property, with the exception of airplanes and motor vehicles licensed by the Division of Motor Vehicles.

FINANCIAL INCENTIVES:

• **Direct Loan Program.** The West Virginia Economic Development Authority (WVEDA) can provide low interest loans to expanding state businesses and to companies locating in West Virginia. Loan proceeds may be used for the acquisition of land, buildings, and equipment. Working capital loans and the refinancing of existing debt are not eligible.

• **Loan Insurance Program.** The WVEDA can provide loan insurance to a commercial bank to assist businesses unable to obtain conventional bank financing. This program insures up to 80 percent of a bank loan for a maximum loan term of four years. The insured portion of any loan may not exceed $150,000.

• **Industrial Revenue Bonds.** The WEVDA can issue taxable or tax-exempt industrial revenue bonds. WVEDA also may assist with obtaining allocation from the statewide cap on tax-exempt bonds: $35 million is annually allocated for small-issue manufacturing bonds; $10 million for qualifying projects in Enterprise Communities, and $55 million for exempt facility projects.

• **Leveraged Technology Loan Insurance Program.** This program expands the loan insurance coverage to 90% for those businesses involved in the development, commercialization, or use of technology-based products and processes. All other terms and conditions are identical to the Loan Insurance Program.

• **Small Business Development Loans.** This program provides loans from $500 to $10,000 to entrepreneurs for new or expanding small businesses. The program seeds pilot revolving loan funds leveraged with local dollars and provides linkages through technical assistance from local Small Business Development Centers and other entities.

• **The Governor's Guaranteed Work Force Program (GGWFP).** The GGWFP is a nationally recognized award-winning customized industry-specific training program. The program provides business and industrial job training assistance to companies guaranteeing that a qualified work force will be available. The program assists both new companies entering the state and existing companies that are either expanding operations or requiring skill enhancement due to technological innovation.

SUCCESSFUL INCENTIVES:

• **Super Tax Credit.** Mentioned earlier under tax incentives.

• **Governor's Guaranteed Work Force Program.** Mentioned earlier under financial incentives. Since its beginning 425 companies and over 58,000 employees have benefited from the program.

Contact:

Manager of Research
West Virginia Development Office
Room 504, Building 6
Capitol Complex
Charleston, WV 25305
(304) 558-2234

WISCONSIN

LEGISLATIVE TIMELINE:

1990: Created the Recycling Loan Program to encourage new or expanding businesses to make products from recycled materials.

1991: Appropriated $300,000 for economic development planning and implementation grants for northern Wisconsin communities; made available $1.2 million in loans for businesses on Native American reservations.

1993: Added two new development zones with $3 million in new taxes credits, created a residence tax credit in the zones, and funded two minority business-development incubator grants.

1995: Created an enterprise development zone program in which individual project can be designated as development zones and receive tax credits. Provided $1.6 million for the Minority Business Development Fund for the next two fiscal years, and appropriated almost $700,000 to fund rural economic development efforts.

1996: Increased the number of special development zones to 20 and boosted the maximum total tax credits that may be claimed in all zones to $33.1 million.

1999: Created a Brownfields Grant Program under which the Dept. of Commerce may award a grant of up to $1.2 million for the redevelopment of brownfields and related environmental pollution investigation.

TAX INCENTIVES:

- **Corporate income tax.** 7.9 percent. Plus a surtax set annually by the Department of Revenue to finance a special recycling fund.

- **Personal income tax.** 4.9 to 6.93 percent.

- **Sales and use tax.** 5.0 percent.

- **Property Tax Exemption for Machinery and Equipment Used in Manufacturing.** Until 1974, machinery and equipment (M&E) used directly and exclusively in manufacturing was subject to general property taxation. This was viewed as an impediment to the continued expansion of business in the state, and as a disincentive to firms contemplating moving into Wisconsin. The 1973-75 state budget act exempted M&E used in manufacturing from personal and real property taxes, effective with the 1974 property tax assessment.

- **Property Tax Exemption for Merchants' and Manufacturer's Inventories.** Tax relief for property taxes on merchant's and manufacturers' inventories has been an important goal since the early 1960s. The inventories tax was viewed as inequitable because businesses differ in their annual inventory cycle, making a fixed date of assessment a poor measure of average inventory levels. In addition, taxing inventories penalizes businesses for storing products in Wisconsin. To relieve the personal property tax on inventories, a state credit on inventory taxes was allowed beginning in 1962. The credit originally amounted to 50 percent of the tax levied.

- **Property Tax Exemption for Pollution Abatement Equipment.** Certain facilities used to treat wastes are exempt form general property taxation. Waste materials include particulates, gas, solids, liquids, and other superfluous products of a manufacturing process. Qualifying facilities must remove, alter, or store waste materials. The exemption is claimed by filing a form with the Department of Revenue (DOR) listing the location, cost, and other pertinent information about the facility. The department is authorized to consult with the Department of Natural Resources (DNR) and the Department of Health and Social Services (DHSS) to determine whether a particular facility qualifies.

- **Property Tax Exemption for Computer Equipment.** The 1997-99 state budget act exempted computer equipment owned by businesses form personal and real property taxes (effective Jan. 1, 1999). This exemption reduces the property tax burden on employers. To avoid an adverse effect on local taxes, special payments are made to affected municipalities and counties to compensate for the lost tax base.

- **Sales Tax Exemption for Manufacturing Machinery and Equipment.** Wisconsin allows a comprehensive sales and use tax exemption for purchases of machinery and equipment used directly and exclusively in a manufacturing process. Manufacturing is defined as the production of a new article using machinery. The new article must be of a different form or have a different use or name than the material it was created from. Machinery and equipment used in activities such as the storage or delivery of finished products, or research and development, are not exempt.

- **Research Expenditures Credits**. A nonrefundable research expenditures credit for non-capital expenditures related to research activities conducted in Wisconsin is available to corporations. Unused amounts of the credit can be carried forward for up to 15 years. The credit is patterned after the federal Research Credit and is equal to 5 percent of the excess of qualified research expenses for the current year over a based period amount. Qualified research expenses include in house expenses for the taxpayer's own research (wages, supplies, and computer use charges) and 65 percent of amounts paid or incurred for qualified research done by a person other than an employee of the taxpayer.

- **Research Facilities Credit**. This credit applies to capital investments in R&D facilities in Wisconsin. The credit is equal to 5 percent of the costs incurred to construct and equip new research facilities in Wisconsin or to expand existing facilities. The credit covers only investments in tangible, depreciable property which is not replacement property. As with the credit for non-capital R&D expenditures, credit claims cannot exceed the current year's tax liability. However, unused amounts of the credit can be carried forward for 15 years.

- **Sales Tax Credit for Fuel and Electricity Used in the Manufacturing Process**. The corporate income and franchise tax credit for sales tax paid on fuel and electricity used directly in manufacturing operations was enacted in 1972. Fuel and power purchases are not covered by the exemption for inputs to the production process because of the administrative and cost problems for utilities preparing energy bills in selectively exempting direct energy usage (e.g., distinguishing between energy used to run machines versus providing plant lighting). Businesses claiming the credit are responsible for determining the portion of total utility costs attributable to manufacturing processes. The allocation is usually made on the basis of engineering studies of the power requirements of qualified equipment. The credit is equal to 100 percent of the sales tax paid. It is not refundable, but unused amounts may be carried forward to up to 15 years to offset income and franchise tax in future years.

- **Deduction for Corporate Dividends Received**. A deduction is allowed for dividends received from subsidiaries in which the parent company owns at least 70 percent of the voting stock. The rationale for the deduction is that corporations are required to treat their investment income, including dividends, as business income subject to the multi-state apportionment formula. In case of dividends received from unitary subsidiaries, the transactions do not constitute the realization of income, but merely the transfer of funds among branches of a unitary business entity. It is argued that similar transfers of funds among unincorporated divisions are not singled out for taxation.

- **Community Development Zone Program**. A non-refundable jobs credit of up to $6,500 for new full-time jobs being created and filled by members of target groups. Eligible target groups include:
    - W-2 participants
    - Dislocated workers
    - Federal Enterprise Community residents
    - Vocational rehabilitation program referrals
    - Vietnam era veterans
    - Ex-felons
    - Youth from low-income families

A non-refundable jobs credit of up to $4,000 for new full-time jobs being created and filled by Wisconsin residents who are not members of the target groups includes the following limitations:
    - The actual amount of jobs credits is dependent upon wages and benefits.
    - Wages must be at least 150 percent of federal minimum wage.
    - Full-time job means regular, non-seasonal, and required to work 2,080 hours per year.
    - One-third of the allocated jobs credits must be claimed for jobs that are filled by target group members.

- **Enterprise Development Zone**. The 1995-97 state budget act established up to 50 enterprise development zones in the state. Eligible businesses locating in the zones would be able to claim up to $3 million worth of tax credits. The available tax credits include all of the existing credits under the Community Development Zone Program. Each enterprise development zone will have a minimum of one business eligible to claim the available tax benefits and will be site specific.

FINANCIAL INCENTIVES:

- **The Community Development Block Grant For Economic Development (CDBG-ED)**. The CDBG-ED program was designed to assist businesses that will invest private funds and create jobs as they expand or relocate to Wisconsin. The Wisconsin Department of Commerce awards the funds to a general purpose unit of government (community) which then loans the funds to a business. When the business repays the loan, the community may retain the funds to capitalize a local revolving loan fund. This fund can then be utilized to finance additional economic development projects within the community.

Since 1982, the Wisconsin Department of Commerce has made more than 324 CDBG-ED awards in excess of $113 million which have in turn leveraged $340 million in private investment.

- **Major Economic Development (MED) Program**. The MED program is designed to assist businesses that will invest private funds and create jobs as they expand in or relocate to Wisconsin. Since 1986, the Wisconsin Department of Commerce has made more than 85 awards in excess of $38 million which have in turn leveraged $820 million in private investment and created or retained more than 19,000 jobs in Wisconsin.

  To be eligible for consideration under the MED program, the project must:
  1. Involve significant capital investment relative to the state of Wisconsin as a whole, or
  2. Involve the retention or creation of a significant number of jobs in the political subdivision where the project is located.

- **Customized Labor Training (CLT) Program**. The CLT program was designed to assist companies that are investing in new technologies or manufacturing processes by providing a grant of up to 50 percent of the cost of training employees on the new technologies. The program's primary goal is to help Wisconsin manufacturers maintain a workforce that is on the cutting edge of technological innovation. Any business making a firm commitment to locate a new facility in Wisconsin or expand an existing facility within the State which is upgrading a product, process or service that requires training in new technology and industrial skills is eligible.

  Since its inception in 1983, the CLT program has provided more than $52 million to over 175 Wisconsin businesses who have in turn trained in excess of 42,000 employees.

- **Technology Development Fund (TDF) Program**. The TDF program was established in 1984 to assist Wisconsin businesses research and development technological innovations that have the potential to provide significant economic benefit to the state. In order to achieve its goals, the TDF program is structured so that Commerce shares in both the risks and benefits associated with project.

- **Rural Economic Development Microloan (RML) Program**. The RML Program is designed to provide working capital or fixed asset financing for businesses. Since it's inception in 1990, the RML program has provided more than $1.4 million to over 110 Wisconsin businesses. Eligible activities include: construction, working capital, acquisition of existing businesses, land, buildings and equipment.

- **ISO 14000 Training Program**. The ISO 14000 Training program was designed to assist companies that are attempting to obtain ISO 14000 certification. This pilot program provides 50 percent of eligible costs up to $5,000 to train employees on new environmental management systems. The program's primary goal is to help Wisconsin manufacturers maintain their competitive edge by obtaining the ISO 14000 certification. The award will be provided in the form of a forgivable loan, with the understanding that if ISO 14001 certification is obtained within two and one-half years, the loan will be forgiven.

- **The Enterprise Development Zone Program**. This program provides tax incentives to new or expanding businesses whose projects will effect distressed areas. Based on the economic impact of a proposed business project, the Department of Commerce will be able to designate an enterprise development zone. A zone is "site specific" and applies to only one business. The maximum amount of credit per zone is $3.0 million. Zones can exist for up to seven years. The Department can vary zone benefits to encourage projects in areas of high distress. The Department can designate up to 50 zones.

OTHER INCENTIVES:

- **Export Assistance**. The Wisconsin Department of Development allows up to $5,000 to reimburse company expenses for trade shows.

- **Child Care Development Early Planning Grant Fund (CEPG)**. The CEPG program was established to stimulate the start up of employer sponsored on-site or near-site child care facilities. Locating a childcare facility within an industrial park or near a major employer will help reduce the barriers faced by W-2 participants and low-income individuals. The goal of the program is to develop a coordinated effort between employment, transportation and childcare services in an effort to enhance the attraction and retention of employees in positions that provide a living wage as well as skill development and career advancement opportunities. To accomplish this goal, the program provides financial assistance to employers so that they may obtain professional services necessary to determine the feasibility of a proposed childcare.

Contact:

Phil Albut
Deputy Secretary
Wisconsin Department of Commerce
P.O. Box 7970
Madison, WI 53707
(608) 267-0770

WYOMING

TAX INCENTIVES:

• **Corporate income tax.** None.

• **Personal income tax.** None.

• **Sales and use tax**. 4.0 percent.

FINANCIAL INCENTIVES:

• **Community Development Block Grant Program**. This program provides grants to local governments for community facilities such as senior centers; water, sewer, and streets; community centers; day care; ADA compliance; medical clinics and mental health centers.

• **Energy Conservation Programs**. This program includes the following:
   – Grants to not-for-profit schools and hospitals.
   – Training seminars for building maintenance personnel in pneumatic controls and efficient boiler operation fields.
   – Access to Petroleum Violation Escrow funds to be used for the demonstration of off-the-shelf energy efficiency demonstrations.
   – Access to many funding mechanisms available on a competitive basis from the U.S. Department of Energy.
   – Low interest loans for the implementation of energy conservation measures.

• **Rural Rehabilitation Fund**. This program includes the following:
   – Scholarships for the University of Wyoming and community colleges.
   – Assistance for youth leadership programs.
   – Funds to local organizations to improve the facilities, grounds or buildings on public property in Wyoming communities.

OTHER INCENTIVES:

• **Trade Show Incentive Program**. The Trade Show Program attends numerous industry trade shows to promote Wyoming. The Trade Show also assists Wyoming businesses with the costs of attending national out-of-state trade shows.

Contact:

Steve Achter
Director of Capital, Infrastructure and Community Development
Wyoming Business Council
214 W. 15ᵗʰ St.
Cheyenne, WY 82002
(307) 777-2800

LEGISLATIVE TIMELINE:

1990: Removed the sunset clause for the state's Investment Fund Committee and appropriated $1.5 million for a state-funded economic development loan program.

1991: Passed a new development-financing measure that allows the state to purchase up to 50 percent of an industrial revenue bond issued by a business involved in manufacturing processing.

1992: Approved an expansion of state fund investments in municipal or county industrial development bonds and changed the Community Development Block Grant rules to allow for float loans, loan guarantees and job training.

1993: Increased the state sales tax to 4 percent from 3 percent.

1995: Authorized a phased deregulation of infrastructure long-distance telephone service.

1996: Created the Wyoming Partnership Challenge Program that provides state loans to local economic development organizations. The maximum loan amount is $250,000 and local groups must provide matching funds.

1997: Increased Wyoming Community Development Authority's project financing, and eligible loans by $300 million.

1998: Created the Wyoming business council — 15 members appointed by the governor with consent of the Senate.

GUAM

1997: Guam's captive insurance law was created in order to make easier the formation of a captive company in Guam and to create the environment conducive to captive companies.

1998: As an amendment to Public Law 23-109, which provides 100 percent abatement of gross receipts taxes on insurance premiums and other revenues and rebates on all income taxes of an insurance underwriting entity, Public Law# 24-266 was enacted, which authorizes additional benefits to insurance underwriters and similar tax incentives for Guam-based trusts.

TAX INCENTIVES:

• **Corporate income tax.** N/A.

• **Personal income tax.** N/A.

• **Sales and use tax.** N/A.

• **Income Tax Rebate:**
    1. Up to 75 percent for a maximum of 20 years, extendable. Corporation must be engaged in an approved venture.
    2. Up to 100 percent for a maximum of 20 years, for hotel developers who advance $5 million to the Housing Fund.
    3. 100 percent for a maximum of 20 years, for affordable housing developers.
    4. 100 percent for a maximum of 20 years, extendable, for Guam-based trusts.
    5. 100 percent for a maximum of 20 years, extendable, for commercial insurers, reinsurers, captive insurers

• **Dividend Tax Rebate:**
    1. Up to 75 percent for a maximum of 5 years for shareholders of a Qualifying Certificates Beneficiary, including Subchapter S corporation.
    2. 100 percent of the income tax withheld from non-resident shareholders of QC Beneficiary, for a maximum of 20 years, extendable. (for insurance and trusts domiciled on Guam)

• **Rental Income Rebate:** For a lessor of land, buildings, machinery/equipment to a hotel/tourist facilities developer who is a QC beneficiary: Up to 50 percent for a maximum of 5 years; and up to 25 percent, for a maximum of the next 5 years (subject to sunset provision valid through January 1, 2002 or as extended).

• **Capital Gains Rebate:** For a seller of land and other real property to a hotel/tourist facilities developer who is a QC beneficiary: Up to 50 percent in any tax year, and part of which falls within the sunset provision period ending January 1, 2002 or as extended.

• **Real Property Tax Abatement:** 100 percent, for a maximum of 10 years, to owners of property used for the approved venture.

• **Gross Receipts Tax Abatement:**
    1. 100 percent for a maximum of 20 years, on insurance premiums to commercial insurers, reinsurers and captive insurers.
    2. 100 percent for a maximum of 20 years, to any developer of affordable housing (min. 25 units)
    3. 100 percent for a maximum of 24 months, extendable for cause, to suppliers of building materials, supplies; contractors for labor/supervision furnished after 8/17/98 to the approved venture.

4. 100 percent for a maximum of 10 years, on income derived from lease of land, building, machinery or equipment to approved venture.

5. 100 percent for a maximum of 10 years, on income from sale of alcoholic beverages and petroleum products manufactured in Guam.

- **Use Tax Exemption:** Up to 24 months, extendable for cause, to owner of hotel/tourist facilities identified in the QC.

FINANCIAL INCENTIVES:

- **The Guam Development Fund Act (GDFA)**. Provides financing (direct and guaranteed loans) in areas of agriculture, aquaculture, manufacturing, tourism, commercial support industries and any other industry that GEDA's board of directors determines will improve the island's economy.

- **The Agriculture Development Fund**. This offers low interest loans to bonafide commercial farmers and agricultural related businesses.

- **The Chamorro Heritage Foundation Program**. Provides loans or grant for activities that preserve, develop and enhance the Chamorro culture and heritage of the indigenous people of Guam.

- **The Micro Enterprise Development Program (MDP).** Provides financial assistance to establish, stabilize and expand micro-enterprises, with funds from the U.S. Department of Housing and Urban Development Community Development Block Grant administered by the Guam Housing and Urban Renewal Authority.

OTHER INCENTIVES:

- **Foreign Investment**. Tax incentives: Although most of GEDA's incentive programs are for local and foreign investors alike, the following benefits are for non-residents only:
  - Rebates of 100 percent of the income tax withheld from dividends paid to shareholders of qualified insurance underwriters.
  - Rebates of 100 percent of the income tax withheld from the beneficiaries of a Guam-based trust on payments or distributions made to the beneficiaries from such a Guam-based trust.

Both of these benefits are valid for up to 20 years, renewable for additional 20-year periods as long as the beneficiaries remain in good standing under the laws of Guam and under the rules and regulations of the Authority.

- **Reverse Trade Missions:** Selected potential investors will be invited as official guests of the Government of Guam to experience "Destination Guam" firsthand.

- **Insurance Underwriters Incentives.** (Reinsurers, commercial insurers and captive insurers):
  - 100 percent abatement of gross receipts taxes on insurance premiums and other revenues.
  - 100 percent rebate on all income taxes resulting from the operation of an insurance underwriting entity.
  - Rebates on dividends tax to shareholders of qualified insurance underwriters:
    - 75 percent for resident shareholders for 5 years.
    - 100 percent of income tax withheld from non-resident shareholders for 20 years.

- **Guam-Based Trusts Incentives**. One hundred percent rebate of all income tax paid by a Guam-based trust on all earnings from either inside or outside of Guam. One hundred percent rebates on income tax withheld on payments to non-resident beneficiaries of Guam-based Trusts.

- **Day Care Facilities Assistance**. Through GEDA's Financial Assistance program, eligible applicants may receive direct financing from GEDA, or loans from a private lending source with a GEDA guarantee up to 90 percent of the loan.

- **Regulatory Relief**. GEDA administers a Special QC program for Foreign Sales Corporations and Guam-based Trusts, which would allow the beneficiaries to enjoy the tax incentives without the regulatory restrictions placed on regular QC holders (captive insurance companies will soon be included in this category).

SUCCESSFUL INCENTIVES:

- **GEDA's QC Program**. This program has been the catalyst in attracting investments to Guam with major emphasis on increasing local employment. In 1996 and 1997, QC recipients provided 4,407 and 4,305 employment opportunities respectively, representing 8 percent of the total civilians employed each year on Guam. The majority of the QC recipients have been hotels and tourist-related facilities.

Contact:

Mrs. Leigh Leilani Lujan
Industry Development Manager
Guam Economic Development Authority
5th Floor, ITC Building, 590 S. Marine Drive
Tamuning, GU 96911
(671) 647-4332

PUERTO RICO

LEGISLATIVE TIMELINE:

1987: Passed the Puerto Rico Tax Incentives Act to promote economic development.

1990: Amended the Puerto Rico Tax Incentives Act to include the canning of fish as an eligible activity to receive incentives.

1998: Passed the 1998 Tax Incentives Act. This reduced corporate income tax to a minimum of 2 percent to a maximum of 7 percent.

TAX INCENTIVES:

• **Corporate income tax**. The Tax Incentive Act of 1998 provides for a maximum corporate income tax rate of 7.0 percent; rates for some companies are as low as 2.0 percent.

• **Personal income tax**. Puerto Rican residents are exempt from federal income taxes on Puerto Rico source income. However, they are subject to Puerto Rico income tax up to a maximum rate of 33.0 percent.

• **Sales and use tax**. No sales and use tax; excise tax averaging 5.0 percent payable one time on certain articles imported into or sold, consumed, used, transferred, or acquired in Puerto Rico. Excise tax is levied on certain transactions and provides for oil import fees. Numerous exemptions, including products or supplies used in manufacturing.

• **Puerto Rico's 1998 Tax Incentive Act**. The cornerstone of this act is a dramatically reduced corporate income tax. Qualified local, foreign and mainland companies now enjoy anywhere from a maximum 7 percent tax rate — a virtual 50 percent reduction compared to the previous Tax Incentives act of 1987 — to a minimum 2 percent.

• **Manufacturer's Tax Exemption**. Manufacturers in Puerto Rico enjoy a 100% exemption from excise taxes on raw materials and machinery and equipment. Also, qualified companies are exempted from excise taxes on fuels for power co-generation and on chemicals used to treat their wastewater.

• **Initial Construction or Start-Up Tax Exemption**. Qualified businesses are exempt from real and personal property taxes during the initial construction or start-up period, as well as during the first year of operations. In subsequent years of operation, the qualified business receives a 90 percent property tax exemption. These businesses are also exempt from any property tax on intangible assets, such as patents, production licenses, trademarks, and what not.

• **Personnel Management Tax Exemption**. Qualified companies can enjoy a "super-deduction" of the costs of training aimed at increasing productivity and quality control, improving worker communications and enhancing management. This tax deduction may be 200 percent of the excess of these expenses over the three-year average annual training costs, if any incurred from 1995 through 1997.

FINANCIAL INCENTIVES:

• **Puerto Rico offers the following Financial Incentives:**
  – Cash grants for training, building improvements and other start-up costs, based on jobs created and regional development zone location of the operation.
  – Wage incentives – Subsidies for employment of welfare recipients.
  – Low interest industrial revenue bonds (AFICA is the Spanish acronym)

– Special Fund for research and development, financing of management buy-outs of tax-exempted businesses, financing of strategic industries and risk-sharing programs with small business.

– Loans, guarantees and investments by the Economic Development Bank (for smaller businesses) and the Government Development Bank for Puerto Rico (for larger enterprises and infrastructure projects)

– Special "Venture Capital Initiative" (VCI) package: includes package of loans and/or investments and R&D grants.

– Rental of Puerto Rico Industrial Development Company (PRIDCO) factory space at below-market rates.

– Foreign trade zones.

OTHER INCENTIVES:

• **PRIDCO Overseas Offices**. PRIDCO and other Puerto Rico government entities have offices in overseas and US locations to promote trade, tourism and investment. However, incentives offered do not discriminate by the nationality of the investor.

• **PROMOEXPORT**. A public corporation, is responsible for administering all export assistance programs, setting up trade shows at different world locations, and facilitating the financing of exports. The Government of Puerto Rico, is dedicated to boosting exports by encouraging more local businesses to export as well as diversifying their exports destinations. Currently, 88 percent of Puerto Rico's exports go to the US market.

• **Regulatory Relief**. The current administration started various deregulatory initiatives in 1993. It has adopted Uniform Commercial Code to facilitate the business transactions environment. The Authority for Permits and Regulations of the Government of Puerto Rico has also created a one-stop-shop where they can process all the necessary permits to begin any economic enterprise.

• **Public/Private Partnerships**. The Government of Puerto Rico has various programs that create partnerships with the private sector that are administered by government institutions such as:

1. The Government Development Bank AFICA program for Puerto Rico tax exempt industrial revenue bonds, as well as financing for privatization and infrastructure projects.

2. The Economic Development Bank offers financing to small businesses and collaborates with the Puerto Rico Industrial Development Corporation in the Venture Capital Initiative that develops public/private financing packages for high technology venture capital financing.

3. Special Fund money may be used for R&D, management buy-outs, venture capital enterprises, financing of strategic industries and risk-sharing programs with small business.

SUCCESSFUL INCENTIVES:

• **Sara Lee Corporation Expansion**. In February 1999, the Sara Lee Corporation announced plans to expand its Branded Apparel manufacturing facilities in Puerto Rico. With an investment of approximately $45 million over the next three years, Sara Lee will add 2,000 high-tech manufacturing jobs at its Branded Apparel manufacturing operations there. The Executive Director of the Puerto Rico Industrial Development Company (PRIDCO) says "We believe the combination of our skilled work force and aggressive incentives program makes Puerto Rico an ideal place for companies such as Sara Lee to compete in today's global market."

• **Pharmaceutical Plants**. Due to PRIDC's aggressive incentives, in Puerto Rico there are 79 pharmaceutical plants operating on the island with employment of over 22,000 persons, according to the 1997 Manufacturing Census of the Department of Labor and Human Resources.

• **Foreign Trade Zones**. In February 1999, the US Foreign-Trade Zones Board approved the expansion of the foreign-trade zone system in Puerto Rico, making it the most unique and comprehensive, non-contiguous foreign-trade zone in the United States. The new system, which applies foreign-trade zone status to most industrial parks, buildings and land owned by the Puerto Rico Industrial Development Company, will allow companies to obtain significant new financial savings opportunities when locating manufacturing and distribution operations on the island.

Contact:

John R. Stewart, Jr., Ph.D.
Economic Consultant
Puerto Rico Industrial Development Company
335 F.D. Roosevelt AVE.
Hato Rey, PR 00918
(787) 758-4747

APPENDIX A

YEAR-BY-YEAR HIGHLIGHTS OF LEGISLATIVE ACTIONS ON BUSINESS INCENTIVES

• 1990

In 1990, many states continued to offer tax exemptions. Legislation tended to target **certain industries or businesses:**

✓ **Iowa** provided a 10 percent income tax credit for investments by an individual firm in a qualified corporation or seed-capital fund.

✓ **New Mexico** exempted companies that invested $50 million or more in equipment in a new facility from paying sales tax on that equipment.

✓ **Utah** exempted from the sales tax pollution-control facilities, aircraft parts and equipment installed in Utah and sales of aircraft manufactured in Utah.

Several states established **new economic development organizations or programs:**

✓ **Delaware** enhanced the state's Small-Business Revolving Loan to provide credit enhancements that banks can access as collateral in making loans.

✓ **Florida** established the Florida Seaport Transportation and Economic Development Trust Fund, which provides matching grants to finance port facilities and port transportation projects.

✓ **Kansas** established the Community Strategic Planning Assistance program to award grants for the development of countywide economic development strategy plans.

✓ **North Carolina** provided funding for an Industrial Building Renovation Fund to create jobs in 50 of North Carolina's 100 counties.

✓ **Virginia** created the Rural Economic Development Planning Grant Fund to assist local governments in rural areas in identifying and evaluating public industrial sites.

✓ **Wisconsin** created a Recycling Loan Program to encourage new or expanding businesses to make products from recycled materials.

Examples of **high-tech** incentives:

✓ **Indiana** implemented the Indiana Strategic Development Fund designed to provide matching funds to industry groups to promote technological development.

✓ **West Virginia** authorized the creation of High-Tech 2000 research zones and parks in which businesses are eligible for deferral of all state corporate net income tax, business and occupation tax, business franchise tax or other state income tax liability for the initial business start-up period.

Examples or **research and development** incentives:

✓ **Illinois** passed the Technology Advancement and Development Act, encompassing several programs to directly fund research in Illinois universities and nonprofit research laboratories, with the goal of finding new ways to keep state businesses competitive.

✓ **Maryland** created the Maryland Venture Capital Trust to stimulate the commercialization of research and development in order to create and sustain businesses throughout the state.

Legislatures in two states expanded **bonding** capacity to stimulate economic development:

✓ **Mississippi** added $18 million in bonding authority to the Economic Development Highway Fund for building highways, or sections of highways, for adequate access to economic-development projects.

✓ **New York** passed a constitutional amendment to increase the state Job Development Authority's bonding capacity from $600 million to $900 million.

Five state legislatures acted on **enterprise zones:**

✓ **Alabama** instituted an enterprise-zone program in economically distressed areas and offered tax credits.

✓ **California** expanded the state's enterprise-zone program, authorizing the creation of 15 additional zones.

✓ **Missouri** amended state enterprise-zone legislation to authorize the formation of five new zones, increasing the state's total number of zones to 38.

✓ **Oklahoma** consolidated enterprise-zone designation criteria, providing additional flexibility in venture-capital investment and enhancing confidentiality of business information received by government agencies.

✓ **Virginia** expanded the enterprise-zone program.

Two states passed **business-incubator** programs:

✓ **Nebraska** passed the Small-Business Incubator Act to allow governments, educational institutions and other organizations to designate vacant space in public buildings as incubator space for new business development.

✓ **North Carolina** expanded the existing business-incubator program to allow for participation by communities of all sizes.

• 1991

Examples of **new tax incentive** programs:

✓ **Georgia** granted employers a $150 income tax credit for each employee completing an employer-provided basic skills education program.

✓ **Indiana** permitted local governments to grant a tax abatement for new manufacturing equipment for five or 10 years.

✓ **Kentucky** passed a corporate tax incentive measure to help land a United Airlines facility.

✓ **Louisiana** enacted a development-incentive law that provides a $750 tax credit against the state income tax and corporate franchise tax for employment of each previously unemployed person in a newly created full-time job.

✓ **Massachusetts** repealed a 5 percent tax on some 600-business services.

✓ **Mississippi** extended a $500 income-tax credit per employee for corporations establishing their regional or national headquarters in the state.

✓ **New Hampshire** provided tax credits for job creation and capital investment and reduced the effective rate of the business-profits tax for expanding firms. Companies that register a net gain in employment will be entitled to a tax credit equal to 15 percent of the compensation paid to new employees during the taxable period.

✓ **Nebraska** passed Local Option Municipal Development Act, which allows the use of municipal general tax revenues for local economic development activity.

✓ **Nevada** approved tax abatement for businesses that create 50 or more jobs or $500,000 or more in capital investment.

✓ **New Mexico** provided a limited exemption of commercial property from local property taxes for certain types of business facilities.

✓ **North Carolina** expanded the number of counties eligible for the Jobs Tax Credit Program from 25 to 33 counties.

✓ **North Dakota** increased tax exemptions for new and expanding businesses.

✓ **Oklahoma** provided a 20 percent tax credit for investments in qualified venture-capital companies.

✓ **South Carolina** extended the jobs tax credit to tourism facilities and agricultural developments.

✓ **Tennessee** passed a pollution-control tax exemption.

Examples of **financial incentive** measures:

✓ **Delaware** adopted the Greer Industry Initiative that makes certain companies involved in recycling eligible for technical and financial assistance.

✓ **Florida** enacted the Enterprise Florida Program to leverage both public and private resources to attract and retain industry.

✓ **Maine** established the Economic Opportunity Fund to provide loans to municipalities for public and private investments to stimulate economic growth.

✓ **Montana** passed the Micro-business Development Act, which provides a total of $3.2 million in $20,000 loans for businesses that have fewer than 10 employees and gross less than $500,000 annually.

✓ **Oregon** strengthened a number of business-financing programs and added a new entrepreneurial-development loan for start-up businesses.

✓ **Pennsylvania** passed legislation authorizing millions of dollars in low-interest loans as an incentive to encourage the location of new companies in the state.

✓ **Texas** approved the Rural Economic Development Act to expand assistance beyond industrial and manufacturing enterprises.

✓ **Utah** established a $10 million Industrial Assistance Fund to grant qualifying companies loans or other financial assistance to establishing, relocating or developing industry in the state.

✓ **Washington** passed the Pacific Northwest Economic Region bill, which addresses regional strategies to boost export trade, tourism, environmental industries, value-added products and regional recycling.

Examples of legislation to expand **training** programs:

✓ **Kansas** approved the Kansas Investments in Lifelong Learning Program, to permit eligible businesses to enter into an agreement with educational institutions to establish training projects for employees in new jobs.

✓ **West Virginia** passed the Guaranteed Workforce Program, which provides one-stop shopping for all economic development related job-training needs.

Examples of legislative actions on **enterprise zones:**

✓ **Illinois** authorized the addition of six enterprise zones, bringing the total to 88 enterprise zones in the state.

✓ **Missouri** provided for the designation of 50 enterprise zones, an increase from the previous limit of 32.

✓ **Rhode Island** enacted a major enterprise-zone bill that sets up a series of investment-tax credits against the corporate-income tax for businesses establishing operations in designated zones.

• 1992

In 1992, additional states joined the large group of states offering business incentives for certain **targeted industries or businesses:**

✓ **Alaska** expanded the Limited Business Partnership Law to encourage more investments from out of state.

✓ **Arizona** designated military reuse zones that offer property and income tax incentives to eligible businesses locating in the zones.

✓ **Colorado** allowed sales tax exemptions for railroad equipment.

✓ **Connecticut** broadened sales and property tax exemptions for manufacturing machinery and equipment.

✓ **Delaware** provided tax credits for new job creation and financial assistance for job training.

✓ **Hawaii** appropriated funds to attract international technologies and businesses.

✓ **Louisiana** created an incentive program to lure aerospace companies to the state.

✓ **Maryland** provided financing to technology-based companies.

✓ **Michigan** expanded tax credits for small businesses.

✓ **Missouri** provided special assistance for the state's defense contracting firms.

✓ **New Mexico** reduced the tax rate for telecommunications companies.

✓ **Oklahoma** provided a sales tax exemption for telecommunications services.

✓ **South Carolina** provided tax credits for research and development jobs.

✓ **South Dakota** provided venture capital for new businesses.

Several states created **organizations or programs** to further expand their job-creation activities:

✓ **Kentucky** passed legislation establishing the Kentucky Economic Development Partnership to head the state's economic development efforts.

✓ **Minnesota** created Advantage Minnesota, a nonprofit public corporation designed to market the economic potential of the state.

✓ **New Hampshire** passed a measure that restructured the Business Investment Trust to better serve small and medium businesses.

✓ **Virginia** created the $4.5 million Governor's Economic Development Contingency Fund to be used at the discretion of the governor to attract industrial prospects and secure expansion.

✓ **West Virginia** created a $10 million Jobs Investment Trust to provide businesses and college students with an opportunity to develop innovative economic-development programs and investment opportunities.

✓ **Missouri** permitted municipalities to issue revenue bonds for the purchase, construction, extension or improvement of distribution facilities.

✓ **New Jersey** approved a measure to issue $200 million in private-sector investment. The fund includes a statewide lending pool for small and medium businesses, an export-import fund, money for economic development infrastructure and funds to renovate schools.

✓ **Texas** authorized issuing revenue bonds in an unlimited amount for any eligible project.

✓ **Wyoming** approved an expansion of state-fund investments in municipal or county industrial development bonds.

• 1993

In 1993, the trend toward creating **new economic development organizations continued**:

✓ **Arizona** created the Environmental Technology Manufacturing Assistance Program.

✓ **Delaware** created a Capital Access Program.

✓ **Florida** created Technology and Innovation Partnerships.

✓ **Michigan** created the Jobs Commission.

✓ **Mississippi** created the Rural Economic Development Assistance Program.

✓ **Missouri** passed the Omnibus Economic Development Act, a major initiative to help existing Missouri companies expand and lure small- to medium-sized companies to the state.

✓ **Oklahoma** created the Quality Jobs Program.

✓ **Pennsylvania** created a public/private economic development partnership.

✓ **Rhode Island** created the Office of Defense Economic Adjustment to help Rhode Island companies make the transition to a post-defense-dependent economy.

✓ **Texas** created the Smart-Jobs Fund that offers grants for new job training.

✓ **Vermont** passed the Economic Progress Act to add new economic incentives.

Many state legislatures acted on **business-incentive programs**:

✓ **Connecticut** created a $60 million fund to improve regional infrastructure and a loan program for small businesses.

✓ **Georgia** changed the state's Job Tax Credit Program, allowing businesses locating in designated distressed urban areas to receive an annual $2,000 tax credit for each new job created.

✓ **Iowa** eliminated the property tax on new manufacturing machinery used for recycling plastic waste.

✓ **Illinois** authorized corporate-income tax credits of up to 20 percent of the cost of providing cooperative vocational education programs for youth.

✓ **Indiana** expanded to small businesses the income-tax credit for investing in economically disadvantaged areas.

✓ **Kansas** approved a new program authorizing tax incentives to manufacturing investing in facilities, equipment or employees.

✓ **Kentucky's** new tax incentive programs were tapped by Ford Motor Co., International Paper and Canadian steel manufacturers, Dofasco and Co-Steel, who located or expanded in the state.

✓ **Maryland** broadened the current sales and use-tax exemptions for research and development.

✓ **New Hampshire** passed a measure creating a new business-enterprise tax to eliminate loopholes for professional who escape business-profits taxes by claiming profits as salary.

✓ **New Jersey** repealed the business personal-property tax; enacted a 10 percent research and development tax credit; and set aside tax credits for facility investments that create jobs.

✓ **North Carolina** extended the job creation tax credit to 17 more counties, bringing the total to 50.

✓ **Ohio** passed the Ohio Jobs Bill to encourage creation of high-quality employment by providing job-creation tax credits, encouraging research and development, and promoting export industries.

✓ **Tennessee** passed the new Jobs Tax-Credit Bill, which provides incentives of up to $3,000 for a variety of companies that create new employment.

Five state legislatures acted on **enterprise zones**:

✓ **Nevada** enacted enterprise-zone legislation.

✓ **New York** passed legislation creating a linked-deposits loan program and expanding the existing economic-development zones program.

✓ **Oregon** enhanced the existing enterprise-zone program, extending its benefits to seven additional non-urban areas.

✓ **Virginia** increased from 19 to 25 the number of enterprise zones.

✓ **Wisconsin** added two new development zones.

• 1994

In 1994, several states established or expanded economic development **organizations and programs**:

✓ **Florida** created the Qualified Target Industry Tax Refund Program that provides a tax refund for new jobs created in Florida through the expansion of existing state businesses or the location of new companies and the Qualified Defense Contractor Tax Refund Program that provides a tax refund for jobs created in the defense industry.

✓ **Kansas** expanded the Export Loan Guarantee Program to increase the limit on loan guarantees from 30 percent to 50 percent of the current balance in the fund.

✓ **Kentucky** established the Kentucky Research and Technologies Infrastructure that consists of research centers to provide research, development and technology transfer to businesses on a fee-for-service basis.

✓ **Maryland** created the Defense Adjustment Loan Program to make low-interest loans to new or existing companies in communities suffering dislocation due to defense downsizing.

✓ **Massachusetts** established the Massachusetts Manufacturing Partnership to help state firms penetrate export markets by providing technical assistance, management advice, market research and strategic planning services.

✓ **Missouri** authorized the Missouri Tech. Corp., to make venture capital investments.

✓ **Nebraska** created the State Unemployment Insurance Trust Fund, interest from which will be used for training, retraining and upgrading of worker skills.

✓ **North Carolina** appropriated $7 million to the state's Industrial Recruitment Competitive fund under which grants are available to communities for infrastructure, relocation expenses or equipment costs for new or expanding businesses.

✓ **Oklahoma** refined the Quality Jobs Program, which included an expansion of the types of businesses that qualify for the incentive.

✓ **Texas** created the Texas Leverage Fund to allow eligible cities to leverage their economic development sales-tax collections by providing easy-to-access capital with favorable terms through locally formed industrial development corporation.

✓ **Utah** amended the Industrial Assistance Fund to make businesses with five to 100 employees that establish operations in economically disadvantaged rural areas, eligible for reimbursement of part or all of their relocation costs.

✓ **West Virginia** created the Office of Business Registration to provide one-stop shopping for new and expanding businesses.

Several **tax incentives** measures were enacted by state legislatures:

✓ **Alabama** reduced the state's corporate income-tax rate and the 20% floor on the depreciated value of commercial personal property to 10 percent by tax year 2000.

✓ **California** passed a 6 percent tax on purchase of manufacturing made after Jan. 1, 1994; making it's existing research and development tax credit permanent.

✓ **Colorado** added enterprise-zone tax credits to trucking companies and adopted a law designed to attract the consumer credit-card industry.

✓ **Iowa** enacted the New Jobs and Income Program that allows a complete exemption from property taxes for up to 20 years, that doubles job-training funds, offers an investment tax credit of 10 percent and provides a 6.5 percent research and development tax credit to companies creating at least 50 high-paying jobs with a minimal capital investment of $10 million.

✓ **Georgia** approved the Business Expansion and Support Act to provide a statewide job tax credit for new jobs.

✓ **Illinois** extended the research and development tax credit to Dec. 31, 1999 and provided additional funding for the state's industrial training program.

✓ **Indiana** approved the Economic Development for a Growing Economy tax-credit program to assist companies that are creating new jobs by locating or expanding in the state.

✓ **Ohio** provided a nonrefundable corporate franchise income-tax credit for company purchasing new manufacturing machinery or equipment for use in an Ohio production facility.

✓ **Michigan** lowered property taxes by an average of 30 percent and capped business property taxes for school purposes at 24 mills.

✓ **Minnesota** eliminated the sales tax on special tooling equipment and enacted a gradual reduction in the sales tax on replacement equipment to 2 percent from 6 percent by 1999.

✓ **Mississippi** eliminated the capital-gains tax and authorized a tax credit for companies using Mississippi ports.

✓ **New Hampshire** reduced corporate income taxes to 7 percent from 7.5 percent.

✓ **New Jersey** reduced the corporate tax rate by 0.397 percent and enacted a sizable income tax cut.

✓ **New York** created a tax credit for wages paid to new employees in areas that qualify for designation as economic–development zones.

✓ **North Dakota** approved additional tax exemptions to help lure a $245 million corn processing plant to the state.

✓ **Pennsylvania** enacted a bill that gradually reduces the state's corporate income tax to 9.99% from 12.25 percent.

✓ **South Carolina** reduced to 40 the number of jobs necessary for a corporate headquarters to qualify for credit against the state corporate income tax can passed legislation that allow part-time jobs to count towards job totals for qualification for property-tax abatement.

✓ **South Dakota** extended the sales and use tax and contractors' excise-tax refund or credit to all large facilities and lowered the threshold for eligibility.

✓ **Tennessee** revised the franchise –tax credit to expand the types of businesses that qualify, permit the credit to be taken sooner, delete the requirement tat 25 new jobs must be added every year that the credit its taken and extend the credit carry-over to 15 years.

✓ **Virginia** provided a one-time income tax credit of $1,000 per new job, in excess of 100 jobs, created by new or expanding businesses in Virginia.

✓ **Washington** approved a tax credit to high-tech firms for research and development and deferred sales taxes for those firms' investments in buildings, machinery and equipment.

Enterprise zone actions:

✓ **New Jersey** added 10 new zones to the urban enterprise-zone program.

✓ **Oklahoma** modified its enterprise zone law to allow any city or town within a county already designated as an enterprise zone to also be designated as an enterprise zone.

• 1995

The number of states acting on their **enterprise-zone** programs increased in 1995:

✓ **Arkansas** included biotechnology firms in the state's enterprise zone program.

✓ **Colorado** established enterprise-zone credits to encourage economic development in disadvantaged areas of the state.

✓ **Connecticut** increased the number of enterprise zones.

✓ **Michigan** created an enterprise-development zone program in which individual projects can be designated as development zones and receive tax credits.

✓ **Missouri** passed a measure that allows enterprise zones to request a seven-year extension beyond the 15-year limit and permits eligible taxpayers to receive additional credits.

✓ **New Jersey** added 10 new zones to the urban enterprise-zone program.

✓ **South Carolina** created a new enterprise-zone program that offers significant tax credits and other benefits to encourage economic development in rural and underdeveloped areas, as well as, areas where significant job losses have recently occurred.

✓ **Wisconsin** created an enterprise-development zone program in which individual projects can be designated as development zones and receive tax credits.

Several states initiated **new business-incentive programs**:

✓ **Alabama** revised its economic-development incentives program, allowing new and expanding industries to write off 5 percent of their construction costs each year for 20 years against their state income taxes.

✓ **Alaska** enacted several new economic-development laws that target oil, mining and high tech industries.

✓ **Arizona** passed a $341.7 million tax-relief package, including reductions in income and property taxes.

✓ **Georgia** expanded the eligibility for investment and job tax-credits. It also agreed to shift $12.5 million to a new grant program designed to make communities more attractive to new business.

✓ **Illinois** increased the state's manufacturing machinery purchaser's credit from 15 percent to 25 percent.

✓ **Kansas** reduced the rate on unemployment taxes for new employers and placed a two-year moratorium for existing employers with a positive balance.

✓ **Nebraska** approved the Quality Jobs Act, which authorizes a wage-benefit credit to new employees of approved companies in Nebraska that either add at least 500 new jobs and $50 million in new investment or 250 jobs and $100 million in new investment.

✓ **Nevada** approved a new sales- and use-tax abatement on manufacturing equipment and machinery.

✓ **New York** enacted a reduction in the personal income tax to be phased in over three years and cut various business taxes, including the petroleum business tax on aviation fuel.

✓ **North Carolina** cut individual and corporate income taxes by $380 million and repealed the intangible tax and reduced unemployment insurance taxes for the third year in a row.

✓ **Ohio** created a nonrefundable 7.5 percent corporate-franchise or state income-tax credit for manufacturing machinery and equipment.

✓ **Maine** enacted several tax relief measures to benefit business, including the business machinery and equipment tax program, a cap on income taxes and a phase-out of recycling fees.

✓ **Oregon** enacted a $266 million income tax cut and extended several key business tax credits, including those for pollution control facilities, reclaimed plastic, business energy and research and development.

✓ **Oklahoma** expanded financial incentives available under the Quality Jobs Program.

✓ **Rhode Island** reduced the corporate-income tax rate by 0.25 percent for every 10 jobs a company creates by the end of 1997.

✓ **Tennessee** exempted certain finished goods from the franchise tax minimum measure and apportionment formula.

✓ **Utah** broadened the manufacturers' sales-tax exemption to include the purchase of replacement manufacturing equipment.

✓ **Virginia** passed the Major Business Facility Job Tax Credit, which provides a one-time tax credit of $1,000 per each new job in excess of 100, or 50 jobs if the facility is in an enterprise zone or economically distressed area.

✓ **Washington** provided enhanced tax incentives by creating the Distressed-Areas Program and the High-Technology Program.

• 1996

In 1996, states continued to create **additional business incentives**:

✓ **Alaska** passed a tax incentive program for the mining industry; corporate-income tax rebates for up to five years will help offset the cost of mineral exploration.

✓ **California** approved a 35% increase in research- and development-tax credits and a 5 percent corporate and business-tax cut.

✓ **Colorado** modified several tax credits for businesses including: the sales and use-tax for machinery and machine tools used in manufacturing; a new credit of 10 percent for qualified job training and school-to-work programs in enterprise zones.

✓ **Connecticut** voted to phase the "S" corporation tax over the next five years. Under the measure small businesses will receive a 10 percent tax break in 1997 and the tax will be eliminated entirely in 2001.

✓ **Georgia** passed a measure that made job tax credits more easily available to businesses that relocate or expand in Georgia.

✓ **Illinois** extended for seven years the Illinois Replacement Investment Tax Credit, which was due to expire at the end of 1996.

✓ **Iowa** made the New Jobs and Income Program available to some companies investing $3 million and creating 15 new jobs.

✓ **Kentucky** passed a law that will allow tax credits for private investment in tourism projects and set up a new exemption to the sales tax for manufacturing processors.

✓ **Louisiana** approved tax credits for eligible companies that participate in the Louisiana Quality Jobs Program.

✓ **Maine** passed a measure that provides for $11 million in proposed bonds to be used to provide financing to small businesses and changed the state's tax increment financing program to allow businesses that create 15 or more jobs over two years to get a tax break.

✓ **Maryland** enacted the Job Creation Tax Credit Act to benefit business and industry that create 60 new full-time jobs in a two-year period and pay at least 150 percent of the federal minimum.

✓ **Montana** passed a new law that provides infrastructure loans to new companies that employ at least 50 workers.

✓ **Nebraska** amended the Quality Jobs Act, giving companies the option of taking a wage-benefit credit that can be applied against state income-tax liability.

✓ **New York** created the Jobs Now Program designed to help attract major new businesses creating at least 300 jobs.

✓ **North Carolina** passed the William S. Lee Quality Jobs and Expansion Act that provides for several tax reductions and credits. The law includes a new investment tax credit to 7 percent of the excess value of machinery and equipment placed in service in North Carolina by new and expanding firms.

✓ **Oklahoma** authorized two new tax incentives to increase the manufacture and export of value-added agricultural products in Oklahoma.

✓ **Pennsylvania** created the $25 million Opportunity Grant Program.

✓ **Rhode Island** extended the Job Development Act of 1994, providing a permanent reduction in the corporate-tax rate for companies creating jobs.

✓ **South Dakota** passed a tax incentive that exempts the international sale of agricultural and industrial equipment from the gross receipt tax.

✓ **Washington** extended the existing sales or use tax exemption on manufacturing machinery and equipment to cover items used for research and development of new products.

State legislatures acting on **enterprise zones**:

✓ **Alabama** enacted tax exemptions for businesses that employ at least 1,200 people and make capital investments and improvements of at least $75 million within an enterprise zone from utility gross receipt tax, utility gross receipt service tax, state and local sales and use tax and income tax.

✓ **Arizona** modified the state's enterprise-zone program and extended it to 2001.

✓ **Michigan** approved establishing as many as nine tax-free "Renaissance Zones," the first such initiative in the nation. In the zones, taxes waived include both city and state personal income tax, the single-business tax, state and local school-operating taxes, local-property taxes and local-utility taxes.

✓ **South Carolina** approved the Rural Development Act under which the entire state is designated as an enterprise zone.

✓ **Utah** expanded the enterprise-zone program to include 17 counties and many cities.

✓ **Wisconsin** increased the number of special development zones to 20 and boosted the maximum total tax credits that may be claimed in all zones to $33.1 million.

• 1997

In 1997, the following states initiated **new business incentives**:

✓ **Arkansas** passed an act to provide for agricultural and economic development through biotechnology.

✓ **Colorado** House Bill 97-1152 allows an income tax credit equal to 10 percent of the total qualified investments in a school to career program.

✓ **Florida** created the High Impact Performance Incentive (HIPI) to provide large incentives for major investments in certain high impact sectors, such as silicon wafer production and automotive and aircraft assembly.

✓ **Guam** a captive insurance law was created in order to make the formation of a captive easier and to create the environment conducive to captive companies.

✓ **Illinois** passed an enterprise zone tax break that enables municipalities to make certain tax exemptions.

✓ **Indiana** passed a Brownfield revitalization zone tax abatement.

✓ **Iowa** authorizes a county to designate up to 1 percent of its total area as an enterprise zone for a period of 10 years.

✓ **Kansas** amended the law governing the High Performance Incentive Program making more options for eligibility.

✓ **Louisiana** created the Tri-State Delta Economic Compact to be composed of Louisiana, Arkansas, and Mississippi for the purpose of promoting the economy of the delta region by providing job opportunities.

✓ **Maine** passed an Act to encourage the development of High-technology Industry in the State.

✓ **Maryland** enacted a 10 percent personal income tax reduction and an expansion of the sales tax exemption for manufacturing property purchases.

✓ **Massachusetts** passed an act deregulating the electric utility industry and enhancing consumer protections therein.

✓ **Minnesota** appropriated more than $135 million for economic and community development purposes.

✓ **Mississippi** increased bonding by $110 million for Mississippi Major Economic Impact Act and authorizes an additional $20 million in bonds for economic development projects under the Economic Development Act.

✓ **Missouri** expanded the duties of the Agriculture and Small Business Developemnr Authority to provide assistance to businesses involved in processing, manufacturing, and exporting Missouri's agricultural products by granting partial loan guarantees.

✓ **Montana** passed an Act that allows the Department of Commerce to establish a foreign capital depository to attract legally derived foreign capitol for investment, revenue enhancement, and other economic development purposes.

✓ **Nevada** passed a bill to encourage certain types of industry to locate or expand their businesses within the state with certain abatements, exemptions and deferrals of taxes.

✓ **New Hampshire** established the Northern New England Interstate Commission on Economic Development which shall not become effective until Maine, New Hampshire, and Vermont have adopted it.

✓ **New Mexico** amended Development Training by moving industrial development training program to Economic Development Department form State Department of Education.

✓ **North Dakota** amended seed capital investment tax credit provisions to eliminate the requirement of gross sales receipts of less than $2 million in the most recent year.

✓ **Oregon** passed House Bill 2143 which provides added property tax abatement and corporate income tax exemptions for companies locating in enterprise zones with chronic high unemployment.

✓ **Pennsylvania** amended the Job Enhance Act by establishing the Export Financing Loan Fund and the Family Savings account program to provide financial assistance to small businesses.

✓ **Puerto Rico** passed the Puerto Rico Tax Incentives Act to promote economic development.

✓ **Rhode Island** raised the R&D credit to 22.5 percent. Established an Investment Tax Credit where manufacturers investing in worker training will be able to take a 10 percent credit on all purchased or leased equipment. In addition, appropriated $2.7 million for the Slater Innovation Partnership (for cellular medicine).

✓ **South Dakota** revised the sales and use tax and contractors' excise tax refund for new agriculture facilities worth $4.5 million plus.

✓ **Utah** passed energy Savings Tax Credit Extension; increases the maximum amount allowable as a credit for residential energy systems.

✓ **Wyoming** increased Wyoming Community Development Authority's project financing, and eligible loans by an additional $300 million.

• 1998

In 1998, the following states initiated **new business incentives**:

✓ **Alaska** established a grant program to aid the development of new businesses in the state.

✓ **Colorado** created an income tax credit for alternative fueling facilities.

✓ **Connecticut** provided funds for remediating "Brownfield" sites and enacted laws limiting the liability of developers who remediate these sites up to specified standards.

✓ **Florida** created an investment tax credit on the Florida's corporate income tax of up to 5 percent of an investment over $50million for up to 20 years for industries in designated HIPI sectors. Exempted accounts receivable and certain other business assets from the intangibles tax.

✓ **Guam** passed Public Law#24-266, which authorizes additional benefits to insurance underwriters and tax incentives for Guam-based trusts.

✓ **Hawaii** passed Regulatory Flexibility Act that requires review and reduction of regulatory impact in rules and waver/reduction in penalties.

✓ **Illinois** made Economic Development Grants available to local governments and nonprofit organizations to promote Illinois localities as business sites.

✓ **Iowa** recognized that an Iowa agricultural industry finance corporation is a private business corporation and not a public corporation or instrumentality of the state.

✓ **Kansas** abolished the privilege tax on Kansas insurance companies and expanded the magnitude of the premium tax.

✓ **Kentucky** created the Kentucky Investment Fund Program to assist investment fund managers.

✓ **Maine** passed an act to reduce income and property taxes.

✓ **Maryland** enacted an enhancement of the property tax exemption for biotechnology and computer software used in manufacturing.

✓ **Massachusetts** passed an act to eliminate discrimination against hiring women on state construction projects.

✓ **Michigan** allowed 85 communities in the state to exempt the personal property of certain businesses.

✓ **Minnesota** appropriated over $1.5 million for economic development projects.

✓ **Mississippi** passed Small Enterprise Development Finance Act that allows the bonding authority to be a total of $140 million outstanding at any time. Increased bond money for Mississippi Business Investment Act to a maximum of $254.8 million.

✓ **Missouri** authorized tax credits and other incentives for economic development.

✓ **Nebraska** amended the Quality Jobs Act allowing a company 6 years instead of 4 to meet the requirements of the levels of employment or investment.

✓ **New Mexico** made industrial development training appropriation of $6,070,000.

✓ **Oregon** modified the Oregon Economic Development Department's mission statement to state, "Assist Oregon business and governments to create economic opportunities and build quality communities throughout Oregon." The new focus will enable the department to be more flexible and responsive to the needs of Oregon communities and business which will focus department efforts on solving problems rather than just running programs.

✓ **Pennsylvania** created "Keystone Opportunity Zones" that provide tax exemptions, tax deductions, tax abatements, and tax credits.

✓ **Puerto Rico** passed the 1998 Tax Incentives Act. This dramatically reduced corporate income tax to a minimum of 2 percent and a maximum of 7 percent.

✓ **Rhode Island** enacted a wholesale and retail inventory tax phase out on wholesale and retail inventories over a ten year period for every municipality. The Jobs Development Act was extended to allow corporate income tax rate reductions for jobs created before July 2001.

✓ **South Dakota** authorized the formation of limited liability companies and reduced residential property taxes by five percent for a total reduction of 25% in the last three years.

✓ **Utah** created Rural Enterprise Zones that allow Indian Tribes to apply for enterprise zone designation.

✓ **Wyoming** created the Wyoming business council – 15 members appointed by the governor with consent of senate.

• 1999

In 1999, the following states initiated **new business incentives**:

✓ **Alabama** created a fund in which tobacco revenues will be deposited and the funds would be used for the issuance of bonds in limited amounts for purposes of economic development and industrial recruitment.

✓ **Arizona** extended the corporate income tax credit for construction materials from December 31, 1999 to December 31, 2004 (i.e. five years).

✓ **Arkansas** revised existing business identified programs to include high-tech, knowledge-based industries, reduced capital gains taxes and created small business loan programs.

✓ **California** passed a bill that is intended to help start a secondary market for economic development loans in order to make those loans available to small businesses.

✓ **Colorado** created an exemption of farm equipment from the state sale and use tax.

✓ **Connecticut** expanded the Department of Labor's job-training program and the Connecticut Development Authority's job-training financing program to include businesses involved in certain kinds of manufacturing and research and development.

APPENDIX A - YEAR-BY-YEAR HIGHLIGHTS OF LEGISLATIVE ACTIONS ON BUSINESS INCENTIVES

✓ **Delaware** passed an Act that will reduce the gross receipts tax rate on manufacturing activities by 25 percent.

✓ **Florida** streamlined and refocused Enterprise Florida, Inc., the state's private/public economic development entity and primary economic development organization.

✓ **Hawaii** passed Act 105 Authorized issuance of revenue bonds to assist high tech industry.

✓ **Idaho** appropriated an additional $122,300 to the Department of Commerce for fiscal year 1999, totaling $24 million for 1999.

✓ **Illinois** passed the Micro-Enterprise and Self-Employment Assistance Act.

✓ **Indiana** created incentives for high growth companies with high skilled jobs, information and high technology infrastructure.

✓ **Kansas** expanded the type of businesses that may qualify for tax incentives associated with the High Performance Firms Incentives Program.

✓ **Louisiana** provided that a cooperative economic development project may be undertaken by the state or any agency or corporation acting on behalf of the state, with prior written approval of the commissioner of administration.

✓ **Maryland** enacted the One Maryland Economic Development Program for Distressed Counties creating a loan program for distressed counties.

✓ **Missouri** made changes to various economic development programs including tax credit programs and enterprise zones.

✓ **Montana** reduced the current minimum loan limit for the Mt. Board of Investment Infrastructure Loans from $500,000 to $250,000 and the job creation threshold from 50 jobs to 15 new jobs.

✓ **Nebraska** amended the Employment Expansion and Investment Incentive Act in order to redefine the terms of the original act.

✓ **Nevada** passed a measure to allow the Director of Nevada's Department of Business and Industry to finance the acquisition, refurbishing, replacement, and installation of equipment for a project.

✓ **New Hampshire** established a division of travel and tourism development within the department of resources and economic development.

✓ **New Mexico** made Industrial Development Training Appropriation of $6.16 million. Reduced Oil and Gas Severence Tax Rate and an exemption for first two years of ail and gas production.

✓ **New York** passed an act that provides tax incentives in New York city for the creation of private sector jobs.

✓ **North Carolina** amended the William S. Lee Act to extend sunset from 2002 to 2006 and by providing additional tax incentives.

✓ **North Dakota** passed a bill that provides for a beginning entrepreneur loan guarantee program.

✓ **Ohio** passed an act that allows municipal corporations, counties, townships, the state, and certain persons and private entities to enter into cooperative economic development agreements.

✓ **Oklahoma** passed a corporate income tax credit for investment, made in a new or expanding facility.

✓ **Oregon** passed House Bill 2804 creating the Oregon Internet Commission to examine policies concerning Internet commerce.

✓ **Pennsylvania** amended the Tax Reform Code. Providing for a tax credit for coal waste removal and for ultra-clean fuels, reducing the capital stock and franchise tax, and eliminating utilities gross receipts tax on natural gas.

✓ **Rhode Island** passed a bill where insurance companies were allowed an Investment Tax Credit to be applied against Gross Premium Tax.

✓ **Tennessee** created the Tennessee Forest Industries Economic Development and Taxpayer Act which increases state expenditures to produce environmental impact studies.

✓ **Texas** passed an act exempting certain purchases of machinery and equipment used for research and development from sales and use taxes.

✓ **Utah** modified the individual income tax and corporate franchise and income tax credits for research activities and research equipment and allows certain taxpayers to make an irrevocable election to be treated as a start-up company for purposes of calculating the base amount.

✓ **Virginia** passed an Amendment that expanded the research and development investment tax credit.

✓ **West Virginia**, in order to attract new business and industry makes it necessary to promote adequate higher education, arts, sciences and tourism facilities, including infrastructure.

✓ **Wisconsin** created a Brownfields Grant Program under which the Department of Commerce may award a grant of up to $1.2 million for the redevelopment of brownfields and related environmental pollution investigation.

Source: Compiled by The Council of State Governments from CSG's 1999 national survey of state economic development and business-incentive leaders (50 states and three territories responding).

APPENDIX B

STATE JOB TRAINING PROGRAMS

The following states have job training programs. These programs provide grants and other financial assistance to businesses for entry-level skills training and skills upgrade training for new, displaced or existing workers. Training may be conducted on-site or in a classroom setting.

State	Program	Description
ALABAMA	The Alabama Industrial Development Training Program	Provides free job training for companies if certain qualifications for starting wages and job creation are met. Support for on-the-job training is available to companies that meet other criteria.
ARIZONA	The Workforce Recruitment and Job Training Grant Program	Provides grants for short-term training for new employees. The training must be job and business specific. The program is funded annually at $4.5 million. Fifteen percent of the fund goes to businesses with fewer than 100 employees and 15 percent of the fund for businesses located in a rural community.
ARKANSAS	The Existing Workforce Training Program (EWTP)

The Arkansas Industrial Development Commission Industry Training Program (ITP) | Provided to manufacturing industries an Alabama for upgrading workforce skills. The program is administered by the Department of Higher Education, the Vocational-Technical Division of the Department of Education and the Arkansas Industrial Development Commission. The focus of this program is to upgrade skills specific to a company's current workforce at any level.
Provides intensive pre-employment training for Arkansas workers to meet the increasing technical employment needs of the state's new and expanding industry. AIDC provides training on the company's equipment at its site, or if its in the construction phase, at an off-site facility. |
CALIFORNIA	The Employment Training Panel (ETP)	Assists businesses in acquiring and retaining a highly skilled workforce to increase competitiveness and productivity. The ETP is a program supported by California employers through a small contribution to the California Employment Training Fund.
COLORADO	The Colorado FIRST and Existing Industries Programs	Offer short-term, fast track job training assistance to qualified Colorado employers. Customized job training assistance is available to new and existing businesses that create primary jobs in the manufacturing and business service sectors.
CONNECTICUT	Connecticut Job Training Finance Program	Encourages banks to make loans up to $250,000 to manufacturers to train their production workers. Connecticut Development Authority provides a grant of the lesser of 25 percent of the loan or $25,000 upon completion of training, which is used to pay down the bank loan.
DELAWARE	Venture Capital Program	The Delaware Economic Development Office has access to more than 60 recognized educational resources to provide company-specific skill training. Training contracts may be arranged with Delaware colleges, vocational schools, special ized training centers and independent agencies that provide business, industrial and service-related instruction.
FLORIDA	Quick Response Training Program

The Seaport Employment Training Grant Program | Provides rapid, effective start-up training tailored to benefit specific companies. Quick Response is administered by the Department of Commerce, in cooperation with community colleges, vocational-technical centers, state universities and private institutions.
Funds for job skills training programs designed to improve the movement of cargo or passengers. |
| GEORGIA | Quick Start | Provides complete training services free-of-charge to companies opening new facilities in Georgia or expanding existing operations. Training is customized to each company's specific needs and focuses on entry-level job skills. |
| HAWAII | The Employment and Training Fund (ETF) | Assists qualified businesses in recruiting, hiring and training employees quickly, with the assistance of state and local resources and services. The program is administered by the Department of Labor and Industrial Relations. |
| IDAHO | The Workforce Development Training Fund

The New Industry Training | Provides skills training necessary for specific economic opportunities and industry expansion initiatives. It also upgrades the skills of currently employed workers who are at risk of being permanently laid off.
Provides customized job training for new and expanding industries. The State Department of Employment assists in recruiting, screening and testing potential trainees and pays for qualified instructors. |
ILLINOIS	The Industrial Training Program (ITP)	Assists Illinois companies in training new workers or upgrading the skills of existing workers. ITP grants may be awarded to individual companies, multi-company efforts and intermediary organizations offering multi-company training.
INDIANA	Training 2000	Indiana's Training 2000 Program is designed to provide financial assistance to new and expanding industries committed to training their workforce. Companies can receive reimbursement not to exceed $200,000 for retraining existing workers.
IOWA	New Jobs and Income Program	The Iowa New Jobs and Income Program (NJIP) provides a package of tax credits and exemptions to businesses making a capital investment of at least $10.38 million and creating 50 or more jobs meeting wage and benefit targets.
KANSAS	Kansas Industrial Training (KIT)
Kansas Industrial Retraining (KIR)

State of Kansas Investments in Lifelong | Provides pre-employment training for new an expanding businesses creating at least five jobs.
Provides on-the-job training for restructuring companies whose employees are likely to be displaced due to obsolete or inadequate job skills. This program requires matching funds from the company.
Provides pre-employment training for new and expanding businesses, or consortiums of business, that are creating large Learning (SKILL) number of new jobs or new jobs paying above average wages. |
| KENTUCKY | The Bluegrass State Skills Corporation (BSSC) | BSSC, and independent dejure corporation within the Cabinet for Economic Development, provides grants for customized skills training of workers for new, expanding and existing businesses and industries in Kentucky. |
| MARYLAND | The Maryland Industrial Training Program (MITP)
The Partnership for Workforce Quality (PWQ) | MITP provides incentive grants for the development and training of new employees informs locating or expanding their workforce in Maryland.
The rapid rate of technological change and increasing domestic and international competition demand a skilled workforce. PWQ targets training grants and technical assistance to resident Maryland manufacturing and technology companies to upgrade the skills of the existing workforce. |

APPENDIX B - STATE JOB TRAINING PROGRAMS

State	Program	Description
MASSACHUSETTS	Corporation for Business, Work, and Learning	The Corporation provides a variety of worker training services including support for defense firms seeking to enter commercial markets and support for firms adding jobs and developing new training methods.
MISSISSIPPI	Basic Skills Training Tax Credit	Provides a tax credit to new or existing businesses that pay for certain basic skills training or retraining for their employees. The credit is equal to 25 percent of qualified training expenses. Training programs must be certified by the state Department of Education to qualify for this credit.
NEVADA	Customized Job Training	Nevada offers a customized job training program to qualified businesses that meet established criteria. This program may be used prior to a plant opening and up to 90 days following.
NEW HAMPSHIRE		New Hampshire offers subsidized training to privately owned companies through state technical colleges and institutes.
NEW JERSEY	Workforce Training Grants	New Jersey, through its nationally recognized Workforce Development Partnership, offers customized skills training, education and support services to workers and employers.
NORTH DAKOTA	The Job Training Partnership Act (JTPA)	JTPA provides eligible individuals with an opportunity to get training or retraining so they may gain the skills necessary to obtain employment. There are several ways in which a person may become eligible for JTPA.
RHODE ISLAND	Job Development and Training	The Rhode Island Job Training Tax Credit allows companies to take a tax credit up to $5,000 per employee over any three year period against their state business tax. The tax credit is equal to 50 percent of approved worker training expenses up to $5,000 per individual employee over any three-year period. Up to $1,000 of the $5,000 may be for employee wages. Plans must be filed with the Rhode Island Human Resources Investment Council for approval prior to the training.
SOUTH CAROLINA	Workforce Training	The State of South Carolina, through its highly regarded network of Technical Colleges, will recruit, screen, test and train workers needed to fill new manufacturing jobs. This training is done in concert with the company's human resources department and is designed specifically to meet the needs of the company.
SOUTH DAKOTA	Workforce Development Program	The South Dakota Workforce Development Program is an opportunity to extend training and educational resources so that South Dakota employers will be provided with a well-trained and skilled workforce. Training is provided in conjunction with an educational institution approved by the Workforce Development Coordinator. Technical instructors, curriculum materials, instructional materials and equipment are available through the coordinating educational institution to help deliver quality programs.
TENNESSEE	Appalachian Regional Commission Program (ARC)	All 50 Appalachian counties are eligible. Eligible activities include: infrastructure projects (water, wastewater, roads, rail) required to secure the creation, expansion or retention of job opportunities; job training programs; basic skills development in reading, writing, computation and computer literacy; housing projects; and, multi-jurisdictional programs in enterprise development assistance demonstration projects. State maximum ability to pay is $500,000.
TEXAS	Smart Jobs Fund	The Smart Jobs Fund provides grants to employers to train their employees. The fund is a business incentive program designed to increase the competitiveness of Texas businesses in the global economy. The program is "employer driven," which means the employer determines which employees they will train, what type of training will be performed, and who will administer the training. The legislature has appropriated $108 million for the 1998-99 biennium. The maximum grant amount available to a single employer is $1.5 million per state fiscal year.
VERMONT	Workforce Development Tax Credit	A person may receive a credit against income tax liability in the amount of 10 percent of his/her qualified training, education and workforce development expenditures. A 20% credit may be taken for qualified training, education and workforce development expenditures for the benefit of welfare to work participants.
VIRGINIA	Governor's Opportunity Fund	The Governor's Opportunity Fund supports economic development projects that create new jobs and investment in accordance with criteria established by state legislation. Funds can be used for such activities as site acquisition and development; transportation access; training; construction and build-out of publicly owned buildings; or grants and loans to industrial development authorities.
WASHINGTON	Employee Training Business and Occupation Tax Credits	A B&O tax credit is available to businesses which have received approval for the Distressed Area Sales and Use Tax Deferral/Exemption Program and provide employee job training to their employees at no cost to the employee. The maximum annual credit a business may use is $5,000. The credit is computed by multiplying the approved training cost by 20 percent.
WEST VIRGINIA	The Governor's Guaranteed Work Force Program (GGWFP)	The GGWFP is a nationally recognized award-winning customized industry-specific training program. The program provides business and industrial job training assistance to companies essentially guaranteeing that a qualified work force will be available. The program assists both new companies entering the state and existing companies that are either expanding operations or requiring skill enhancement due to technological innovation. The GGWFP can provide up to $1,000 of training assistance per employee and will guarantee the training to the satisfaction of the customer.
WISCONSIN	ISO 14000 Training Program	The ISO 14000 Training program was designed to assist companies that are attempting to obtain ISO 14000 certification. This pilot program provides 50 percent of eligible costs up to $5,000 to train employees on new environmental management systems. The program's primary goal is to help Wisconsin manufacturers maintain their competitive edge by obtaining the ISO 14000 certification. The award will be provided in the form of a forgivable loan, with the understanding that if ISO 14001 certification is obtained within two and one-half years, the loan will be forgiven.
WYOMING	Community Development Block Grant Program	Provides grants to local governments to provide job training programs.

Source: Compiled by The Council of State Governments from CSG's 1999 national survey of state economic development and business-incentive leaders (50 states and three territories responding).

STATE ENTERPRISE ZONE PROGRAMS

The following states offer special business incentives for companies that locate in designated geographic locations referred to as enterprise zones. These zones are typically economically distressed areas; however, states utilize different economic criteria when offering incentives to businesses located in or moving to these zones.

State	Program	Description
ALABAMA	Enterprise Zone Credit	Twenty-seven Enterprise Zones across the state encourage economic growth in areas considered to have depressed economies. Each area offers innovative packages of local tax and non-tax incentives to encourage businesses to locate in their Enterprise Zones.
ARIZONA	Enterprise Zone Program	The program has two incentive components (At least 35 percent of the workforce must be hired within the boundaries of the zone in order to qualify for either incentive). In addition: 1) Income Tax Credits are available to any non-retail business that creates net new quality jobs. A "quality job" is full-time and permanent, pays on hourly wage above a certain level and provides at least 50 percent of the health insurance costs for the employee. Businesses can receive up to $3,000 in tax credits per job retained over three years. A five-year carry forward is allowed for unused credits. 2) Property Tax Reclassification is available to manufacturing businesses that either women or minority owned or "independently owned and operated" and "small." These businesses must make at least a $2 million investment in fixed capital assets. All property is reclassified from a 25 percent assessment ratio to a 5 percent assessment ratio for five years.
ARKANSAS	Arkansas Enterprise Zone Program Incentives	The Enterprise Zone Program offers three incentives: (1) a state income tax credit for each new position or job created based on the average wage of new workers multiplied by 100. In areas with unemployment rates equal to or in excess of 50 percent of the state's average unemployment rate for the previous calendar year. The above formula used is 400 times the average hourly wage. The cap is $6000 per employee in high unemployment counties. Cap is $3000 per in other counties; (2) a refund of sales and use taxes on the purchase of materials used in construction of a new facility or expansion of an existing facility; and (3) a refund of sales and use taxes on machinery and equipment to be used in connection with the business. To qualify for the Arkansas Enterprise Zone Program, a company must meet job creation criteria and prove the new employees are Arkansas residents during the year in which the credits are earned.
CALIFORNIA	Enterprise Zones	These provide the following various tax credits and benefits: I) Tax credits for sales or use taxes paid on up to $20 million of qualified machinery purchased per year. II) A hiring credit of $26,894 or more for each qualified employee during the employee's first 60 months on the job. III) A 15 year carryover of up to 100 percent of net operating losses. IV) Expensing up to $40,000 of certain depreciable property. V) Lender interest income deductions for loans made to zone businesses. VI) Preference points on state contracts.
COLORADO	Enterprise Zone Credits	The Enterprise Zone includes the following credits: Three percent investment tax credit, $500 job tax credit, double job tax credit for agricultural processing, $200 job tax credit for employer health insurance, research and development tax credit, credit to rehabilitate vacant buildings, credit for contributions to zones, ten percent job training credit, Exemption from state sales and use tax for manufacturing and mining equipment, and local government tax incentives.
CONNECTICUT	Targeted Investment Community (TIC) Benefits	(Any community with an Enterprise Zone) 80% for 5-year real property and personal property tax exemptions for manufacturers. Forty percent to 80 percent for 5-year real property and personal property exemptions for service facilities, depending on amount invested. Fifty percent to 80 percent for 5-year tax exemption for personal property when part of a process technology upgrade, depending on the asset acquired.
	Enterprise Corridor Zone Benefits	Selected communities bordering Route 8 and I-395 are eligible for full Enterprise Zone Level benefits.
DELAWARE	Targeted Area Tax Credits	Firms which qualify as a Targeted Industry and locate in one of the targeted areas qualify for corporate income tax credits of $650 for each new employee and $650 for each new $100,000 investment.
FLORIDA	Florida Enterprise Zone Program	The Florida Enterprise Zone Program provides a credit against either its sales or corporate income tax to a business located within or hiring from within the zones. There are also credits for building materials used in the zone and other activities in the zone.
GEORGIA	Job Tax Credit	Effective January 1, 1999, job tax credits are available to businesses of any nature, including retail businesses, in counties recognized and designated as the 40 least developed counties. Counties and certain census tracts in the state are ranked and placed in economic tiers using the following factors: 1. Highest unemployment; 2. Lowest per capita income; 3. Highest percentage of residents whose incomes are below the poverty level; and 4. Average weekly manufacturing wage.
HAWAII	Enterprise Zone Program	Established to increase business activity and create jobs in areas with above normal unemployment and/or below average income levels.
ILLINOIS	Corporate Income Enterprise Zone Incentives	These incentives include a 0.5 percent investment tax credit; a $500 per job, jobs tax credit; a deduction for dividends paid by a corporation operating in an Illinois enterprise zone; and a deduction for interest paid on loans to businesses operating in an Illinois enterprise zone.
	Sales Tax Enterprise Zone Incentives	These exemptions include: a sales tax exemption for building materials to be used in an enterprise zone if bought in the municipality or county which created the zone; a sales tax exemption for materials consumed in a manufacturing process; and, a utility tax exemption on gas, electricity, and telephone.

APPENDIX C - STATE ENTERPRISE ZONE PROGRAMS

State	Program	Description
IOWA	Enterprise Zone Program	Eligible businesses locating or expanding in an Enterprise Zone area may receive property tax exemptions and expanded state tax credits. Twenty-eight counties and eighteen cities qualify for the program under the 1997 law's provisions by having areas which meet legislative definitions of economic distress.
KANSAS	Enterprise Zone Incentives	Enterprise zone incentives are available to qualifying businesses throughout the state, based on the location of the facility, the type of facility (manufacturing, non-manufacturing or retail), the capital investment and the number of jobs created. A sales tax exemption is available on the materials, equipment and services purchased when building, expanding or renovating a business facility. State income tax credits are available for job creation and capital investment.
KENTUCKY	Enterprise Zone Program	State and local tax incentives are offered to businesses located or locating in zones, and some regulations are eased to make development in the area more attractive. A zone remains in effect for 20 years after the date of designation.
LOUISIANA	Enterprise Zones	Qualified businesses locating or expanding in Louisiana enterprise zones are eligible for a one-time tax credit of $2,500 for each net new employee added to the payroll. The credit may be used to satisfy state income and corporate franchise tax obligations. If the entire credit cannot be used in the year claimed, the remainder may be applied against the income tax or franchise tax for the succeeding 10 taxable years, or until the entire credit is used, whichever occurs first.
MARYLAND	Enterprise Zone Tax Credits (Property and Income Tax Credits) Enterprise Zone "Focus Area" Tax Credits	Maryland was a pioneer in the development of enterprise zones. It was one of the first states to enact its own enterprise zone program, and to designate zones. Advantages of a Maryland enterprise zone location include: • Property tax credits — Ten-year credit against local property taxes on a portion of real property improvements. • Credit is 80 percent the first five years, and decreases 10 percent annually thereafter to 30 percent in the tenth and last year. • Income tax credits — One- to three-year credits for wages paid to new employees in the zone. The general credit is a one-time $500 credit per new worker. For economically disadvantaged employees, the credit increases to a total of $3,000 per worker distributed over three years. • Priority access to Maryland's financing programs — There are thirty-five Maryland enterprise zones. The Maryland General Assembly has passed legislation to create "focus area" within enterprise zones. This legislation became effective October 1, 1999. "Focus areas" are especially distressed portions of enterprise zones. Businesses in these "focus areas" receive new and enhanced tax credits.
MASSACHUSETTTS	Economic Development Incentive Program (EDIP)	This program was initiated to stimulate economic development in distressed areas, attract new businesses and encourage existing business to expand in Massachusetts. There are 33 designated Economic Target Areas throughout Massachusetts. Certified projects within Economic Opportunity Areas can qualify for additional investment incentives, including a 5 percent state investment tax credit, a 10% abandoned building tax deduction, priority for state capital funding and municipal tax benefits that include a special tax assessment and tax increment financing.
MICHIGAN	Michigan Renaissance Zone Program	Michigan's Tax-Free Renaissance Zones are regions of the state designated as virtually tax free for any business or resident presently moving in to a zone. The zones are designed to provide selected communities with the most powerful market based incentive — No Taxes — to spur new jobs and investment.
MINNESOTA	Enterprise Zone Program	The Enterprise Zone Program provides tax credits to qualifying businesses which create investment, development, job creation or retention in the Enterprise Zone cities. Tax credits are allocated by the State to Enterprise Zone cities and businesses that apply for tax credits through the city Enterprise Zone coordinator. The type of tax credits include: property tax credits, debt financing credit on new construction, sales tax credit on construction equipment and materials, and new or existing employee credits.
MISSISSIPPI	Economic Development Highway Program	Assist political subdivisions with the construction or improvement of highway projects that encourage high economic benefit projects to locate in a specific area. A high economic benefit project is any new private investment of $50 million or more by a company in land, buildings or depreciable fixed assets, or an investment of at least $20 million by a company that has statewide capital investments of at least $1 billion.
MISSOURI	Enterprise Zone Credit	You may be eligible for this credit if you established a new facility or expanded an existing facility in an enterprise zone and created new jobs and new investment.
NEBRASKA	Enterprise Zone Act	The Enterprise Zone Act provides tax credits for qualifying businesses that, during any tax year, increase investment by at least $75,000 and increase net employment by an average of full-time positions during a taxable year. Credits may be used to reduce a portion of the taxpayer's income tax liability or to obtain a refund of sales-and-use taxes paid.
NEW JERSEY	Urban Enterprise Zone	In promoting growth and development within the state's economically distressed areas, New Jersey has created 27 Urban Enterprise Zones (UEZ's). Companies that locate within one of the designated zones and create jobs are eligible for a number of benefits and zone incentives.
NEW MEXICO	Enterprise Zones	The Enterprise Zone was enacted to stimulate the creation of new jobs and revitalize economically distressed areas. It authorizes local governments (municipality, county, Indian nation, tribe or pueblo), based on public input, to designate as an Enterprise Zone an area within its jurisdiction not exceeding 25 percent of its land area or encompassing more than 25 percent of its population.
NEW YORK	Economic Development Zone (EDZ) Investment Tax Credit EDZ Employment Incentive Credit	A credit against the corporation franchise tax or personal income tax is available for new capital invested in buildings and/or depreciable tangible personal property used primarily in production by manufacturing, processing, assembling, pollution-control and certain other activities in a designated Economic Development Zone. An additional credit, at 30 percent of the Zone Investment Tax Credit is deductible from the tax payable in each of next three years succeeding the firm's eligible investment, if the firm maintains an average employment in the Zone of 101 percent of the average number of employees employed by the taxpayer in the Zone in the year immediately preceding the year of the eligible investment in the Zone.

State	Program	Description
NEW YORK (continued)	EDZ Wage Tax Credit	A credit against the corporation franchise tax, personal income tax, insurance tax or bank tax is available to eligible firms who create full-time jobs in Economic Development Zones.
	EDZ Capital Credit	A credit is allowed against the corporation franchise tax or the personal income tax for up to 25 percent of any of the following investments or contributions: Investments in or contributions to EDZ capital corporations; Qualifying investments in certified Zone businesses that employ no more than 250 persons within New York State (not counting general executive officers), investments made by or on behalf of a partner proprietor or stockholder in the business are not eligible for the credit; cash contributions to community development projects in an EDZ.
	EDZ Sales/Use Tax Credit	Purchases of building materials that will become an integral part of non-retail commercial or industrial real property located in an economic development zone are exempt from the State sales/use tax and may also be exempt from the local sales/use tax if a local law authorizes such an exemption.
	EDZ Real Property Tax Credit	Under Section 485-e of the Real Property Tax Law, businesses or homeowners constructing, reconstructing or improving real property located within an economic development zone may be eligible for a partial exemption from real property taxes for up to ten years.
NORTH CAROLINA	Development Zone Enhancements	Taxpayers located in development zones gain additional tax credit enhancements. The taxpayer must already qualify for credit under Article III A of the Act.
OHIO	Enterprise Zone Program	This includes local and state tax incentives for businesses that expand or locate in Ohio. In municipalities, up to a 75% exemption of the value of real property improvements and/or new tangible personal property for up to 10 years. In unincorporated areas, incentives can be up to a 60 percent exemption of the value of new real and/or personal property for up to 10 years. Business must agree to retain or create employment and establish, expand, renovate or occupy a facility in an Enterprise Zone. Retail projects are not eligible.
OKLAHOMA	Enterprise Zones	Enterprise Zones can be designated in either disadvantaged counties, cities or portions of cities. These zones provide extra incentives for business. Double the Investment/New Jobs Tax Credit is allowed and low interest loans may be made available through enterprise district loan funds.
OREGON	Enterprise Zone Program	If you locate your facility in an enterprise zone, new construction and most of the equipment installed in the plant would receive a 100% property tax abatement for a minimum of three years. Manufacturing and distribution companies are eligible activities.
PENNSYLVANIA	Enterprise Zone Credit	These credits are available to businesses making investments in the rehabilitation, expansion, or improvement of buildings or land in enterprise zones. Businesses that are interested must develop a plan that describes their activities, the benefits that will result, a budget itemizing costs, and make a commitment to avoid dislocation of current residents.
RHODE ISLAND	Enterprise Zones Tax Incentives	A business which has been certified by the Enterprise Zone Council is allowed a credit against chapters 44-11, 44-14, 44-17 and 44-30; Rhode Island General Laws. The credit is 50 percent of the Rhode Island salaries and wages paid only to those newly hired enterprise job workers comprising the employees included in the "5 percent growth test" used for certification by the council.
SOUTH CAROLINA	Economic Impact Zone Investment Tax Credit	In order to help offset the impact of federal downsizing in the state, legislation was passed to spur economic growth in 26 of the state's 46 counties surrounding the Charleston Naval Base, Myrtle Beach Air Force Base and the Savannah River Site. This legislation allows manufacturers locating in "Economic Impact Zones" a one-time credit against the company's corporate income tax of up to 5 percent of the company's investment in new production equipment. The actual value of the credit depends on the applicable recovery period for property under the Internal Revenue Code.
TENNESSEE	Enterprise Zone Contributions	Corporations are entitled to reimbursements of up to 50 percent of their excise tax payments for net new employment in an enterprise zone ($1,000 per new employee) and for 1.3 percent of the purchase price of industrial machinery for use in such a zone. If the reimbursement on account of industrial machinery exceeds the 50 percent limit, it may be carried forward for two years.
TEXAS	Enterprise Zone Program	Enterprise projects are eligible for a refund of state sales or use taxes paid on machinery and equipment, building materials, labor for the rehabilitation of existing buildings, and electricity and natural gas purchased for use in the enterprise zone. The refund is based on $2,000 for each permanent job the project creates or retains during the five-year designation period. The maximum number of jobs for which a refund may be received is based upon commitments made in the project application. Each project is limited to a maximum refund of $1.25 million, or $250,000 per year over the five-year period.
UTAH	Enterprise Zones	The act passed by the Utah State Legislature provides tax credits for manufacturing companies locating in rural areas that qualify for assistance. A $750 tax credit is given for all new jobs created plus a credit of $1,250 for jobs paying at least 125 percent of the average wage for the industry. In addition, investment tax credits are available for all investment in new plant and equipment as follows: 10 percent for first $100,000; 5 percent of next $250,000. Tax credits can be carried forward for 3 years. Enterprise Zones benefits are only available in certain non-metro counties.
VIRGINIA	Enterprise Zone Program	Qualified businesses locating or expanding in an enterprise zone are eligible for the following incentives: A 10-year general credit against state tax liability; a credit against state tax equal to 30 percent of qualified zone real property improvements is available for rehabilitation projects investing at least $50,000 or an amount equal to the current assessed value of the real property, whichever is greater; large projects that invest at least $100 million and create at least 200 jobs are eligible for a negotiable credit of up to 5 percent of the total investment (real property, machinery and equipment); and, businesses creating new, full-time positions are eligible to receive grants of up to $500 per person filling a position and up to $1,000 per zone resident filling a position for three years.

APPENDIX C - STATE ENTERPRISE ZONE PROGRAMS

State	Program	Description
WASHINGTON	Distressed Area Business and Occupation Tax Credit	A $2,000 or $4,000 (if wages and benefits exceed $40,000) credit against the business and occupation tax is available for each new employment position created and filled by certain businesses located in eligible areas.
WISCONSIN	Enterprise Development Zone	The 1995-97 state budget act established up to 50 enterprise development zones in the state. Eligible businesses locating in the zones would be able to claim up to $3 million worth of tax credits. The available tax credits include all of the existing credits under the Community Development Zone Program. Each enterprise development zone will have a minimum of one business eligible to claim the available tax benefits and will be site specific.

Source: Compiled by The Council of State Governments from CSG's 1999 national survey of state economic development and business-incentive leaders (50 states and three territories responding).

APPENDIX D

SELECTED PUBLIC/PRIVATE PARTNERSHIP PROGRAMS

Several states have entered into partnerships with the private sector to promote economic development. These partnerships typically involve state financial backing for private lending institutions or venture capital firms to promote high risk lending to businesses that would otherwise be unable to secure conventional financing.

State	Program	Description
ALABAMA	The Retirement Fund	The Retirement Systems of Alabama is a public/private partnership that totals $22 billion for the Public Pension Fund.
ARIZONA	The Governor's Strategic Partnership for Economic Development (GSPED)	The Governor's Strategic Partnership for Economic Development (GSPED) is a public/private partnership that enhances the competitiveness of Arizona's economy through export-driven industry clusters and linking activities with workforce development.
ARKANSAS	The Arkansas Capital Corporation (ACC)	The Arkansas Capital Corporation (ACC) is a privately owned, non-profit organization established in 1957 to serve as an alternative source of financing for businesses in Arkansas. Its main goal is to improve the economic climate in the state by providing long-term, fixed-rate loans to Arkansas businesses. As a preferred lender for the Small Business Administration, ACC makes loans to existing operations and business start-ups for everything from new construction and equipment to working capital. ACC loans may be used in combination with bank loans, municipal bond issues, or other sources of financing.
DELAWARE	Delaware ACCESS Program	The Delaware Access Program is designed to give banks a flexible and extremely non-bureaucratic tool to make business loans that are somewhat riskier than a conventional bank loan, in a manner consistent with safety and soundness. It is designed to use a small amount of public resources to generate a large amount of private bank financing, thus providing access to bank financing for many Delaware businesses that might otherwise not be able to obtain such access.
FLORIDA	Enterprise Florida Innovation Public/Private Partnership	The Innovation Partnership is a nonprofit corporation that centers on the creation and expansion of innovative, technology-based firms in the state such as biochemical, computer, microelectronics and software development. The partnership provides seed capital, expertise and direct production problem assistance. The partnership created Innovation and Commercialization Corporations (ICCs), which provide management, financial and marketing services for the commercialization of technologies developed at universities, federal laboratories and private firms.
HAWAII	Strategic Development Corporation	The Hawaii Strategic Development Corporation provides equity funding to private limited partnership venture capitalists who, in turn, invest in Hawaii companies.
INDIANA		The Indiana Department of Commerce partners with public utilities to promote economic development.
KANSAS	Kansas Venture Capital, Inc. (KVCI)	The KVCI is a state-wide risk capital system designed to meet the special needs of businesses throughout Kansas. The system seeks to create private risk capital for investment in smaller Kansas businesses. All funds invested by KVCI must be invested in Kansas businesses solely for the purpose of enhancing productive capacity within the state, or for the purpose of adding value to goods or services produced or processed within the state. Most corporate businesses that meet the Small Business Administration's definition of a small business qualify for KVCI assistance. Any type of business can apply to the KVCI for assistance.
MAINE	Maine & Company	Maine & Company, a private non-profit corporation dedicated to attracting new businesses into the state, oversees the Maine Investment Exchange (MIX). MIX is a joint venture project created by private businesses from throughout Maine. Their mission is to provide a regularly scheduled forum to bring together providers of risk capital with qualified entrepreneurs seeking capital. The monthly forum provides for prospective investors to hear several presentations given by qualified entrepreneurs seeking investment capital. Investors include: personal investors, personal advisor, venture capital firms, corporations and banks.
MASSACHUSETTS	Capital Access Program	The program provides participating banks with a cash collateral guarantee. The program is designed to encourage banks to makes loans to small businesses and is available to Massachusetts companies with annual sales less than $5 million that have borrowing needs up to $500,000.
	Massachusetts Capital Resource Company	This private company established in conjunction with the state acts as an economic catalyst by providing capital to businesses throughout the commonwealth.
	Massachusetts Business Development Corporation	This private corporation under state charter provides loans to firms unable to obtain full financing from conventional lenders.
MICHIGAN	Capital Access Program	Participating banks throughout Michigan offer the Capital Access Program directly to companies that need credit enhancement. Similar to loan loss reserve fund, the bank, company and the Michigan Economic Development Corporation place a small percentage of the loan into a reserve that makes it possible for the company to receive fixed asset and working capital financing.
MINNESOTA	Capital Access Program	This program is used to encourage loans from private lending institutions to businesses, particularly small-and medium sized-businesses, to foster economic development. When loans are enrolled in the program by participating lending institutions, the lender obtains additional financial protection through a special fund created by the lender, borrower and the State. The lender and borrower contribute between 3 percent and 7 percent of the loan to the fund. The amount of funds contributed by the borrower/lender must be equal; however, the funds contributed by the bank may be recovered from the borrower as additional fees or through interest rates.

APPENDIX D - SELECTED PUBLIC/PRIVATE PARTNERSHIP PROGRAMS

State	Program	Description
MISSISSIPPI	The Mississippi Department of Economic and Community Development (MDECD) International Development Division	The MDECD and local economic development organizations partner frequently on business recruitment and expansion projects. The public/private partnership also includes: individual businesses participating in foreign investment and trade missions, business leaders serve on Workforce Development Councils (created under the Workforce and Education Act of 1994) to help direct worker training efforts; MDECD and universities are partnering with companies in the MS Space Commerce Initiative to build a remote sensing based industry sector in the state; State agencies and universities partner with private sector controlled non-profit technology development corporations.
MISSOURI	Missouri FIRST Linked Deposit For Small Businesses	The State Treasurer has reserved a portion of available linked deposit funds for small businesses. State funds are deposited with participating lending institutions at up to 3% below the one-year Treasury Bill rate, with the lender passing on this interest savings to the small business borrower. A company must have less than 25 employees, be headquartered in Missouri, and be operating for profit. Small Business MISSOURI FIRST Linked Deposit loans are available for working capital. The maximum loan amount is $100,000.
MONTANA		The State Commerce Department Regional Development Officers assist clients with finding private capital.
NEBRASKA	The Nebraska Investment Finance Authority (NIFA)	The Nebraska Investment Finance Authority (NIFA) provides low interest financing for eligible industrial projects. NIFA was created by state law, and its Board of Directors is chaired by the Director of the Department of Economic Development. The Department of Economic Development also uses Nebraska's Community Development Block Grant (CDBG) funds to provide loan guarantees for bank financing of projects it favors.
NEW JERSEY	Statewide Loan Pool for Business	The Statewide Loan Pool for Business targets businesses that create or maintain jobs; are located in a financially targeted municipality; or represent a targeted industry such as manufacturing, industrial, agricultural or one of the other sectors targeted for assistance by the EDA. Through an arrangement between EDA and New Jersey banks, loans from $50,000 up to $1 million for fixed assets and up to $500,000 for working capital are available.
NEW YORK	Project Long Island New York-Interamerican Commerce for Consulting Engineers (NYICCE) NYSERNet New York State's Energy Research and Development Authority (NYSERDA) Emerging Industry of NYS	Project Long Island was begun last year by the LIA to identify and strengthen the high technology manufacturing industries already on Long Island that have the best chance of rapid growth and rapid job creation during the next five years. The industries are biotechnology/bioengineering, emerging electronics, graphic communications, medical imaging and health information systems, and computer software. This is a trade development initiative including partnerships between ESD, the American Consulting Engineers, and it's New York member organization, the Consulting Engineers Council of New York State, Inc., the New York Association of Consulting Engineers, Inc., The US Department of Commerce and the Pan-American Federation of Consulting Engineers. The three year initiative is designed to build business relationships between consulting engineering firms in New York and Latin America to increase exports of their services. This program advances network technologies and applications that enable collaboration and promote technology transfer for research and education, expand these to government, industry, and the broader community. NYSERDA provides grants to NYS firms seeking to develop or commercialize innovative products or processes that will lead to improvements in energy or waste minimization. This six-member association (NY Biotechnology Association, NY New Media Assoc., Photonics Development Corp. Environmental Business Association of NYS, NY Software Industry Association, Aerospace Diversification & Defense Conversion Association) represents the dynamic high technology sectors of NYS's economy. Each partially funded by ESD are involved in a number of initiatives to facilitate the job growth and economic prosperity of their constituents.
NORTH CAROLINA		These partnerships are a joint public/private economic development initiative comprised of North Carolina counties. The counties of North Carolina have been organized into seven regional partnerships for economic development. North Carolina's regional partnerships enable regions to compete effectively for new investment and to devise effective economic development strategies based on regional opportunities and advantages.
OKLAHOMA	Capital Access Program	The Oklahoma Capital Investment Board manages this easy-to-use economic service that encourages additional business lending activity. It provides a "credit insurance" reserve for Oklahoma banks through a fee-matching arrangement for loans enrolled in the program. It gives banks additional resources to finance economic development and community reinvestment activities.
OREGON	Capital Access Program	The Capital Access Program is designed to increase the availability of loans from banks to small businesses in Oregon. The program provides a form of loan portfolio insurance so lenders may make business loans that carry higher than conventional risks, but that are within the soundness and safety requirements of federal and state banking regulations.
PENNSYLVANIA	Team Pennsylvania	Team Pennsylvania, headquartered in Harrisburg just minutes from the State Capitol's Complex, is a dynamic public-private partnership that brings together Pennsylvania's businesses, its government and community and economic development leaders. Guided by a board of directors chaired by Governor Ridge, Team Pennsylvania builds a vision for the future in the Commonwealth by providing the resources businesses need to launch or expand business success in the Commonwealth.
PUERTO RICO	The Government Development Bank The Economic Development Bank	The Government Development Bank's Low interest industrial revenue bonds (AFICA is the Spanish acronym) AFICA program for Puerto Rico tax exempt industrial revenue bonds, as well financing for privatization and infrastructure projects. The Economic Development Bank offers financing to small businesses and collaborates with the Puerto Rico Industrial Development Corporation in the Venture Capital Initiative that develops public/private-financing packages for high technology venture capital financing. Special Fund money may be used for research and development, management buy-outs, venture capital enterprises, financing of strategic industries and risk-sharing programs with small business.

State	Program	Description
TEXAS		These partnerships are through the Texas Capital Access Fund, Texas Linked Deposit Fund, and the Industrial Revenue Bond Program.
VIRGINIA	Job Training Partnership	The Virginia Economic Development Department is an authority that can partner with private sector to support economic development.
WASHINGTON	The State Business Development Team	The state Business Development Team works in partnership with local Economic Development Councils, local and state government agencies, port authorities, and utility companies on business development activities such as arranging site visits by potential business investors, and assisting businesses in accessing local business recruitment incentives.

Source: Compiled by The Council of State Governments from CSG's 1999 national survey of state economic development and business-incentive leaders (50 states and three territories responding).

APPENDIX E

A COMPARISON OF STATE TAX RATES

	Corporate Income Tax (Percent)	Personal Income Tax (Percent)	General Sales and Use Tax (Percent)
ALABAMA	5.0	2.0 - 5.0	4.0
ALASKA	1.0 - 9.4	None	None
ARIZONA	9.0 (a)	2.9 - 5.2	5.0
ARKANSAS	1.0 - 6.5	1.0 - 7.0	4.625
CALIFORNIA	8.84 (b)	1.0 - 9.5	6.0
COLORADO	5.0	5.0	3.0
CONNECTICUT	10.5 (c)	3.0 - 4.5	6.0
DELAWARE	8.7	3.1 - 6.9	None
FLORIDA	5.5 (d)	None	6.0
GEORGIA	6.0	1.0 - 6.0	4.0
HAWAII	4.4 - 6.4 (e)	2.0 - 10.0	4.0
IDAHO	8.0 (f)	2.0 - 8.2	5.0
ILLINOIS	7.3 (g)	3.0	6.25
INDIANA	7.9 (h)	3.4	5.0
IOWA	6.0 - 12.0	0.36 - 8.98	5.0
KANSAS	4.0 (i)	3.5 - 7.75	4.9
KENTUCKY	4.0 - 8.25	2.0 - 6.0	6.0
LOUISIANA	4.0 - 8.0	2.0 - 6.0	4.0
MAINE	3.5 - 8.93 (j)	2.0 - 8.5	6.0
MARYLAND	7.0	2.0 - 4.95	5.0
MASSACHUSETTS	9.5 (k)	5.95	5.0
MICHIGAN	(l)	4.4	6.0
MINNESOTA	9.8 (m)	6.0 - 8.5	6.5
MISSISSIPPI	3.0 - 5.0	3.0 - 5.0	7.0
MISSOURI	6.25	1.5 - 6.0	4.225
MONTANA	6.75 (n)	2.0 - 11.0	None
NEBRASKA	5.58 - 7.81	2.51 - 6.68	5.0
NEVADA	None	None	6.5
NEW HAMPSHIRE	7.0 (o)	(x)	None
NEW JERSEY	(p)9.0 (p)	1.4 - 6.37	6.0
NEW MEXICO	4.8 - 7.6	1.7 - 8.5	5.0
NEW YORK	9.0 (q)	4.0 - 7.125	4.0
NORTH CAROLINA	7.25 (r)	6.0 - 7.75	4.0
NORTH DAKOTA	3.0 - 10.5 (s)	2.67 - 12.0	5.0
OHIO	5.1 - 8.9 (t)	0.713 - 7.201	5.0
OKLAHOMA	6.0	0.5 - 7.0	4.5
OREGON	6.6 (a)	5.0 - 9.0	None
PENNSYLVANIA	9.99	2.8	6.0
RHODE ISLAND	9.0	(y)	7.0
SOUTH CAROLINA	5.0	2.5 - 7.0	5.0
SOUTH DAKOTA	None	None	4.0
TENNESSEE	6.0	(z)	6.0
TEXAS	(u)	None	6.25
UTAH	5.0 (a)	2.3 - 7.0	4.75
VERMONT	7.0 - 9.75 (a)	(aa)	5.0
VIRGINIA	6.0	2.0 - 5.75	3.5
WASHINGTON	None	None	6.5
WEST VIRGINIA	9.0	3.0 - 6.5	6.0
WISCONSIN	7.9 (y)	4.9 - 6.93	5.0
WYOMING	None	None	4.0
PUERTO RICO	2.0 - 7.0 (w)	(bb)	None
GUAM	N/A	N/A	

Key:
(a) Minimum tax is $50 in Arizona, $10 in Oregon, $250 in Rhode Island, $100 in Utah and $250 in Vermont.
(b) Minimum tax is $800. The tax rate on S-Corporations is 1.7 percent.
(c) Or 3.1 mills per dollar of capital stock and surplus (maximum tax $1 million) or $250. Tax rate is scheduled to fall to 7.5 percent after 1999.
(d) Or 3.3 percent Alternative Minimum Tax. An exemption of $5,000 is allowed.
(e) Capital gains are taxed at 4 percent. There is also an alternative tax of 0.5 percent of gross annual sales.
(f) Minimum tax is $20. An additional tax of $10 is imposed on each return.
(g) Includes a 2.5 percent personal property replacement tax.
(h) Consists of 3.4 percent on income from sources within the state plus a 4.5 percent supplemental income tax.
(i) Plus a surtax of 3.35 percent (2.125 percent for banks) taxable income in excess of $50,000 ($25,000).
(j) Or a 27 percent tax on Federal Alternative Minimum Taxable Income.
(k) Rate includes a 14 percent surtax; minimum tax of $456.
(l) Michigan imposes a single business tax (sometimes described as a business activities tax or value added tax) of 2.3 percent on the sum of federal taxable income of the business, compensation paid to employees, dividends, interest, royalties paid and other items.
(m) Plus a 5.8 percent tax on any Alternative Minimum Taxable Income over the base tax.
(n) A 7 percent tax on taxpayers using water's edge combination. Minimum tax is $50; for small business corporations, $10.
(o) Plus a 0.25 percent tax on the enterprise base (total compensation, interest and dividends paid). Business profits tax imposed on both corporations and unincorporated associations.
(p) The rate reported in the table is the business franchise tax rate; there is also a net worth tax at rates ranging from 0.2 to 2 mills. The minimum tax is $200. Corporations not subject to the franchise tax are subject to a 7.25 percent income tax.
(q) Or 1.78 mills per dollar of capital (up to $350,000); or 5 percent of the minimum taxable income; or a minimum of $1,500 to $$325 depending on payroll size.
(r) Rate decreases 7.0 percent for 1999.
(s) Or 6 percent Alternative Minimum Tax. Minimum tax is $50.
(t) Or 5.82 mills time the value of the taxpayer's issued and outstanding share of stock; minimum tax is $50.
(u) Texas imposes a franchise tax of 4.5 percent of earned surplus.
(v) Plus a surtax set annually by the Department of Revenue to finance a special recycling fund.
(w) The Tax Incentive Act of 1998 provides for a maximum corporate income tax rate of 7 percent; rates for some companies are as low as 2 percent.
(x) State income tax is limited to dividends and interest income only.
(y) 27.0 percent federal tax liability.
(z) State income tax is limited to dividends and interest income only.
(aa) 5 percent federal tax liability.
(bb) Puerto Rican residents are exempt from federal income taxes on Puerto Rico source income. However, they are subject to Puerto Rico income tax up to a maximum rate of 33%.

Source: Compiled from The Council of State Governments' *The Book of the States 1998-99,* and various other sources.

Center for Leadership, Innovation & Policy

CSG establishes the Center for Leadership, Innovation & Policy

To expand quality programs and services into the 21st century, The Council of State Governments proudly announces the establishment of the Center for Leadership, Innovation & Policy. CLIP will serve the state government community by promoting policy development and leadership training and by recognizing innovative state programs. With CSG's multibranch membership and regional leadership conferences as a foundation, CLIP is uniquely positioned to develop and execute critical state problem-solving initiatives with intergovernmental, philanthropic and corporate partners.

CLIP now houses the national Innovations Awards Program, the Henry Toll Fellowship Program and CSG's national policy research activities. Through the center's four policy groups — Corrections & Public Safety, Environmental Policy, Health Capacity and State Trends — CLIP seeks to maximize public and private resources to assist state officials in developing and implementing effective policies, practices and programs. To enhance CSG's current state programs and services, CLIP will focus on developing new products to benefit state officials.

For more information, please visit our Web site at www.csg.org/clip.

CLIP Staff

Robert Silvanik
Director
(859) 244-8250
silvanik@csg.org

Development

Catherine McKinney
Development Officer
(859) 244-8217
cmckinn@csg.org

Leadership & Innovation

Debbie Powell
Program Planning Coordinator
(859) 244-8249
dpowell@csg.org

Policy

Dr. Keon S. Chi
Senior Fellow
(859) 244-8251
kchi@csg.org

Bert Harberson
Manager, National Institute for State Conflict Management
(859) 244-8228
bharberso@csg.org

Lynn Cunningham
Logistics and Development Assistant
(859) 244-8018
lcunningham@csg.org

Trina Hembree
Executive Director, National Emergency Management Association
(859) 244-8233
thembree@csg.org

Marcia Hensley
Administrative Secretary, National Emergency Management Association
(859) 244-8162
mhensley@csg.org

Cindy J. Lackey
Senior Policy Analyst
(859) 244-8163
cindyl@csg.org

Karen Marshall
Senior Policy Analyst
(859) 244-8234
kmarshal@csg.org

Trudi Matthews
Health Policy Analyst
(859) 244-8157
tmatthews@csg.org

Malissa McAlister
Environmental Policy Analyst
(859) 244-8243
mcalister@csg.org

Magdalena Mook
Policy Analyst
(859) 244-8199
mmook@csg.org

John J. Mountjoy
Regional Coordinator
(859) 244-8256
jmountjoy@csg.org

Electronic Commerce: Revenue Implications for States

Thirteen million U.S. households spent $20 billion on online retail purchases in 1999. By 2004, those figures are expected to reach 49 million and $184 billion, respectively. This dramatically expanding volume of online retail sales makes the decision of whether to tax electronic commerce critical to state and local governments' tax revenues. With so much at stake, e-commerce taxation is clearly the definitive federalism issue of our times.

To learn more about this pressing topic, state officials now can turn to *Electronic Commerce: Revenue Implications for States.* In addition to laying out the arguments for and against e-commerce taxation, this easy-to-read primer briefly reviews the rise of Internet commerce and the federal actions that have limited state and local authority to tax e-commerce. It also outlines possible sales tax reforms that states could use to ease the administrative burden of paying these taxes.

Electronic Commerce: Revenue Implications for States (Order #ecommerce00) is available for $20 by calling the CSG publication sales department at 1-800-800-1910 or by visiting the CSG online store at www.csg.org.

The Council of State Governments
P.O. Box 11910
Lexington, KY 40578-1910
(859) 244-8000